Praise in *The Faerie Queene*

Praise in *The Faerie Queene*

Thomas H. Cain

University of Nebraska Press
Lincoln and London

The publication of this book was assisted by a grant from the Andrew W. Mellon Foundation.

8 21. 309
S748c
c. 1

Publishers on the Plains

UNP

Parts of chapters 1, 2, and 7 have been previously published, in different form, as "The Strategy of Praise in Spenser's *Aprill*," *Studies in English Literature*, 8 (1968): 45–58; and "Spenser and the Renaissance Orpheus," *University of Toronto Quarterly*, 41 (1971): 24–47.

Library of Congress Cataloging in Publication Data

Cain, Thomas H
  Praise in The faerie queene.

  Includes bibliographical references and index.
  1. Spenser, Edmund, 1552?–1599. The faerie queene.
2. Praise in literature. I. Title.
PR2358.C3   821'.3   78–8962
ISBN 0–8032–1405–7

For my mother and in memory of my father

Contents

Illustrations

Preface

Scholars could once conveniently invoke such formulas as "mere flattery" or "fulsome rhetoric" to dismiss the encomiastic literature of earlier periods as a subject for serious investigation. Recent work on the funeral elegy, the court masque, and the royal entry, however, recognizes the pervasive role of official praise in Renaissance culture. In the case of *The Faerie Queene*, its encomiastic character has always received lip service in the scholarly commentary and even in the lecture room: every student of literature knows that it was composed to honor England's great queen and that the Faery Queen is, in some sense, Elizabeth herself. But there has as yet been no sustained investigation of *how* Spenser's epic operates, in one of its many functions, as a poem of praise. In the present study, I attempt to describe *The Faerie Queene* as encomium.

Because Spenser's encomium of Elizabeth develops in three stages, I have followed a chronological organization based on three dates: 1579, when *The Shepheardes Calendar* announces a neo-Virgilian poet whose offering of pastoral praise is an earnest of heroic praise to come; 1590, when the first three books of *The Faerie Queene* fulfill that promise; and 1596, when the last books of the poem show signs of the foundering of praise and the frustration of the poet. Because the nature of encomium varies from book to book of *The Faerie Queene*, each chapter deals with a distinctive facet of praise. To most readers, of course, *The Faerie Queene* appears to be mainly an allegorical romance. To find its encomiastic phenomena one must delve a little below the poem's surface, and it is at this level that most of my discussion of praise occurs. The approach taken is, broadly speaking, that of historical criticism, with attention paid to Spenser's inventive and often freewheeling use of epideictic rhetoric, cultural and political mythology, iconology, and imitation of other poets. Throughout I have drawn attention to the poet's self-representation, for whenever Spenser praises Elizabeth he concomitantly asserts his role as encomiast, often with implicit reference to the archetypal poet Orpheus; in fact, when praise grows attenuated, the figure of the poet increases in prominence. While praise of Elizabeth and others certainly exists elsewhere among Spenser's poems, I have made only incidental reference to these and have confined my subject to praise in the *Calender* and *The Faerie Queene*—two poems which Spenser himself seems to have considered a unit in his canon.

Throughout I have used the text of *The Poetical Works of Edmund Spenser*, ed. J. C. Smith and Ernest de Sélincourt, 3 vols. (Oxford: Clarendon Press, 1909–10), with one noted exception. I have, however, altered the letters *i*, *u*, and *v* to fit normal usage and abandoned the convention of italicized names to permit my own italicizations where useful. Translations not otherwise attributed are mine, except for those of Aristotle, Quintilian, the *Herennius*-rhetor, and the *Homeric Hymns*, which are taken from the Loeb Classical Library editions.

The figures in the text are reproduced with the cooperation and permission of the Huntington Library, San Marino, California, the Library of Congress, the McMaster University Library, Hamilton, Ontario, the Victoria and Albert Museum, and the University of Toronto Library.

Among those to whom I am indebted I must especially thank my students, whose responsive discussions of Spenser have been of the sort that ensures the symbiosis of teaching and research. My colleagues Alvin A. Lee and Chauncey Wood have given encouragement over a long period. Colleagues in other departments of McMaster University—Charles J. Jago, William J. Slater, and G. Derek West—responded helpfully to my queries. A. C. Hamilton of Queen's University read the manuscript twice and commented on it with characteristic generosity. Like all students of Spenser, I have been stimulated by the energy and in-

Preface

sights of current Spenser scholarship and thus regret that one of its main achievements, James Nohrnberg's *The Analogy of "The Faerie Queene,"* appeared too late for me to make such use of its resources as I would have wished. I am grateful to Yale University for the award of a Morse Fellowship, 1965–66, to the Canada Council for a Leave Fellowship, 1974–75, and to McMaster University for several summer research stipends. The editors of *Studies in English Literature* and the *University of Toronto Quarterly* gave permission to adapt articles of mine originally published in those journals. Finally, to my wife, Emily, and son, Patrick, I am indebted for their forbearance during the summers of composition.

Praise in *The Faerie Queene*

CHAPTER ONE

1579

Laudable Exercises

Spenser's usual term for describing *The Faerie Queene* is praise. Its first stanza announces an intention "to blazon broade" "prayses having slept in silence long." And several of its dedicatory sonnets characterize the poem as encomium. The sonnet to Raleigh, for instance, deferentially makes it a temporary substitute for "thy faire Cinthias praises," while the sonnet to Buckhurst flatters him as a poet "much more fit . . . / Thy gracious Soverains praises to compile." The sonnet to Norris makes the familiar assertion that the muse can "immortalize" heroes' deeds "In her shril tromp, and sound their praises dew." And the sonnet to Essex tells him to expect his portrait among "the last praises of this Faery Queene." Here "praises" apparently is a synonym for the books of the poem, each thought of as an encomium. Similarly, when in *Daphnaida* (1591) Spenser points to his "praises in all plenteousnesse" already addressed to Elizabeth, "That her with heavenly hymnes doth deifie," he refers to the first three books of *The Faerie Queene*, then just published. Finally, when from the vantage point of *Epithalamion*, Spenser summarizes his canon as "prayse" and "complaints," he expresses an attitude toward literature that may be called epideictic—the position that, theoretically, all the genres may be categorized as praise or blame.

The phrases just quoted have implications which I wish to explore in the following chapters. It is of course a commonplace that Spenser's great poem exists to praise Elizabeth and that she is the Faery Queen. But there has been no detailed description of how the poem praises. As I shall show, encomium in *The Faerie*

Queene takes many forms. In the proems Spenser praises Elizabeth directly. He praises her indirectly through her "mirrours more then one," the types of the queen appearing at times in figures like Una, Belphoebe, and Florimell. He praises her "great auncestry" in the idealized history Guyon reads in the House of Alma and makes her its teleological focus. He praises her through her fictive ancestor Britomart and her putative ancestor Arthur. And he praises her as the originator and goal of the poem's heroic quests. All this can be studied from the first three books. But some consideration of the later books is also necessary, for in them encomium falters as the initial ideals of the poem come under question.

When encomium occurs in Spenser, the poet's self-representation usually goes with it. In part this is a manifestation of the humanists' glorification of the poet, often under the image of Orpheus, as a culture hero. But the speaker of praise also advertises his role because encomium expects a reward, and Spenser is a candidate for no less than royal patronage. Among the well-wishers contributing commendatory verses to the poem, one H. B. makes the point baldly: "Faire be the guerdon of your Faery Queene, / Even of the fairest that the world hath seene." Because Spenser tends simultaneously to voice encomium and assert the encomiast's role, discussion of one requires discussion of the other.

Like other Renaissance poets, Spenser composed, in part, by manipulating inherited rhetorical instructions.[1] Among them are precise directions for *laus*, or praise, which Spenser learned at the Merchant Taylors' School and later made the technical basis of his encomiastic practice. Some explanation of these directions appears in this chapter, together with illustration of their use in the *Aprill* ode. But first it is necessary to describe praise and blame as a way of organizing poetry as a whole.

The Epideictic Theory of Literature

The view that all literature is praise or blame arises from a postclassical confusion of poetic and rhetoric. Ancient rhetoric, following Aristotle, has three great categories: deliberative, concerned with persuasion; forensic, with prosecution and defense; and epideictic, with praise and blame. The epideictic or demonstrative oration is a ceremonial performance at which, as Aristotle says, the audience expects a display of ability (*Rhetoric* 1. 3). Indeed, *epideixis*, like its Latin equivalent *demonstratio*, means exhibition. Yet epideictic has a special affinity for the deliberative; "what you might suggest in counselling becomes encomium by a change in the phrase" (*Rhet.* 1. 9). And Quintilian notes that encomium is often advisory, although its main function is "to amplify and embellish its themes" (*Institutio oratoria* 3. 4. 12–16, 7. 1–2). This tension between the ornamental and the instructive runs through the history of epideictic and reemerges in the Renaissance as the tension between literature's functions of delighting and teaching.

Epideictic is the specialty of the sophists, whose tradition parallels the forensically oriented rhetoric of Aristotle, Cicero, and Quintilian. With the sophists verbal display comes to dominate the epideictic, and the epideictic itself begins to dominate rhetoric as a whole. In Greek rhetoric from the second to fourth centuries and Roman rhetoric after Quintilian (commonly called Second Sophistic),[2] the epideictic category expands to include poetry. The second-century pedagogue Hermogenes, for instance, held all literature to be epideictic, including Plato and Homer.[3] This view makes the *Iliad* and *Odyssey* poems of praise.

Poetry and epideictic become even more entwined in medieval rhetoric. For instance, two French treatises describe poetry as ornamentation of encomiastic themes. Matthew of Vendôme's *Ars versificatoria* (before 1175) is an epideictic poetic on the use of verbal figures to amplify seven basic *descriptiones* (e.g. of a pope or king), five praising their subjects and two dispraising.[4] Geoffrey of Vinsauf's *Poetria nova* (ca. 1210) also gives directions for amplification of themes by figures, especially apostrophe and description. C. S. Baldwin notes that Geoffrey's poetic is "mainly the rhetoric of dilation. The sophistic of the ancient encomium, walking the schools once more, is now called Poetria."[5]

Epideictic and poetic come into the Renaissance in their medieval conflation. In fact, one of the earliest humanists, Coluccio Salutati, alters the classical definition of the orator, "vir bonus dicendi peritus" ("a good man, skilled in speaking") to produce a definition of the poet as an epideictic orator: "vir optimus laudandi vituperandique peritus" ("the best man, skilled in praise and blame").[6] Much Italian study of Aristotle's *Poetics* does not free poetry from the grip of the epideictic. Indeed, Averroes' paraphrase of the *Poetics* made in the twelfth century, printed in Latin in 1481, and often reprinted in the sixteenth century, begins by asserting in totally un-Aristotelian fashion that "every poem and all poetic discourse is blame or praise."[7] Since he did not know the Greek poetic and dramatic texts mentioned by Aristotle, Averroes, a Moslem, equated them with the encomium and satire typical of Arabic poetry. Aristotle's tragedy thus becomes praise, and comedy, blame. By the agency of the Averroes Paraphrase, an epideictic notion of genres enters the Renaissance with the apparent blessing of Aristotle.

Among the sixteenth-century Italian critics who viewed poetic and rhetoric as one, several adopted Averroes' construction of the genres, and, in England, Puttenham was its main exponent. His *Arte of English Poesie* (1589) organizes the genres by praise and blame, as well as by decorum based on rank: "The immortall gods were praised by hymnes, the great Princes and heroicke personages by ballades of praise called Encomia, both of them by historicall reports of great gravitie and majestie, the inferiour persons by other slight poems." By "historicall reports" Puttenham means exactly what Spenser means in the Letter to Raleigh by "historicall fiction"—that is, the epic. Thus, in Puttenham's scheme, hymn, ode and epic become genres of praise. His genres of blame include tragedy, which shows great men "the mutabilitie of fortune, and the just punishment of God in revenge of a vicious and evill life," as well as comedy and satire, which rebuke common persons.[8] Sidney in the *Apology* also sees tragedy as blame ("that maketh Kings feare to be Tyrants"), but some Italian critics, following Averroes, saw it as praise.[9] Obviously, theorists with epideictic assumptions about literature forced the various genres into categories of praise and blame with small regard for content.

But all epideictic critics agreed that epic is a genre of praise, as did early commentators on the *Aeneid*. For instance, Fulgentius argues that the *Aeneid* is encomiastic, with each of its main episodes illustrating the hero's exemplary virtues. This approach makes the poem a panegyrical biography of which the *Cyropaedia* was the prototype.[10] In the Renaissance the tradition of an encomiastic *Aeneid* surfaces not only in Puttenham but also implicitly in J. C. Scaliger's massive and influential *Poetices* (1561). His description of Aeneas as the ideal hero whose every venture exemplifies princely virtues, collectively understood as justice,[11] clearly fits the tradition of reading epic as panegyrical biography and also serves literature's didactic end. As Sidney remarks, "The Poet nameth Cyrus or Aeneas no other way then to shewe what men of theyr fames, fortunes, and estates should doe."[12] In other words, the *Aeneid*—the one ancient poem against which every poet among the moderns measured himself—comes into the Renaissance dressed in the colors of didactic praise. Its encomiastic reading derived ultimately from the epideictic's capture of poetry and its didactic reading from the epideictic's affinity for the deliberative.[13]

By appealing to the didactic function of praise, the Renaissance encomiast defended himself against the charge of adulation. Erasmus, accused of flattery when he presented his *Panegyricus* (1504) to Philip of Burgundy, argued that "no other way of correcting a prince is as efficacious as offering the pattern of a truly good prince under the guise of flattery to them, for thus do you present virtues and disparage faults in such manner that you seem to urge them to the former while restraining them from the latter."[14] A century later, Ben Jonson similarly defends his poems for having "prais'd some names too much, / But 'twas with purpose to have made them such."[15] This didactic defense of praise comes from a poet whose nondramatic verse as a whole falls into the epideictic category: *The Forrest* and *Under-wood* are *silvae*, or collections of poems on occasional themes, and the *Epigrammes* express either praise or blame.[16] However, the didactic defense has an attendant problem: it is so easy to invoke in cases of unmerited praise that it seems to license adulation and betray the poet as a sycophant.[17]

Anticipating for a moment, we can see how Spenser avoids Jonson's problem. For a poet cannot flatter if his overt aim is glorification and even deification. Nor, in the poem of 1590, is there much hint of Erasmus's strategy of instructing a prince through praise. Yet nothing pervades the poem more than its deliberative role, obvious from its organization by "legends" of virtues. Spenser manages this role so as to make Elizabeth the source of instruction rather than its object: as a semidivine agent she mediates heavenly virtue to the human hero, and when he experiences his particular virtue in its ideal manifestation, that virtue is identical with her. By such means Spenser realizes the Renaissance sense of the epic as didactic praise. And, in doing so, he makes free use of traditional encomiastic technique.

The Topoi of Praise

There are three rhetorical operations basic to any act of composition: invention, or finding material; disposition, or arrangement of material; and elocution, or expression of material. The epideictic interest in ornamentation of themes puts weight on elocution, but there also comes down from antiquity a special set of topoi, or basic subjects, to examine in the invention of praise, as well as an ideal disposition. Spenser learned these at the Merchant Taylor's School as he progressed through the *Progymnasmata* of Aphthonius, a fourth-century neosophist. After 1546 this textbook in elementary rhetorical composition came into standard use in English schools in Reinhard Lorich's augmented edition.[18] It rigidly prescribed topoi for fourteen themes of increasing difficulty, giving scholia and examples. The eighth—*laus*—presents the traditional topoi for invention of praise and simultaneously fixes their disposition. These topoi are *proemium pro qualitate rei* (a preface emphasizing the exceptional excellence of the subject); *genus* (background), divided into *gens* (race), *patria* (native land), *maiores* (ancestors), and *patres* (parents); *educatio* (upbringing); the major topos of praise *res gestae* (deeds), divided into *animi bona* (virtues, such as prudence), *corporis bona* (physical excellences, such as strength or beauty), and *fortunae bona* (gifts of fortune, such as wealth or office); a *comparatio* elevating the subject of the encomium by favorable or outdoing comparison to someone else; and finally *votum* (a prayer or good wish). Firm time-words fix the order in which these topoi are to be executed: *deinde, post, hinc, postremo.*[19]

Before proceeding further, it will be instructive to see two passages using this set of topoi in the prescribed disposition. The first is an apparently playful sonnet by the Earl of Surrey, written around 1537 and probably addressed to nine-year-old Elizabeth Fitzgerald, daughter of the Earl of Kildare.[20]

From Tuscan cam my ladies worthi race;	*gens*
Faire Florence was sometime her auncient seate;	
The westerne ile, whose pleasaunt showre doth face	*patria*
Wylde Chambares cliffes, did geve her lyvely heate;	
Fostred she was with mylke of Irishe brest;	
Her syre an erle, hir dame of princes bloud;	*patres*
From tender yeres in Britaine she doth rest,	
With a kinges child, where she tastes gostly foode;	*educatio*
Honsdon did furst present her to myn eyen;	
Bryght ys her hew, and Geraldine she highte;	*corporis bona*
Hampton me taught to wishe her furst for myne;	
And Windesor, alas! doth chace me from her sight.	
Bewty of kind, her vertues from above,	*corporis & animi*
Happy ys he that may obtaine her love.	*bona*

The full treatment of *genus* (including *gens, patria,* and *patres*) suits praise of a child, as does the minimization of *res gestae,* turned more to *corporis* than *animi bona.*

In the second example, from Shakespeare's *Troilus and Cressida* (II. 3. 251–67), Ulysses attempts to manipulate Ajax with false praise by using the same topical arrangement.

Thank the heavens, lord, thou art of sweet composure.	*qualitas rei*
Praise him that got thee, she that gave thee suck;	*genus (patres)*
Fam'd be thy tutor, and thy parts of nature	*educatio*
Thrice fam'd beyond, beyond all erudition.	
But he that disciplined thy arms to fight—	
Let Mars divide eternity in twain	
And give him half; and for thy vigour,	*corporis bona*
Bull-bearing Milo his addition yield	
To sinewy Ajax. I will not praise thy wisdom,	*animi bona*

Which, like a bourn, a pale, a shore, confines
Thy spacious and dilated parts. Here's Nestor,
Instructed by the antiquary times:
He must, he is, he cannot but be wise;
But pardon, father Nestor, were your days   *comparatio*
As green as Ajax' and your brain so temper'd,
You should not have the eminence of him
But be as Ajax.

The encomiastic disposition here implies that no material exists to praise Ajax, for Ulysses simply gives the schoolbook directions. He uses *patres* without fitting it with parents' names or qualities. *Educatio*, usually devoted to youthful signs of promise, he comically emphasizes. He introduces *animi bona* only to reject it. And he perversely mismanages *comparatio* to say that if Nestor were as young as Ajax and Ajax as wise as Nestor they would be rather alike. The sophisticated audience of law students for whom Shakespeare probably wrote this play would certainly notice that Ulysses is simply giving the encomiastic recipe while obfuscating its realization or amplification.

Every rhetorician discussing the epideictic insists on the importance of amplification. Among the several meanings of this term two are relevant here: dilation or expansion of topoi; and assertion of the subject's superiority. Properly embellished expansion of given topoi supposedly enhanced the dignity of the subject.[21] To achieve this kind of amplification rhetoricians listed general topoi to be searched, and such lists recur many times in the scholia to Aphthonius. A famous one was Cicero's "seven circumstances" which Thomas Wilson offers in his discussion of the demonstrative oration: "Who, what, and where, by what helpe, and by whose; / Why, how, and when, does many things disclose." He adds that "these places helpe wonderfully to set out any matter, and to amplifie it to the uttermost, not onely in praysing, or dispraysing, but also in all other causes."[22] The Surrey sonnet quoted above amplifies its praise topoi by a single general topos, the "where" of Wilson's list. Amplification in the sense of dilation overlaps to some degree with the stylistic ideal of copiousness *(copia)*, the ability to say one thing many ways. In *De duplici copia verborum ac rerum* (1512), written for Colet's humanist curriculum at St. Paul's, Erasmus devotes the section on copious-

8

ness in praise almost entirely to amplification by means of the topos of comparison.[23] And in Aphthonius, the scholia to *laus* emphasize comparisons for amplification of praise.

But *comparatio* is also the central means of realizing the other and more particularly encomiastic meaning of amplification, the assertion of the subject's superiority (or what we might pejoratively identify as the element of exaggeration in encomium).[24] Even Aristotle insists on the importance to epideictic of demonstrating the subject's superiority by comparing him with illustrious men. When encomiastic rhetoric's emphasis on comparison combines with poetic's demand for decorum, the result is a search in the praise of princes for the most hyperbolic comparisons. Of the three basic kinds of comparison—by greater, by equal, and by less—only comparison by less (*comparatio a minore*) facilitates the outdoing required by royal encomium. The encomiast could realize it in various ways. For instance, Erasmus advocates a kind of composite superiority achieved by drawing each quality from a famous example: "his good fortune and effectiveness from Julius Caesar, his magnanimity from Alexander, his urbanity from Augustus, his statesmanship from Titus Senior, his piety and clemency from Trajan, his disdain for glory from Antoninus."[25] A Latin elegy on Henry V uses just this sort of cumulative outdoing comparison: "In wars he was Mars, in arms tall Hector, in contests Ulysses, in judgments Radamanthus, in quests Charlemagne, and in government St. Louis."[26] Raleigh's "Epitaph upon Sidney" (actually an elegy organized around the Aphthonian disposition of praise topoi) climaxes in a similarly cumulative *comparatio*: "That day their Haniball died, our Scipio fell, / Scipio, Cicero, and Petrarch of our time."[27] For Scaliger, readily available comparisons ("proxima") succeed less well than the farfetched: "longinqua petenda sunt" (*Poetices* 3. 100). It is in the search for "longinqua" that Spenser in *The Faerie Queene* pushes beyond such expected royal comparisons as "more magnanimous than Alexander" to cultic images of the queen as Venus, Diana, and Astraea, and beyond that to deifying icons implying proximity to God himself. To justify such far-reaching hyperbolic comparison he could appeal to Quintilian (*Inst. or.* 8. 6. 67): "When the magnitude of the facts passes all words our language will be more effective if it goes beyond the truth than if it falls short of it."

As another important means of insinuating the magnitude of the subject, the author protests inability or affects modesty. Particularly apt at the beginning (i.e. the exordium of the oration), it facilitates the amplification of the first topos in the Aphthonian disposition, *proemium pro qualitate rei*. Epideictic use of the inability topos goes back to the sophists: Menander recommends a statement that only Homer, Orpheus, or the Muses could do the subject justice.[28] But it also gained support from the ethical argument of classical rhetoric, whereby the speaker presents himself as a good man—the first element in the often repeated definition of the orator, "vir bonus, dicendi peritus." In fact, the directions in *Rhetorica ad Herennium* (3. 6) combine inadequacy and authorial humility: "We shall say that we fear our inability to match his deeds with words; . . . his very deeds transcend the eloquence of all eulogists." As Curtius has shown, the topos of inability develops a special currency in medieval literature.[29] Lydgate uses it heavily.[30] And it is one of Spenser's most characteristic encomiastic devices, as in the opening lines of *The Faerie Queene*.

But affectation of self-disparagement not only serves to elevate the subject of praise: it also draws attention to the speaker himself. It is this paradox inherent in the topos of inability that Spenser particularly exploits. Like most ambitious poets of his day, he assumed that the poet's role was of crucial importance to society and, like them, frequently asserted his own importance by claiming an analogy between himself and Orpheus. For the humanists of the Renaissance, this archetypal master-poet symbolized the values of the literary culture which they promoted; and, because the poems attributed to Orpheus were hymns, the encomiast found identification with him to be especially apt. When we turn to Spenser's initial encomium of Elizabeth in *Aprill*, we will find that three related phenomena occur together: the traditional topoi of praise; the topos of inability, managed so as to make us aware of the encomiast; and his identification with Orpheus. This identification brings to the fore the encomiast's assertion of his powers that is implicit in the topos of inability. Hence, it is important, before reading the April encomium, to understand Orpheus's significance for the Renaissance.

The Renaissance Orpheus

Orpheus came into the Renaissance already heavy with interpretation.[31] The early church fathers saw in him a pagan parallel to David the psalmist and pressed both into service as types of Christ.[32] The Middle Ages inherited as well Boethius's moral allegory of Orpheus as the rational part of man controlling, then ironically yielding to, his sensual and earthbound desires—that is, Eurydice (*Con. phil.* 3. met. 12). In the *Ovide moralisé* Orpheus denotes not only "Jhesu Christ, parole devine, / Le douctour de bone doctrine," but even the pegs of his lyre's seven strings represent Christian teachings.[33] In the medieval popular tradition, Orpheus survived as the musician who enchants: the wonderful "menstrel" of *Sir Orfeo* or the Orpheus submerged in the folkloric figure of the Pied Piper, charmer of rats and children.

But it is the Renaissance humanists who make Orpheus prototype of the compellingly articulate orator or poet. It is the humanists who promote the idea of a primarily literary culture; who shift the emphasis in the trivium from logic to rhetoric; who make the formal oration the goal of education; who equate eloquence and civilization. And it is the humanists who find in Orpheus a convenient culture hero. Very early in the Renaissance Coluccio Salutati can refer possessively to "homo noster Orpheus."[34]

The humanist construction of the Orpheus myth appears in the mythographers Spenser used most heavily, Boccaccio and Natalis Comes. In *Genealogiae deorum* (c. 1370) Boccaccio allegorizes Orpheus as the omnicompetent verbal artist who epitomizes the humanist ideal of eloquence and advertises its power to move men. According to his fanciful etymology Orpheus's name even means eloquence, by derivation from "*aurea phones*, that is, the good voice of eloquence, itself the child of Apollo or wisdom and of Calliope whose name means sweet sound."[35] Although Orpheus's lyre represents the whole "art of rhetoric, made up of no single way of speaking, such as eulogy *(demonstratione)*, but of many," the focus on *demonstratio* (probably meaning demonstrative or epideictic rhetoric in its medieval conflation with poetic) betrays an encomiastic bias in Boccaccio's conception of eloquence.

But it is the effectiveness of Orpheus's words that impress Boccaccio most:

> With [his lyre] Orpheus moves woods whose powerful roots are embedded in the earth, which represent obstinate opinionated men who can be moved from their stubbornness only by the powers of eloquence. He arrests the flow of rivers, that is, impulsive and lustful men who are destined to flow into the sea of unending bitterness unless the powerful pronouncements *(demonstrationibus)* of eloquence confirm them in manly virtue. He tames fierce animals, that is, bloodthirsty men, who can often be restored to mildness and humanity only by some wise man's eloquence. [5. 12]

Boccaccio's Orpheus melds the teaching and delighting powers of the Horatian poet with the suasive powers of the classical orator. He thus provides a ready symbol of the importance claimed by humanist educators for eloquence and literary culture.

Boccaccio attaches one more humanist theme to Orpheus—the poet's quest for enduring fame. He allegorizes the story of how a snake tried to eat Orpheus's head when, torn off by the Bacchantes, it floated with his lyre down the swift Hebrus to the Lesbian shore. Apollo intervened, turning the snake to stone and immortalizing Orpheus's lyre by stellifying it.

> The snake I understand to mean the circling years which (just as they do to anything that remains) tried to devour Orpheus's head—that is, his name or rather those works Orpheus composed by his genius *(ingenio)* while the powers of imagination throve in his head. The snake is said to be turned to stone, however, to show that time can in no way put Orpheus down. Nor has it succeeded even yet, since to this very day Orpheus with his lyre is famous, and he is still acknowledged as the most ancient of the poets. [5.12]

The triumph of Orpheus's works and fame over invidious time conveniently symbolizes the humanist poet's ambition to build his own *monumentum aere perennius*. Even the schoolbooks connect the cult of fame with Orpheus, for instance, Raphael Regius's gloss on "Rhodopeius . . . vates" *(Met.* 10. 11–12) in sixteenth-century editions of Ovid: "Orpheus poeta Thracius: cuius Hymni in plerosque Deorum etiam nunc extant"—"whose hymns to most of the gods *exist even now*."[36] The awed sense that the most ancient poet's poems still exist is precisely attuned to the Renaissance poet's own desire for permanent fame.

Natalis Comes' *Mythologiae* (1551) interprets Orpheus in terms that advertise the humanist poet's conception of his role. Three aspects of Comes' treatment are noteworthy. First is his clear euhemerism. His Orpheus is definitely a human poet deified in reputation "because he was a man of brilliant verbal and poetic skill."[37] Second, Comes sees in Orpheus the genius of civilization as opposed to barbarism, and that genius is verbal. In fact, civilization itself orginates with Orpheus:

> Before Orpheus came among mortal men, they were barbaric, living without chosen customs or laws, roaming the fields like wild animals, without so much as a roof over their heads. But Orpheus's words and the sweetness of his speech *(orationis)* had so great an effect that he converted men to a gentler way of life, calling them together into one place, teaching them to build cities, to keep civil laws, and to accept the institution of marriage. Such was believed to be the vocation of ancient poets and is intrinsic to the art of poetry. [7. 14]

Thus, the archetypal poet becomes a Logos figure from whose word the order of society proceeds. Comes is not urging the social usefulness of poetry but rather asserting society's dependence on the great poet. Third, Comes measures modern poets against their triumphant archetype and finds them lacking his genius and heroic role:

> For that race of ancient poets knew everything, quite unlike those of our own day who think the whole art of poetry to consist merely of verbal quantities and metric; or who babble away to flatter some important man, hoping to snap up some trivial gift that might pop into his mind. The songs of the ancient poets, on the other hand, were revered like the holiest laws. Cities quarreling over something would commonly take a poet's song as a sentence of the weightiest judgement. In fact, Orpheus's great power of speech was said to be such that, when men were panic-stricken and through some great disaster fallen into despair, he would restore them to their original state and bring their minds peace. *The man who can do things like this is the kind of man the rest of society must acknowledge as superior.* [7. 14]

The contrast between the archetypal superpoet and contemporary versifiers implicitly opens the way for Orpheus's Renaissance successor—the great poet acknowledged and rewarded as such by his society.

The young Ronsard claimed such a role. His "orgeuilleuse aspiration au rôle d'Orphée moderne" declared in *L'Hymne de France* (1549) and his continuing identification with Orpheus indicate, as Eva Kushner shows, "une volonté constante de définir sa vocation poétique."[38] Spenser seizes on the same identification and for similar reasons: to advertise himself as a major poet and to explore the meaning of that role. Although the number of his allusions to Orpheus (some half-concealed) is not great, all except one have direct or implicit reference to himself as poet. The exception, in *The Ruines of Time* (323–36, 603–16), refers to Sidney—significantly, after his death. Important among the half-concealed allusions is the formula of the woods responding to the poet's song. In Spenser's hands it always recalls the effect of Orpheus's music and so becomes a way of asserting the poet's impact.[39] In *Aprill* the formula expands to become the encomium in which Colin as Orpheus charms the external world into configuration around Eliza.

The Aprill *Encomium and the Orphic Poet*

As Hobbinoll and Thenot discuss Colin's talent in the dialogue framing the *Aprill* ode, two parallels to Orpheus appear. First, Hobbinoll's estimate of Colin's songs "wherein he all outwent" evokes Orpheus the supreme poet. Second, Thenot's question, "And hath he skill to make so excellent, / Yet hath so little skill to brydle love?" (19–20) recalls Orpheus's loss of Eurydice through failure to control his own passions—the Boethian allegory that Boccaccio, Salutati, and Comes restate. These allusions anticipate Colin's manifestation as new Orpheus in the encomium Hobbinoll recites. Its outline mirrors Colin's Orphic performance: in the first half he commands figures to assemble and celebrate Eliza; in the second half they appear and crown her with symbolic garlands. That is, Colin's song, like Orpheus's, charms the external world into praising the queen. When the muses he invokes appear, they are led to Eliza by Calliope, mother of Orpheus and muse of epic praise,[40] implying that Colin is a type of Orpheus, that he is an encomiastic poet, and that his encomium here anticipates an epic in praise of Elizabeth. Similarly, the nymphs bearing the olive crown are led by Chloris who, according to Homer, was daughter of Amphion, an Orpheus figure whose song raised the walls of Thebes.[41] When at the end Colin says, "Now ryse up Elisa, decked as thou art, / in royall aray," he portrays the Orphic figure of the masterful poet whose eloquence controls the glory of the great.[42] His "trimly dight" encomium now has the permanence of a *monumentum aere perennius* that Hobbinoll can "recorde" (Lat. *recordari*, remember) and so demonstrates the immortality Colin can give to the queen's "honor and prayse."

E. K. calls the poem one of Colin's "laudable exercises," meaning an exercise in *laus*, and Spenser constructs his encomium by beginning with that schoolbook technique. The praise topoi used are *proemium pro qualitate rei*, *genus*, *res gestae*, *comparatio*, and *votum*—the Aphthonian pattern in its prescribed disposition. Only *educatio* is missing, traditionally the weakest topos. Throughout, the poet uses outdoing and impossible comparisons and the suggestions of inability implicit in them to dignify his subject and amplify his matter. Before discussing Spenser's achievement in this poem, it will be necessary to examine his handling of individual topoi.

The invocation of muses serves as declaration of inadequacy and so automatically elevates the subject's dignity—that is, it is a *proemium pro qualitate rei*. E. K.'s gloss, "as it were an *Exordium ad preparandos animos*," suggests that the nymphs and muses are convoked as well as invoked. Thus, the encomium leads to a panegyric in the etymological sense, a *panēgyris*, or gathering of all together, an assembly to celebrate the subject of praise.[43] In fact, panegyric occurs literally in the ode's second half, as the figures convoked by Colin in the first half arrive and crown Eliza—a scene recalling Botticelli's *Primavera*. In the proem Colin also declares his intention "to blaze / Her worthy praise"—that is, of a level satisfactory to "the quality of the subject." "Blaze," meaning to proclaim as in heraldry, is exactly what Spenser does, especially in the icon of the third stanza, as well as in the second half of the poem—a tableau of coronations. The result is a verbal equivalent to the iconography depicting Elizabeth with symbols of her official attributes and reign. William Rogers's engraving of *Eliza Triumphans*, for instance, shows her crowned, holding the orb of rule and the olive branch of peace, while figures present the palm of victory, the crown of bays, the crown of oak, and the fruits of peace.[44] Further, the outdoing topos "Which in her sexe doth all excell" inaugurates the effort, continuous throughout the poem, to raise the queen above all possibility of comparison. In this case the phrasing borrows Gabriel's salutation of the Virgin Mary, at once reinforced by the epithets "that blessed wight: / the flowre of Virgins." Here Spenser follows the convention which transferred attributes of the Virgin to the Virgin Queen.[45] Such an allusion leads in the poem to the semideification of the queen and in part fulfills the requirement of epideictic rhetoric that encomium be elevated to the maximum.

Following the disposition prescribed by Aphthonius, Spenser proceeds to *genus*, subdivided into parents and race:

> For shee is Syrinx daughter without spotte,   *patres*
> Which Pan the shepheards God of her begot:
>   So sprong her grace   *gens*
>   Of heavenly race,
> No mortall blemishe may her blotte.

E. K. comments on the idealization of Henry VIII as Pan but avoids the touchy question of Anne Boleyn as Syrinx. Such a reading allegorizes too readily, missing the literal sense. For Spenser has distanced *genus* to circumvent questions of taste and realized the topos as a complex metaphor. To begin with, "without spotte" and "No mortall blemishe" borrow further from the Virgin's attributes by making Eliza's birth a variety of Immaculate Conception. At the same time, her "heavenly race" focuses the subtopos *gens* to give Eliza a Platonic origin as one of the celestial Ideas. Further, "Pan the shepheards God" who begets her is literally God or, as E. K. admits, "in some places Christ himselfe, who is the very Pan and god of the Shepheardes." In this particular construction of *patres* Spenser touches on the popular Protestant concept of Elizabeth as God's chosen vessel. Finally, and most important, one must recall that, in Ovid, Pan and Syrinx are notably childless: Syrinx is changed into reeds, and Pan's attempt to rape her is foiled. The only union of Pan and

Syrinx lies in Pan's fashioning from those reeds a set of shepherd's pipes (the syrinx, panpipe, oaten reed, or *avena*), the instrument Colin breaks in *Januarye* as a sign of forsaking poetry. The child of Pan and Syrinx, then, is either the poet's oaten reeds or the poem they produce.

By this development of *genus* Spenser implies that Elizabeth is the force inspiring and creating her own praise, an idea corroborated when the Muses crown her with bays like a poet. But he is also saying something quite different: that, as child of the shepherd's pipes, Eliza is the creature of the poet, begotten by Pan on the syrinx and by Colin on his pipe: only when he articulates her praise can she discern her ideal form and possess enduring fame. The accompanying woodcut portrays this exactly (see fig. 1): at its left Colin piping toward eleven ladies charms them into configuration around the twelfth.[46] Eliza and her group appear in relatively great detail, Colin in little more than outline, thus visualizing the contrast between the simple poet "forswonck and forswatt" and the queen "decked . . . in royall aray." At the same time, the figures of queen and poet share prominence in the graphic arrangement.

Bypassing *educatio*, Spenser arrives at the main encomiastic topos, *res gestae*, here largely realized by emphasis on Eliza's beauty *(corporis bona)*. But he turns each physical attribute in a symbolic direction. In stanza 3 Eliza sits in pastoral enthronement, royally "Yclad in Scarlot like a mayden Queen, / And Ermines white," but wearing a crown "set" not with jewels but with flowers. The scarlet and white adumbrate the queen's virgin-cult, for ermines are an emblem of virginity,[47] and Spenser curiously but precisely gives scarlet the same association here. But they are also the colors of England and Saint George, whose day falls in April. Her crown intersperses bay leaves of victory with a seasonally impossible mixture of flowers (primroses and daffodils of early spring with the damask roses of early summer), thereby hinting that Eliza's regime recalls the unfallen and seasonless Eden. (Another seasonally comprehensive garland appears, with the same meaning, in stanza 12.)[48] Eliza herself becomes a "sweete Violet," a charming touch that typifies the mixture of exaltation and familiarity in this ode.

The fourth stanza continues the topic *res gestae*, realized with great economy by comparison ("Like Phoebe fayre") and inter-rogative topoi of outdoing ("Where have you seene the like, but there?"). Spenser begins a blazon, or praise of beauty by enumer-ated parts of the body, but he soon deflects it from *corporis* to *animi bona* so that royal virtues like "heavenly haveour" replace physical details—strikingly in the lines on Eliza's complexion: "The Redde rose medled with the White yfere, / In either cheeke depeincten lively chere." Instead of conventional roses and lilies, Spenser has focused on the union of York and Lancaster that created the Tudor peace of which Elizabeth is symbol and custo-dian.[49]

In the Aphthonian disposition *comparatio* follows *res gestae*. Spenser amplifies the comparison with an anecdote based on the venerable sun-king metaphor. Phoebus looks out but, when he sees "how broade her beames did spredde," withdraws, not dar-ing "His brightnesse compare / With hers, to have the over-throwe." This is the ultimate stroke in topoi of outdoing: Eliza has put the sun in the shade by becoming the sun's sun. (The woodcut shows the defeated sun sinking behind a hill.) The pro-cess for elevating encomium has reached full extension but with an erotic touch as well, for "her beames" evokes the Neoplatonic and Petrarchan image glorifying a lady's glance.

In the next stanza, Cynthia, similarly challenged, quickly finds herself "dasht." Spenser has to compare Eliza to both sun and moon because, in imperial iconography, they respectively sym-bolize the virtues of justice and mercy proper to an emperor (as the Isis Church episode in *The Faerie Queene* shows). More im-mediate to the present poem, however, is Colin's overtly wary refusal to compare Eliza and Cynthia further because similar "follie great sorow to Niobe did breede," "Warning all other to take heede." This passage strikes an odd sour note. An obvious explanation lies in the popular fear in the 1570s of the queen's projected French marriage, so that too great comparison to the virgin Diana might be inappropriate. In fact, the *Calendar* was published when the prolonged and desperately controversial mar-riage negotiations with Alençon were in full swing. We may also note that, in spite of Spenser's refusal to "match her with Latonaes seede" (Apollo and Diana), he has already made pre-cisely these comparisions.

C. S. Lewis wished "that critics had devoted less time to praising this ode and more to explaining its structure."[50] Once one is aware of the patterned encomium, in fact, an intricate structure becomes discernible.

Colin's ode consists of thirteen stanzas. The stanza at its center serves as fulcrum. By recapitulating *genus*, its first part—"Pan may be proud, that ever he begot / such a Bellibone"—gives a peroration to the completed encomium. If the conceit of Pan and Syrinx makes Eliza the creature of the poet's art, then the encomium epitomizes what that art can do. The second part of the ode translates this technical encomium into an action, anticipated in the last half of the pivotal stanza. Here, laudable exercise yields to more intimate celebration, and Colin appears as "her shepherds swayne" to honor his own creature, now translated by his successful art into "my goddesse plaine." In fact, the central stanza sums up the Virgo-Venus paradox often applied in Elizabeth's praise: by recalling Eliza's miraculous begetting, its earlier part epitomizes the analogy between her and the Virgin (as well as Diana) in the encomium just ended; and in its latter part Colin's language of love anticipates the analogy between Eliza and Venus in the rest of the ode. In "my goddesse plaine," the possessive "my" expresses both fealty and proprietorship and the bold "Albee forswonck and forswatt I am" not so much inadequacy as inadequacy transcended.[51]

The last six stanzas that balance the six-stanza encomium offer a kind of mobile tableau, like the masques presented to Elizabeth in her progresses. As such, they contrast with the static unveiling of Eliza as icon in the encomium. Colin now takes on the role of visionary, or *vates*, rather than an artificer, or *poeta*; in fact, the section begins in the eighth stanza with "I see" and proceeds to envision a literal panegyric, a celebration brought on by the Orphic incantation of the encomium. Spenser thus implies that the poet's vision is impossible without the poet's art, although when achieved it complements and fulfills that art. Here for the first time in the canon one can observe Spenser's interest in the creative act and particularly the interdependence in it of conscious artistry and the mysteriously generated afflatus that goes beyond skill and makes the poet a spectator. Even the management of verbs reflects the distinction between *poeta* and *vates*. In the ode's first half, Colin, speaking as maker, uses imperatives ("Helpe me to blaze"); but, as the second half begins, he shifts to the admiring spectator's role and speaks in indicatives ("I see Calliope") and interrogatives ("And whither rennes . . . ?"). The last three stanzas, however, return decisively to the imperative ("hye you there") as the *poeta* reasserts his role, to which Thenot aptly responds, "was thilk same song of Colins owne making?" The correct answer is both yes and no.

Spenser builds his interaction of *poeta* and *vates* into the subliminal structure of Colin's ode by making the details of each half reflect the details of the other. He does this in two simultaneous patterns: in the first, the halves parallel each other; in the second, they are symmetrical. These two patterns are described in the schemes that follow.

The first shows how stanzas 1–6 match stanzas 8–13 in parallel series, so that stanza 1 matches stanza 8, stanza 2 matches stanza 9. To effect this parallelism Spenser sometimes matches stanzas by subject, sometimes by images or phrases (often placed in corresponding lines).

stanza 1	stanza 8
Muses invoked	Muses come with bays

stanza 2	stanza 9
l. 1, Muses' "silver song" pipes of Pan (the syrinx)	l. 1, Graces' dance "the Instrument" (Colins's pipes)
l. 7, "So sprong her grace" Eliza as Virgin Mary: "flowre of Virgins," "without spot"	l. 7, "She shalbe a grace" Eliza as fourth grace, that is, Venus
ll. 8–9, "Of heavenly race"	l. 9, "reigne with the rest in heaven"

stanza 3	stanza 10
l. 1, "See, where she sits"	l. 1, "And whither rennes"
l. 3, "a mayden Queene"	l. 3, "Ladyes of the lake" (that is, nymphs of Diana)
ll. 5–6, "a Cremosin coronet" of flowers	ll. 5–6, "a Coronall" of olive
l. 7, "Bay leaves" (crown of victor)	l. 7, "Olives bene for peace"

stanza 4	stanza 11
"Like Phoebe fayre"	"Let none come there, but that

"Her heavenly haveour, her princely grace"

Virgins bene"

"rudenesse" of shepherd girls

ll. 7–8, "Her modest eye / Her Majestie"

ll. 7–8, "Binde your fillets faste, / And gird in your waste"

stanza 5	stanza 12
Sun outdone *(comparatio)*	but flowers match her *(comparatio)*
ll. 7–9, "Let him, if he dare, / His brightnesse compare/ With hers"	ll. 7–9, flowers "Shall match with the fayre flowre Delice" (pun on *flos lucis*, flower of light)

stanza 6	stanza 13
l. 1, "Shew thy selfe Cynthia with thy silver rayes"	ll. 1–2, "Now ryse up Elisa . . . in royall aray"
l. 5, "But I will not match her"	l. 5, "I feare, I have troubled"

Coincident with this piece of patterning is another that works not in parallel series but symmetrically to match stanzas 1–6 with stanzas 13–8 so that stanza 1 matches stanza 13, stanza 2 matches stanza 12. Thus:

stanza 1	stanza 13
invocation of nymphs and muses	dismissal of nymphs and muses
"Ye dayntye Nymphs"	"ye daintie Damsells"
"Hether looke, / At my request"	"I feare, I have troubled your troupes to longe"
"Helpe me to blaze / Her worthy praise"	"Let dame Eliza thanke you for her song"

stanza 2	stanza 12
l. 3, "The flowre of Virgins"	ll. 3–4, "Sops in wine, / worne of Paramoures"
ll. 3–4, "may shee florish long, / In princely plight"	l. 3, "Coronations"—a pun on carnation and Lat. *corona*, crown
Elisa is "the Flowre of Virgins"	Elisa is "the fayre flowre Delice"

stanza 3	stanza 11
l. 1, "she sits upon the grassie greene"	l. 1, shepherdesses "that dwell on the greene"
l. 3, "like a mayden Queene	l. 3, "none . . . but that Virgins bene"
l. 9, "Embellish"	l. 9, "For more finesse"

stanza 4	stanza 10
ll. 1–2 "Tell me, have ye seene her angelick face, / Like Phoebe fayre?" (question)	ll. 1–2, "And whither rennes this bevie of Ladies bright, / raunged in a row?" (question)
Phoebe (Diana)	nymphs (Diana's associates)
ll. 5–6, red and white roses: Tudor peace	ll. 6–7, olives of peace

stanza 5	stanza 9
Phoebus	the Graces
l. 5, "another Sunne belowe"	l. 5, "a fourth grace" (l. 9) "in heaven"

stanza 6	stanza 8
l. 1, Cynthia withdraws from Eliza	l. 1, Calliope approaches Eliza
l. 1, "with thy silver rayes"	l. 2, "where my Goddesse shines"
l. 8, "makes dayly mone"	l. 8, "sing all the way"

In the center of both patterns is the seventh stanza, devoted partly to summation of Eliza's praise and partly to Colin's self-assertion as poet.

It is to be noted that the correspondences in the second half poem depend not on the praise topoi themselves in the first half but on their amplification. Even though the triple coronation in the second part implies *res gestae*—victory (bays), peace (olives), and popular affection (English flowers) and suggests the triple crown of the Imperial Virgin, successor to a line of antipapal emperors[52]—it arises not so much from the praise topoi as from the Pindaric tradition practiced by poets like Ronsard and reduced to prescription by Scaliger who, in his discussion of panegyric, stresses coronation, especially with wreaths (*Poetices* 3. 108).

One may ask why, in the calendar scheme, Spenser assigns Eliza's praise to April. By traditional etymology, April is the month of Venus and of flowers, as Isidore points out (*Etymologiae* 5. 33): "April is named after Venus or Aphrodite . . . or else from the fact that in this month everything opens (*aperiuntur*) into flower." The most recondite gesture of praise in the poem rests on this double etymology as realized in the garlanding sequence of the twelfth stanza. It begins with flowers associated with Venus, columbine and pinks "worne of Paramoures." These match the virginal flower-imagery of the symmetrically related stanza 2, and, in fact, the Venus-Virgo paradox is epitomized here by "loved Lillies." But the later flowers of the list draw closer to Eliza who, in the concluding *comparatio*, is herself the final flower:

> The pretie Pawnce,
> And the Chevisaunce,
> Shall match with the fayre flowre Delice.

In "flowre Delice" there is a triple pun: *flos deliciae*, flower of delight; *flos lucis*, flower of light; and *fleur de lis*, iris, with adversion to the French claim in the queen's title (and to the Virgin through the basic meaning, lily flower). "Pawnce," or pansy, derives (as the pronunciation suggested by the nonce-spelling indicates) from French *pensée*, thought. No flower called "Chevisaunce" is known, but Spenser uses the word four times elsewhere to mean enterprise. Together these three allegorical flowers create an association of thought, action, and (if we take E. K.'s sense, *flos deliciae*) pleasure. These are exactly the complementary options of the *triplex vita* presented by Ficino: *contemplativa, activa, voluptuosa*. Minerva, Juno, and Venus, the three goddesses among whom Paris chose, are for him an allegory of the *triplex vita*, and by praising Lorenzo dei Medici for his universality in choosing all three, Ficino made available to the Renaissance a new formula for encomium of princes. The Hampton Court portrait in which Elizabeth subsumes the virtues of all three goddesse follows this convention exactly.[53] Here Spenser manages the disarmingly naive garlanding sequence to compliment Eliza as embodiment of the threefold ideal life. But he does so in the process of working out the Venus- and flower-etymologies for April. In fact, the flower *comparatio* is somewhat weighted to favor Venus: it requires both pansy and chevisaunce to "match" the flower of delight.

If these lines are weighted toward Venus, the closing emblems reaffirm the Virgo-Venus paradox that pervades the encomium. They are borrowed from *Aeneid* 1. 327–28 where Aeneas comes on Venus dressed as a nymph of Diana: "O quam te memorem, virgo? . . . O dea certe!" ("How, virgin, am I to remember you?

Figure 1. The *Aprill* woodcut. Eliza and her ladies, with Colin playing the cornett. From the 1579 quarto of *The Shepheardes Calender*, by courtesy of the Huntington Library.

. . . O, as a goddess surely!") But the impact of the encomium imbues them with new senses (as E. K. reminds us): for Eliza is now the goddess, not Venus dressed as a hunting nymph but a Virgin Queen who is simultaneously Venus and who is erotically joined to her lover England. Citation of Virgil's lines also draws attention to the poet. By making them serve as the shepherds' wondering response to Colin's poem, Spenser not only blatantly salutes his own achievement as Elizabeth's encomiast but also claims an identification of himself with Virgil and so implicitly promises a poem to rival the Roman poet's.

Colin's Pipes

The April ode is a virtuoso piece in which the contrary demands of hymnic and pastoral decorum are set in a delicate tension. An image which neatly indicates this tension appears in its woodcut.[54] Unlike E. K.'s commentary, which sometimes manhandles the poems with reductive readings, each of these woodcuts usually so greatly furthers understanding of the accompanying eclogue that their content seems likely to have originated with

Figure 2. The *Januarye* woodcut. A shepherd with broken bagpipe. From the 1579 quarto of *The Shepheardes Calender*, by courtesy of the Huntington Library.

Spenser himself. Their most subtly managed image is the shepherd's pipe, depicted as at least four different instruments.

The January woodcut shows a shepherd with a broken bagpipe (fig. 2). In medieval iconography bagpipes often connote male sexual invitation (the visual analogy to male genitalia is obvious).[55] Colin's broken bagpipe thus betokens his simultaneous failure as lover and poet.[56] In *December*, pieces of a recorder or even whistle epitomize Colin's failed career as lover and poet. In *August* (3, 6), the lovelorn shepherds appropriately play bagpipes, but its woodcut depicts the shawm (ancestor of the oboe), recognizable because belled at the end and held diagonal to the ground. The shawm appears again in the November woodcut (fig. 3). A ubiquitous popular instrument, it had no special connotation, apart from an association it enjoyed with geese: Michael Praetorius in his *Syntagma musicum* (1615–19) noted that its Latin name was *gingrina* because it cackled (*gingrire*) like a goose.[57] This association nicely sets the shawm players of the woodcuts against Colin who, if released from pastoral, will "sing as soote as Swanne" (*Oct.*, 90). And its commonplace character makes it a ready Renaissance counterpart to the oaten reeds of ancient pas-

PRAISE IN The Faerie Queene

Figure 3. The *November* woodcut. Lovelorn shepherds playing the shawm. From the 1579 quarto of *The Shepheardes Calender*, by courtesy of the Huntington Library.

toral. In *October*, however, an old shepherd crowned with bays offers a young shepherd the actual oaten reeds that symbolize the first stage of the Virgilian career-pattern (fig. 4). (In *Februarie*, 40, Thenot disparages oaten reeds or "pypes made of greene corne.")

The April woodcut shows in the left foreground two shepherds Hobbinoll and Thenot) and in the left foreground a diminutive Colin who pipes toward ladies in court dress with Eliza distinguishable by her scepter (fig. 1). Nine are obviously Muses, singing and playing such recognizable Renaissance instruments as the gamba, lute, and transverse flute. Colin's pipe, which curves slightly upward and enlarges gradually like an ox-horn, has no bell, and is held parallel to the ground, is the cornett (Lat. *cornu*, horn), a wooden horn bound with leather.[58] The cornett was used especially in indoor spectacles for salute (in substitution for the trumpet). In *Gorboduc* (II, dumb show), for instance, there is a direction for a cornett fanfare at a solemn royal entry. And in Marston's *Antonio and Melida* (I. 1) "cornetts sound a sennet" and "a flourish" like trumpets. Cornetts and sackbuts (early trombones) were a familiar combination for music of pomp: Giovanni Gabrieli frequently specifies them in his *Sonate* (now usually per-

Figure 4. The *October* wooduct. Two shepherds, one with the panpipe. From the 1579 quarto of *The Shepheardes Calender*, by courtesy of the Huntington Library.

formed by double brass choir).[59] In his pastoral *Arcadia*, Sanna-zaro excludes the sampogna (an Italian peasant bagpipe) from royal decorum because its "humble sound will be ill heard amid that of the fearsome cornets and the royal trumpets."[60] In their association with the trumpet, cornetts are a Renaissance equivalent to the horns *(cornua)* Isidore describes (in his section on the *bucina*, or trumpet) as identical with Virgil's *classica (Aeneid* 7. 637), so named because "they are used to convoke, and *classicum* derives from *calando* or calling together" (*Etym*. 18. 4). Praetorius also suggests that cornetts are the Romans' *bucinae*, or *cornua*. In fact, among his plates illustrating instruments, that depicting the various cornetts shows them with trumpets and sackbuts (see fig. 5, where nos. 5–9 are cornetts and no. 6 the common cornett, recognizably Colin's instrument in the April woodcut).

The cornett's functions are thus, like the trumpet's, salute and convocation. By elevating the shepherd's pipe to a cornett, the *Aprill* woodcut comes as close as possible to the trumpet, which decorum forbids to pastoral but makes specific to epic, as the beginning of *The Faerie Queene* makes clear: "For trumpets sterne to chaunge mine Oaten reeds."

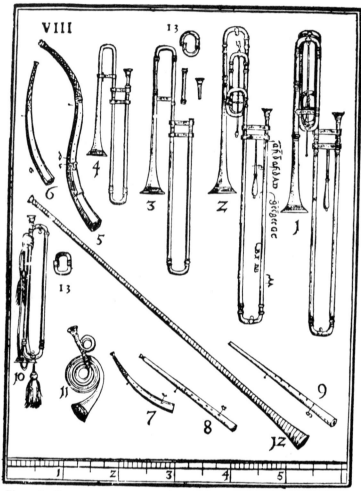

Figure 5. Cornetts, trumpets, and sackbuts. From Michael Praetorius's *Syntagma musicum* (Wolfenbüttel, 1619), by courtesy of the Library of Congress.

The Calender *as Advertisement*

In *Aprill* Spenser uses the Orpheus archetype fully to demonstrate the encomiastic poet's role. But reference to Orpheus is also discernible wherever examination of Colin's status as poet appears.

Spenser never mentions Orpheus by name in the *Calender*, however. Instead, he implies a succession of poets that descends from Orpheus, a scheme of literary history common to many Renaissance critical treatises. This genealogy has three stages: Orpheus, the archetypal poet; then the two Tityri—Virgil, the Roman heroic poet, and Chaucer, the English love poet; and finally Colin Clout, Spenser's pastoral persona. The single direct allusion to Orpheus strikes a typically humanist note: "His musicks might the hellish hound did tame" (*Oct.*, 30). But his descendents' effectiveness is equivocal. Spenser makes the Orphic succession express two contrasting ideas about the poet's power: complaint about its continuous attrition; and proclamation of its rebirth with Orpheus's modern counterpart. This double attitude exactly mirrors the paradox in the encomiast's topos of inability, which combines self-denigration and self-advertisement.

The line of declining poetic power moves from Orpheus's supreme control to the less effective Tityri and the feckless Colin. Virgil, "the Romish Tityrus," inherited something of Orpheus's power, for "the Heavens did quake his verse to here" (*Oct.*, 60). But he was the last heroic poet: the ages following offer neither noble patronage nor heroic subjects worthy of praise (61–78). Attrition of power from Orpheus to Virgil is clear in *The Ruines of Rome* (st. 25) and in the case of the Kentish Tityrus, Chaucer. In *Februarie* he seems to have the Orphic effect: his name evokes praise from both Cuddy and Thenot, and for a moment the conflict of youth and age seems to resolve.[61] But when Thenot tells Chaucer's supposed tale of the oak and the briar, it does not pacify like Orpheus's music but instead exacerbates the conflict, which erupts once more and stops the tale itself. Chaucer appears as debilitated Orpheus again in *June*. His song could not win his lady (unlike Orpheus who won Eurydice with his lyre), but at least he could express disappointed love therapeutically in a poem: "Well couth he wayle his Woes, and lightly slake / The flames, which love within his heart had bredde" (85–86). Furthest from Orpheus's power is the despairing lover, Colin, who complains "I am not, as I wish I were" (105). If only he could inherit a little of Tityrus's "passing skil," says Colin, using the Orpheus formula of woods responding to song, "I soone would learne these woods, to wayle my woe, / And teache the trees, their trickling teares to shedde" (92–95). But Colin lacks Orpheus's touch. He cannot even sing like Tityrus to soothe his grief.[62] And so in *Januarye* he breaks his pipe as a sign of poetic impotence.

But disclaimer of ability is also a conventional exordium available to the encomiastic poet. Colin's protested incompetence and the pseudonym Immerito both suggest that, among other things, the *Calender* serves as an extended inability topos preceding the vast encomium of *The Faerie Queene*. Thus, the theme of Orpheus *manqué* is paradoxical—a gesture of both modesty and self-promotion.

Indeed, the fact of the *Calender* itself belies the protest of inability. Although he had written several poems by 1579, Spenser is careful to publish his pastorals first, conspicuously following Virgil's career, which was paradigmatic in the Renaissance for any poet claiming major status. This career pattern goes back to Petrarch, whose neo-Virgilian bucolics and epic-fragment *Africa* (along with much self-promotion) brought him the offer of the laurel crown from Rome and Paris. From the beginning of the Renaissance, then, a poet who imitated Virgil's career was bidding for official recognition. With the *Calender* Spenser claims that he is the English Virgil, national inheritor of Orpheus's role, just as, in *October*, Virgil is its Roman inheritor. In his preface E. K. repeatedly proclaims Spenser "oure new Poete," an epithet that sets him in competition with Chaucer, the one great English poet to date; at the same time, he hints that, when the New Poet's name "shall be sounded in the tromp of fame," he will eclipse "the olde famous Poete." E. K.'s introduction, arguments, and glosses work directly to promote the New Poet. Some of his glosses are padding, some misleading or misinformed, a few comically redundant (e.g. on "Neighbour towne": "the next towne: expressing the Latine Vicina"); but their cumulative effect makes the *Calender* look like the heavily glossed Renaissance editions of the great classical and a few modern poets. (Mantuan's *Eclogues*, for instance, had acquired glosses by Badius Ascensius and Murmellius, and Ronsard's early poems appeared already glossed by

Marc-Antoine Muret). One glance at the 1579 quarto of the *Calender* makes clear the claim to pseudoantiquity. For the eclogues themselves are printed in Elizabethan blackletter, a deliberately Gothic-looking type used for the sixteenth-century Chaucer folios (the New Poet thus conspicuously resembling the Old Poet), while the arguments and glosses are in a contrasting modern face of Italian derivation. With the glossed *Calender*, Spenser, E. K., and Harvey attempt to launch an unknown as the author of an instant classic.[63]

The idea that Colin prefigures the poet who will culminate Orpheus's line appears not only in *Aprill* but also in *June, August, October,* and *November,* where shepherds recognize Colin's genius as too great for the shepherd world. At the same time, Colin protests his inadequacy (*Januarye, June, December*), thus producing the double effect of humility and advertisement. Both occur in *June* where Colin complains of his "wandering mynde," while Hobbinoll, in an expansion of the Orpheus formula, praises his songs "Whose Echo made the neyghbour groves to ring," and made birds "Frame to thy songe their chereful cheriping, / Or hold theyr peace, for shame of thy swete layes" (52–56). But Hobbinoll has noted that Colin's songs also cause "Calliope wyth Muses moe" to leave Helicon and "Renne after hastely thy silver sound," only "Shepheard to see, them in theyr art outgoe" (57–64). Calliope is Orpheus's mother and muse of "living praises in heroick style" (*Teares of the Muses*, 431). The passage advertises Orpheus's reincarnation in Colin and implies that he will be a poet of encomiastic epic.

In *August, October,* and *November* the retreat of lesser poets before Colin's superior skill heralds him as potential Orpheus. In *August* the poetasters Perigot and Willye cap verses to produce a giddy rondelay on unrequited love, characterized by naive oxymorons like "hey ho heavie cheere." But Colin's solemn sestina on the same subject puts Perigot and Willye in their places as mere rhymesters and simultaneously advertises Colin as a major poet excelling in technically difficult forms (Perigot admires "ech turning of thy verse"). Significantly, Colin's demand that the birds proportion their "yrksome yells" to his complaint is a variant of the Orpheus formula. This is a more assertive posture than that of the paralyzed poet of *June,* unable to "learne these woods, to wayle my woe." And, from the shepherds' perspective, Colin appears as a figure of great success. For Cuddy's ability to "rehearse" the sestina acts out the Renaissance poet's claim that his poems will endure. And Willy's promise, even before hearing the sestina, to crown Colin by proxy (144–45), anticipates official acclaim.

November temporarily goes beyond the pessimistic stasis of *June,* where Colin wishes for "some little drops" of Chaucer's skill. Here, the poet Thenot retreats in silence before the master-poet Colin, from whom "little drops" fall on lesser poets: "The kindlye dewe drops from the higher tree, / And wets the little plants that lowly dwell" (31–32) says Thenot, respectfully, of the Heliconian Colin, "sovereigne of song" and "watered at the Muses well." Thus, Colin has deposed the Kentish Tityrus. The Colin of *November* is also superior in several ways to the same figure in *August:* his ability to compose has returned, and he can now improvise a formal elegy on the spot; it is known that his poem will be a *monumentum* of "endles sovenaunce" that will "aye remaine" (4–5) even before it is composed; and, in the woodcut, the lesser poet Thenot is seen rewarding a shawm-playing Colin with the laurel crown itself.

But pastoral is essentially literature of stasis. As such, it is the natural generic opposite of epic (a polarity Spenser exploits in Book VI of *The Faerie Queene*). When action impinges on pastoral, it is either recounted (as in the fable of oak and briar or Diggon's story of Roffy's fortunes) or foretold (as in *October* or Virgil's fourth *Eclogue*). Sitting and rising formulas intermittently remind us of its sedentary character: "Sitte we downe here under the hille" (*Sept.*, 52); "Up Colin up, ynough thou morned hast" (*Nov.*, 207). Cuddy has sat so long listening to Thenot's fable "That graffed to the ground is my breche" (*Feb.*, 242); and Eliza herself "sits upon the grassie greene" (*Apr.*, 55). Even sheep rearing seldom invades pastoral's dolce far niente, except as a concluding formula (for example, *June,* 117–20); it is surprising to hear so much as that "the Ladde can keepe both our flocks from straying" (*Maye*, 173).[64] In fact, Spenser exploits pastoral's static character to achieve a subtle variety. Stasis in the first four eclogues, for instance, modulates fom Colin's frustration to the implacable opposition of *iuventus* and *senectus* to the sharing of sexual ignorance to the permanent lay of Eliza. But this modulation does not imply progress: readers who try to find subliminal narrative development in the affair of Colin and Rosalind only betray discomfort with the genre. *December* confirms the *Calender's* static nature for, in both form and subject, it restates *Januarye*. In it Colin's situation as poet and lover is the same as in the first eclogue; now clearly subordinate to the annual cycle, he prepares to die with the dying year. But, by making *December* recapitulate *Januarye*, Spenser also hints that the annual cycle is about to begin again. In fact, *December* is exactly twice as long as *Januarye*,[65] suggesting that it potentially holds the succeeding January inside itself. As the envoy declares, the poem is "a Calender for every yeare." The inexorable repetitiveness inherent in the calendar design is thus a structural reflection of the pastoral stasis.

But the two eclogues preceding *December* offer visions of escape. These emerge not through any evolution in the poem but in reaction to its immobile and nonteleological character. In *November* the Christian consolation of Dido's elegy transcends temporal repetition by envisioning an eternal pastoral with "The fieldes ay fresh, the grasse ay greene" (189). And in *October* the stasis of pastoral as a generic trap for the poet yields momentarily to the vertical image of Colin liberated and composing a heroic hymn.

In *October* the line of descent from Orpheus through Virgil to Colin is a line of poets of praise. It begins as Piers attempts to persuade the young poet Cuddy that he has Orphic potential like "the shepheard" whose "musicks might the hellish hound did tame" (28–30). (This unmistakable allusion to Orpheus is Spenser's invention and not in his main source, Mantuan's fifth *Eclogue*). When Cuddy complains that poetry lacks reward, Piers directs him to heroic praise of "fayre Elisa" and her knights. Cuddy recognizes the career model of "Romish Tityrus," at whose heroic praises "the Heavens did quake" just as Hell yielded to Orpheus's hymn. The woodcut depicts the Virgilian paradigm by showing an aged Piers as Virgil crowned with laurel and offering Cuddy the pastoral oaten reeds (fig. 4). On a hill behind

Piers-Virgil is an empty classical temple and an Italianate palace (cf. "Princes pallace," 80, 81). Several figures admire the temple, but one moves resolutely toward it and another climbs its steps. In the woodcut Cuddy rejects Piers's offer by pointing out the figure approaching the temple. In the poem he demurs because he can discern no contemporary material for the heroic poem and hence no relevance in the Virgilian career, for the age of the praiseworthy subject and the generous patron has gone by. Together Piers and Cuddy present the two aspects of the epideictic: Piers sees *laus*, Cuddy, *vituperatio* ("mens follies," 75). At this impasse the dialogue focuses on Colin who, both agree, is the one living poet capable of heroic praise and thus of rescuing the poetic art: "For Colin fittes such famous flight to scanne" (88). Where Cuddy sees possible satire, Colin sees an "Immortall mirrhor"—an image of Eliza immune to calendrical time—whose apotheosis will declare him successor to the hymnic poet Orpheus and the heroic encomiast Virgil. Obviously, the figure ascending to the temple of fame is Colin.

Spenser presents the Virgilian model here because Virgil was born in October. October is the tenth month, and it is the tenth stanza that introduces "the Romish Tityrus" (55).[66] Virgil's birthday was the ides, or mid-point, of October and allusion to him occupies the two middle stanzas (55–66). But October is also the wine-making month. When Cuddy takes the hint and describes his imaginary version of Colin's flight, he intemperately bungles the tradition that a modicum of wine aids imagination (Alciati's "Vinum acuit ingenium"):[67] "when with Wine the braine begins to sweate, / The nombers flowe as fast as spring doth ryse" (107–8). Cuddy's vatic spree, however, is comically brief and only reasserts the pastoral stasis into which he falls back. But his ersatz *enthousiasmos* defines by contrast the extra-pastoral character of Colin's flight "above the starry skie" (94).

Enthousiasmos or *furor poeticus* or inspiration (what we might call the unconscious element in creativity) is one of Spenser's preoccupations. The only thing known about his lost treatise, *The English Poete*, is that it spoke of "celestiall inspiration" "at large" (Argument to *October*). Here "teach," "lyftes," and "cause" imply that Elizabeth herself is the source of *enthousiasmos:* not only Colin's subject but also the power speaking through him (the word's root meaning suggests a god—*theos*—possessing a spokesman). By "immortal mirrhor" Spenser probably means Elizabeth as Venus Coelestis, who, according to Ficino, "dwells in the highest, supercelestial zone of the universe, i.e., in the zone of the Cosmic Mind, and the beauty symbolized by her is the primary and universal beauty of divinity."[68] The mirror Colin admires is clearly supercelestial, drawing his imagination *"above* the starry skie,"* that is, the *coelum stellatum*, or sphere of fixed stars beyond the planetary spheres and, in Ptolemaic cosmology, adjacent to the empyrean and divine primum mobile itself. This passage leads directly to the first lines of the epic where a poet emerges who has risen above "lowly Shepheards weeds" and begins deifying an empress.

The pairings of Orpheus and Colin is built into the patterning of *October* which (like the April ode) simultaneously matches stanzas in arrangements that are both symmetrical (i.e. sts. 1 and 20, 2 and 19) and parallel (i.e. sts. 1 and 11, 2 and 12). In the symmetrical pattern, stanza 5 on Orpheus matches stanza 16 on Colin's flight. The pairing makes Colin superior to Orpheus, for it recalls the Boethian sense that Orpheus mismanaged *cupiditas* and implies that Colin's "love" for Venus Coelestis who "does teach him climbe so hie" makes him immune to the mere desire for Rosalind, the Venus Vulgaris who left him "with love so ill bedight" (89).[69] Some other features of the patterning are worth noting. Two pairs of stanzas reflect the Virgilian career-model. Stanza 7 involves optimistic ascent from "the base and viler clowne" to "those, that weld the awful crowne," and the symmetrically related stanza 14 pessimistically sees no poetry in "brest of baser birth" or "Princes pallace." And in stanza 10 Cuddy understands how Virgil "left his Oaten reed," but in the matching parallel, stanza 20, he chooses to retreat to "our slender pipes." The question of reward (the main concern in Mantuan's fifth *Eclogue*, which Spenser uses heavily here) occurs twice in the symmetrical pattern: Cuddy's unrewarded peacock-poet in stanza 6 is matched in stanza 15 by Colin as transcendent singing swan. More important, the central pair of stanzas (10 and 11) focuses on Maecenas—Virgil's patron now "yclad in claye." The implication

CHAPTER TWO

1590

The Proem
to the Poem

The Faerie Queene is usually read as a romantic epic and an allegory—terms that unarguably account for many of its features. But Spenser himself insists that it is also an encomium. In fact, by reiterating Elizabeth's praise in all six of its proems, he imputes an encomiastic motive to each successive book. He also uses the proems to Books II–VI to announce the moral themes of those books. But the proem to Book I, which serves as preface to the whole work, does not mention Holiness. Instead, it deals almost entirely in praise and so serves to announce the encomiastic strain in the whole poem. Its first stanza asserts that the poem is heroic in genre and encomiastic in intention. The remaining three form a triple invocation—of the Virgin Muse, Cupid, and Elizabeth herself. They anticipate some of the poem's encomiastic strategies, such as Arthur's quest for Gloriana, and culminate in the poet's incantation of an Orphic hymn to England's "Goddesse."

Stanza 1: Virgil, Ariosto, and Spenser

The first stanza of *The Faerie Queene* is a multiple imitation, combining bits from the opening of the *Aeneid* and *Orlando furioso*—for the sixteenth century the most famous ancient and modern heroic poems. Such borrowings announce genre: *The Faerie Queene* is in kind whatever the *Aeneid* and *Orlando* are. But these imitations, by allying Spenser with Virgil and Ariosto, also allow him to go conspicuously beyond them and demonstrate his own uniqueness. Among the elements Spenser adds in each case is encomium. It will thus be useful to examine both imitations in detail.

The following lines begin the *Aeneid* in sixteenth-century editions:

> Ille ego quondam gracili modulatus avena
> carmen, et egressus silvis, vicina coegi
> ut quamvis avido parerent arva colono,
> gratum opus agricolis, at nunc horrentia Martis
> arma virumque cano . . .

[I am that man who once made song on the slender oaten reeds, and when I came out of the woods I taught the nearby ploughlands to yield to the eager peasant—a work that farmers found pleasing; but now I sing of the terrifying arms of Mars and of the hero]

Spenser's adaptations of these phrases in the first four lines of his proem are italicized below:

> *Lo I the man*, whose Muse whilom did maske,
> *As time her taught*, in lowly Shepheards weeds,
> *Am now enforst* a far unfitter taske.
> For trumpets sterne to chaunge *mine Oaten reeds*, . . .

Merritt Y. Hughes has suggested that by imitation Spenser "claims a kind of sonship to Virgil."[1] But the directness of the imitation suggests that Spenser is claiming equality as well: that he is to Britain as Virgil to Rome. This self-proclamation fulfills Piers's prophecy in *October*, but protestation of inadequacy complicates it at once. In fact, Spenser conspicuously insinuates inadequacy topoi into his imitation of the *Aeneid*'s opening. Virgil's "at nunc" leads at once to announcement of heroic subject: "horrentia Martis / arma virumque." But Spenser's corresponding "now" leads not to subject ("Knights and Ladies gentle deeds") but to an inadequacy topos; "am now enforst a far unfitter taske." This manipulation initiates a relentless series of such topoi in all stanzas but the third: "Me, all too meane"; "Thy weaker Novice"; "my weake wit"; "my dull tong"; "my feeble eyne"; "my thoughts too humble and too vile"; "mine afflicted stile." The topos of inadequacy is the most available way of effecting the *proemium pro qualitate rei* which begins the disposition for *laus*. To imitate the

Aeneid's opening implies that *The Faerie Queene* is epic. To add the inadequacy topos implies that the poem is encomiastic. In fact, Spenser at once announces his subject as not Mars's awful arms but "Knights and Ladies gentle deeds; / Whose prayses" he means "To blazon broad." "To blazon" is for Spenser an epideictic verb, meaning to proclaim either praise or blame.[2] Further, Virgil merely lays his shepherd pipe aside. But Spenser replaces "mine Oaten reeds" with "trumpets sterne"—the instrument iconographically associated with both praise and the heroic.[3]

If this imitation of the *Aeneid* proclaims Spenser the English Virgil, his imitation of the *Orlando*'s opening asserts his ascendancy over the most popular sixteenth-century heroic poet. As early as 1580 Harvey reminds Spenser that by his "Elvish Queene" he had "flatly professed" to "emulate, and hope to overgo" the *Orlando*.[4] Certainly Spenser's invention of a new stanza works to his end. In his *Theatrum poetarum Anglicanorum* (1675) Milton's nephew Edward Phillips noted Spenser's stanza to be "but an improvement upon . . . the Ottava Rima"[5]—a rationale surely also apparent to Spenser's contemporaries. To create a unique stanza Spenser takes the ottava rima with its eight lines and three rhymes (a b a b a b c c—that is, *3a*, *3b*, *2c*) and increases its difficulty by keeping to three rhymes, while inventing a more intricate nine-line pattern (a b a b b c b c c—that is, *2a*, *4b*, *3c*), with the ninth line prominent as an alexandrine. Spenser thus deliberately designs his stanza to overgo Ariosto, as well as Boiardo and Tasso who also used the ottava.

In the first stanza Spenser uses only the *Orlando*'s two opening lines: "Le donne, i cavalier, l'arme, gli amori, / le cortesie, l'audaci imprese io canto" ("The ladies, the knights, the arms, the loves, the courteous deeds, the bold exploits I sing"). But he positions his imitation of Ariosto's lines in his own stanza form so as to bespeak superiority. For it is in the fifth line—"And sing of Knights and Ladies gentle deeds"—that Spenser shifts to imitation of the *Orlando*. But the fifth line is also the moment in the stanza's rhyme scheme where it first departs from Ariosto's ottava to become Spenser's more intricate pattern. That is, Spenser conspicuously begins to imitate Ariosto's matter at the exact point where he begins to overgo Ariosto's form. To further the gesture of ascendancy, "Fierce warres and faithfull loves shall moralize my song" recollects "l'arme, gli amori," and (again) "l'audaci imprese io canto," but in the ninth line that caps Ariosto's eight. By ironically setting imitation of matter against novelty of form in his opening stanza, Spenser proclaims himself as the English Virgil who outdoes all the moderns.

Spenser's Proem and Ariosto's

The rest of Spenser's proem shows continual awareness of Ariosto's (*Or. fur.* I. 1–4). Certainly both develop in parallel, from statement of subject to description of erotically impelled hero to praise of patron. But Spenser insistently focuses his borrowings from Ariosto toward encomium. A glance at three of these will illustrate the process.

First, Ariosto's proem has only one protest of inadequacy. He claims only a "minor talent" (" 'l poco ingegno"), which his mistress is gradually eroding, just as love destroyed Orlando. The disproportion between Orlando's madness and the poet's state makes this gesture playfully ironic. The inadequacy topoi in Spenser's proem are equally postured, but, unlike Ariosto, he uses them lavishly to indicate an emphasis on praise. A second example is the poet's claim to novelty of subject. Ariosto promises to tell of Orlando "cosa non detta in prosa mai né in rima" (which Milton will adopt as "things unattempted yet in prose or rhyme"). But Spenser, in the parallel second stanza, claims new material through access to the muse's "scryne" and "The antique rolles, which there lye hidden still, / Of Faerie knights, and fairest Tanaquill." This is an expansion of the idea of praise in stanza 1, where the muse compels the poet to speak knights' and ladies' "prayses having slept in silence long." The parallel is carefully directed toward the idea of praise.

For a third example, we may compare the address of patron (in Spenser's case, potential patron) in the fourth stanza of each proem. Ariosto tells Ippolito d'Este that among the heroes of the poem he will find his ancestor Ruggiero:

> L'alto valore e' chiari gesti suoi
> vi farò udir, se voi mi date orecchio,

> *e vostri alti pensier cedino un poco,*
> sí che tra lor miei versi abbiano loco.

[Of his high valor and his famous deeds I shall help you to learn, if you will give me your ear and yield your high thoughts a little, so that among them my lines may find a place.]

But Spenser asks Elizabeth, whose "true glorious type" is the "argument" of his "afflicted stile," to "*raise my thoughts* too humble and too vile." Ariosto approaches Ippolito with confidence and familiarity and, significantly, without inadequacy topos. But Spenser, taking his cue from "vostro *alti* pensier," creates as great as possible a vertical distance between himself and the queen with epithets expressing her elevation, while the poet affects inadequacy through metaphors of prostration. While Ariosto's presentation bespeaks the deferential and playful courtier, Spenser's is cultic abasement before a divinity. His exaggeration of hierarchical distance is one more strategy for overgoing Ariosto, demonstrating the superiority of his subject, and thus performing the act of amplification central to the epideictic mode.

Spenser also overgoes Ariosto's proem in stanzas 2 and 3 where he introduces Arthur as a hero erotically impelled to discover the Faery Queen—a quest that of course bespeaks Elizabeth's praise. In his proem Ariosto places Ruggiero and Orlando in an epideictic context. He tells his patron that his poem will "name with praise" "quel Ruggier, che fu di voi / e de' vostri avi illustri il ceppo vecchio" (I. 4)—("that very Ruggiero who was the ancient progenitor of you and your famous ancestors"). By making Ruggiero their fictive ancestor, Ariosto can claim that his deeds imply praise of the Este. Rhetorically, this stratagem is a development of encomiastic *genus*. But Orlando's mismanagement of desire makes him a figure of blame: "per amor venne in furor e matto" (I. 2)—("through love he fell into a frenzy and went mad"). Both Orlando and Ruggiero are also Hercules figures, as Ariosto hints by placing their names on either side of his encomiastic address to Ippolito as descendant of Hercules (the favorite hero-archetype of the Renaissance): "generose Ercolea prole, / ornamento e splendor del secol nostro." Ruggiero is the good Hercules who begets a noble family using the name Ercole.[6] But Orlando echoes the tradition of Hercules destroyed by sexual passion. Even the name of the poem invokes Seneca's *Hercules furens*, which takes for its subject Hercules undone by eros.[7]

In his proem Spenser presents Arthur as an erotically motivated and Herculean hero who parallels and transcends both Ruggiero and Orlando. Like Orlando, Arthur is subject to the ambivalent force of Cupid—in his sinister phase armed with "deadly Heben bow,"[8] but in his beneficent phase "Faire Venus sonne." When Cupid "At that good knight so cunningly" (intelligently) did "rove, / That glorious fire it kindled in his hart," he is not the mindless, scatter-shot Cupid, but a noetic energy impelling the hero toward the Virgin Queen. Desire for Angelica undoes Orlando as hero, but desire for Gloriana transforms Arthur into an erotic Hercules whose passion is identical with his virtue.

But Arthur was also, according to official propaganda, a Tudor ancestor. As such, he parallels Ruggiero, the "ceppo vecchio" of the Este. Yet in stanza 2 Spenser surpasses Ariosto's compliment through ancestors by making Arthur's ancient quest, recorded in arcane "antique rolles," a quest for Elizabeth's Faery or ideal type. As "Briton Prince," he exemplifies Britain's longing throughout history for its Faery meaning, "so long / Sought through the world." The poet's sympathy for Arthur's long sufferings expresses the pathos of Britain awaiting the temporal advent of its ideal monarch. Unlike Ruggiero, Spenser's Arthur is not simply an illustrious ancestor but a progenitor whose reason for being lies in his descendant: a deliberate intensification of Ariosto's genetic encomium.

In his demonstration that Spenser was an inquisitive and subtle reader of Ariosto, Paul Alpers remarks that "the opening canto of *Orlando Furioso* . . . is one which Spenser must have known almost by heart and on which he draws time and time again in *The Faerie Queene*."[9] As I have shown, Spenser's effort to overgo the four stanzas beginning that canto relies on an alert search for encomiastic details that admit of amplification and for other elements that he can transmute into praise. But, even while he labors to overgo Ariosto's details, it is from him that Spenser takes license for two major and related ideas: the erotic as a force motivating the epic; and the dynastic romance as a means to

encomium. Praise of a patron through a fictive ancestor originates, as an epic device, with Virgil. As Boccaccio notes in his
Genealogiae (14. 13), Virgil's purpose in praising Aeneas was to
extol the *gens Julia* and so honor Augustus. But Aeneas as national
founder-hero is not erotically impelled: Dido, in fact, threatens
his line. Rather, the erotic as a central epic motivation is peculiar
to the Renaissance, its Ariostan form probably the result of a
deliberate fusion of Virgil's encomiastic hero-ancestor with the
sexual chivalry of medieval romance. Spenser borrows this motivation from Ariosto and takes it so far as to invoke Cupid as the
force energizing the poem's actions.

When in stanza 3 he introduces Mars and Venus, the agent
reconciling them is again the benign Cupid. The image of Mars
"In loves and gentle jollities arrayed, / After his murdrous
spoiles" implies not only that virtue finds fulfillment in Venus's
love, but that English heroism is a response to the queen as Venus
Coelestis—an encomiastic adaptation of the chivalric convention
whereby the hero sublimates worthy sexual desire into "noble
deeds and never dying fame" (III. iii. 1). But the harmonious
union of the contraries "bloudy" Mars and "milde" Venus also
insinuates the tradition that they conceived a daughter, Harmonia.[10] The implicit child is, on the one hand, Elizabeth-
Harmonia: a well-known woodcut depicts her presiding as
primum mobile over the spheres and hence the spheral music.[11]
On the other, Harmonia is the poet's song, analogous to the
spheral harmony: as Comes notes, Orpheus's lyre has seven
strings to imitate the spheres. Again, as in *Aprill*, we confront the
paradox of queen and poet: Elizabeth creates her poem, but her
poet creates her. Of course, Spenser does not mention the child of
Mars and Venus. Instead, invocation of Cupid simply effects
their union, expressed in stanza 4 as the poet's hymn to the
"Goddesse heavenly bright" who stands, like the queen in the
woodcut of the cosmos, outside the turning spheres. The hymn is
a proleptic metaphor for the encomiastic epic to follow. The
poet's praise is thus as much an effect of Cupid as are the heroics
of Arthur and the Faery knights. As Spenser moves into the last
stanza of his proem, Arthur's quest and his own hymn flank
Elizabeth with two archetypes recurrent in his poem, Hercules

and Orpheus, types of the triumphant hero and triumphant poet. Cartari points out the Roman custom of placing statues of Mercury and Hercules on either side of the statue of Cupid, thus emblematizing the centrality of love to both eloquence and fortitude.[12] Spenser's similar arrangement of mythic figures around the energizing force of Cupid also acknowledges the primacy of love as the force behind encomium.

The Muse of The Faerie Queene

Ariosto invokes no muse in the *Orlando* (although the third canto invokes Apollo). But stanzas 2–4 of Spenser's proem invoke the Virgin Muse, Cupid, and the deified queen. Their insistent structural logic appears from the first words of each stanza: "Helpe then, O holy Virgin"; "And thou most dreaded impe"; "And with them eke, O Goddesse." This triple invocation facilitates encomium, for it greatly expands the idea of the poet's inadequacy, suggests the strategy of the hymn, and implies that the subject is three times greater than any attempted before. The muse invoked in stanza 2 particularly fits the encomiastic intention.

> Helpe then, O holy Virgin chiefe of nine,
>   Thy weaker Novice to perforate thy will,
>   Lay forth out of thine everlasting scryne
>   The antique rolles, which there lye hidden still,
>   Of Faerie knights and fairest Tanaquill,
>   Whom that most noble Briton Prince so long
>   Sought through the world, and suffered so much ill,
>   That I must rue his undeserved wrong:
> O helpe thou my weake wit, and sharpen my dull tong.

Whether the muse invoked as "holy Virgin chiefe of nine" is Clio, muse of history, or Calliope, muse of epic, depends on whether one considers *The Faerie Queene* history or epic. On this basis F. M. Padelford argued for Calliope and Josephine Waters Bennett for Clio. H. G. Lotspeich admitted possible ambiguity but felt "fairly certain that Clio was intended." But D. T. Starnes's evidence from sixteenth-century dictionaries such as those of the Stephanus family shows that Spenser's muse is Calliope. He argues effectively that Spenser's contemporaries clearly recognized the poem as heroic; that invocation of the epic muse is hence natural; and that Renaissance lexicographers knew Calliope as " 'praestantissima,' the most excellent of the Muses"—hence Spenser's "chiefe of nine."[13] Starnes's argument is convincing. But no writer on Spenser's muse has noticed that he particularly associates the epic muse Calliope with encomium.

The confusion between Clio and Calliope arises from misinterpretation of Spenser's use of "historicall" in the Letter to Raleigh, and from the similar attributes of Clio and Calliope in *The Teares of the Muses*. When in the Letter Spenser speaks of the "historicall fiction" of his poem, he means heroic narrative and not history in our sense, as he makes clear by claiming to "have followed all the antique Poets historicall" and their successors, and then naming the epicists Homer, Virgil, Ariosto, and Tasso. Spenser also distinguishes between the chronological method of the historian and the artificial method of the heroic poet: "For the Methode of a Poet historicall is not such, as of an Historiographer. For an Historiographer discourseth of affayres orderly as they were donne, accounting as well the times as the actions, but a Poet thrusteth into the middest, even where it most concerneth him, and there recoursing to the things forepaste, and divining of thinges to come, maketh a pleasing Analysis of all."[14] The idea is a commonplace among sixteenth-century Italian literary theorists: that history's natural, chronological, *ab ovo* order distinguishes it from heroic poetry's artificial, plotted, in medias res order.[15] By claiming to begin in medias res, Spenser declares that *The Faerie Queene* is not history as the historiographer would write it but a historical fiction proper to the epic poet. His muse should thus be Calliope.

In *The Teares of the Muses* (1591), Clio and Calliope have similar functions and attributes. Both claim to immortalize men's deeds through the articulation of praise; both have the trumpet as their proper symbolic instrument; both focus on celebration of "auncestrie" (*genus*); and both use epideictic terms to voice the familiar humanist complaint of the neglect of poets and scholars, Clio speaking of blame and Calliope of praise. But only Calliope fuses the ideas of praise and epic, as when she speaks of great men

45

"Whose living praises in heroick style, / It is my chief profession to compyle" (431–32). The phrase "living praises in heroick style" adapts "Carmina Calliope libris heroica mandat" ("Calliope commits heroic songs to writing") from *De inventis musarum*, in Spenser's time considered Virgilian and hence of great authority.[16] These mnemonic verses list the Muses' names and functions in an order Spenser follows in *The Teares*. By adapting Calliope's line to construe "Carmina" as "praises," Spenser deliberately makes Calliope the muse of encomiastic epic—exactly the kind of poem he announces in the first stanza of his proem. For, in spite of qualities common to Clio and Calliope in *The Teares*, only Calliope claims "heroick style." (In *De inventis* as in *The Teares* Clio is in no way associated with epic.) Hence, the muse invoked in stanza 2 of the proem is Calliope.

Spenser's references to Calliope in *Aprill* (100) and *June* (57) show his awareness of the tradition which acknowledges her as supreme muse and muse of encomium. Both references foreshadow *The Faerie Queene*. But because Spenser twice invokes Clio in that poem it is important to understand her interaction with Calliope. In general, the muse in charge remains Calliope unless Spenser announces a shift to Clio for material arranged in the *ab ovo* manner proper to the historiographer.

The first invocation of Clio prefaces Merlin's account of "My glorious Soveraines goodly auncestrie" (III. iii. 4). This chronicle-history proceeds "by dew degrees" from Britomart to Elizabeth, realizing the encomiastic topos *genus* while exactly following what Spenser describes as the historiographer's method. But the reiterated imperative "Begin, O Clio" makes it clear that another muse has heretofore been in charge. This invocation denotes a temporary shift in encomiastic method—from heroic praise to historiographical praise—without implying any change in the poem's generic status as encomiastic epic. Significantly, Spenser embeds this excursus into chronicle-history in that section of *The Faerie Queene* (i.e. III.i–iii) which is most unmistakably organized by the heroic principle in medias res.

That Calliope is in charge of the larger poem is apparent from the Arlo digression in *Mutabilitie* where Spenser again invokes Clio to tell how an Irish *locus amoenus* "Was made the most unpleasant, and most ill. / Meane while, O Clio, lend Calliope thy quill" (VII. vi. 37). While the syntactical ambiguity makes it unclear who is lending a quill to whom, the context removes all ambivalence. Spenser explicitly tells how Arlo declined from "Whylome" (ii. 38) down "to this day" (vi. 55)—i.e. the historiographer's arrangement. So the muse of *The Faerie Queene* is Calliope, who here defers to Clio for a pseudohistorical digression. There can be no doubt that it is Calliope whom Spenser reinvokes at the end of the digression as "thou greater Muse" (vii. 1), the muse traditionally "praestantissima," "chiefe of nine," and hence greater than Clio.

Spenser's precedent here may be Statius, whose *Thebiad* invokes both Clio and Calliope. In the *Aeneid*, however, Virgil invokes Calliope once (9. 525), Erato once (7. 37), but elsewhere simply a muse or muses (1. 8, 7. 641, 10. 163). Similarly, Spenser twice invokes an unnamed muse (I. xi. 7; IV. xi. 9) but Calliope is presupposed. These multiple invocations work tactically to make his poem resemble the *Aeneid*, just as Tasso's make *Gerusalemme liberata* fit his concept of neoclassical epic. At the same time, when we recall the single invocation in *Orlando furioso*—Apollo solicited to facilitate praise of the Este dynasty—then Spenser's reinvocations appear as part of the stratagem insinuating the superiority of *The Faerie Queene* as encomium.

Elizabeth Virgo-Venus as Muse

As well as Calliope, the poet also invokes the subject of praise, the queen herself—explicitly in stanza 4 and implicitly by figure in the invocations of Calliope (st. 2) and Cupid (st. 3). In fact, the three invocations proceed calculatedly from implication to revelation.

The liturgical language of invocation in stanza 2—"Helpe then, O holy Virgin chiefe of nine, / Thy weaker Novice to performe thy will"—indicates the device of transferring the Virgin's epithets to the Virgin Queen. In fact, Spenser places the invocation to parallel Tasso's in the corresponding second stanza of the *Gerusalemme:*

O Musa, tu che di caduchi allori
non circondi la fronte in Elicona,
ma su nel cielo infra i beati cori
hai di stelle immortali aurea corona

[O heavenly muse, that not with fading bays
Deckest thy brow by th'Heliconian spring,
But sittest, crown'd with stars' immortal rays,
In heaven where legions of bright angels sing]

[Fairfax's trans.]

The attributes of heavenly choirs and crown of stars indicate that
Tasso's muse is not, as some editors suggest, Urania (inescapably
one of the Heliconian nine), nor a hypothetical "Christian muse,"
but specifically the Virgin Mary in her state of assumption. The
fifteenth-century *Speculum humanae salvationis* explains that the
attributes of the Virgin of the Assumption are those of the
Woman Clothed with the Sun in the Apocalypse, who conquers
the dragon and ascends to heaven; the half-moon beneath her feet
symbolizes the transitory things of this world (Tasso's "fading
bays") and her crown of stars is the twelve apostles.[17] Spenser
adapts Tasso's Virgin muse to the cult of the Virgin Queen by a
matching invocation. The adaptation implies that the poet who
announces himself as Virgil and overgoes Ariosto means as well
to overgo Tasso. As a stratagem of propaganda the invocation
asserts the superiority of the poet of the Protestant Virgo to the
chief poet of the Counter Reformation.

In this light, the epithet "chiefe of nine" becomes ambiguous:
as well as chief among nine, Calliope as leader of the Muses, it can
also mean as chief over nine, the Virgin Queen herself as tenth
muse. One recalls the woodcut of Eliza presiding over the Muses
in *Aprill*, just as in its text she adds a fourth to the three Graces.
In deliberate contrast to Tasso's Virgin who stands aloof from the
Muses, her brows never crowned with Helicon's fading laurels,
Spenser's "holy Virgin, chiefe of nine" makes all the ancient poetic forces extensions of her power to inspire. The paradox of the
Virgin Queen with the Muses in her train who is simultaneously
Calliope, the muse who praises the queen, is of a piece with the
Aprill paradox where Eliza both creates and receives her own
praise.[18]

IN.SCRINIO PECTORIS.OMNIA

Figure 6. Winged dragon with books falling from a cavity in its breast. From Principio Fabricii's *Allusioni, imprese, et emblemi* (Rome, 1588), courtesy of the McMaster University Library.

Encomium of Elizabeth was a political act. In his adversion to Tasso's invocation, Spenser develops an image of the Virgin Muse's "everlasting scryne" (Latin *scrinium*, chest or coffer) that is both political and encomiastic. For when he asks her to "Lay forth out of thine everlasting scryne / The antique rolles, which there lye hidden still" containing the ancient matters of Faery and Britain, he catches at the canonical formula used to epitomize the papal claim to absolute authority, in particular over the emperor: *in scrinio pectoris omnia* ("all things are in the chest of his breast"). This formula was well-known in sixteenth-century polemic. In his *Delle Allusioni, imprese, et emblemi sopra la vita di Gregorio XIII libri VI*, an emblem book praising the great pope who presided over the mission to England, Principio Fabricii depicts a winged dragon (Gregory's personal device) with books falling from a cavity in its breast (i.e. *scrinium pectoris*—See fig. 6.). But Elizabeth's religious settlement depended on the Henrician Act of Supremacy and its assertion of the supremacy in England of monarch over pope. Its defenders advert sardonically to the *in scrinio* tag in their polemics, the official Anglican apologist John Jewel, for instance, scorning the notion "that all law and right is locked up in the treasury of the Pope's breast."[19] Spenser's appropriation of the formula is also polemical and asserts the Virgin Queen's authority against the pope's. To make her *scrinium* "everlasting" is to dismiss the papal claim as innovative. In fact, this is the first instance in the poem of the antipapalism that colors Books I and V. It is important to remember, however, that the formula is also part of the invocation of the Virgin Queen as muse where the poet appears as a "Novice" just beginning to study antiquities of Faery and Britain that have always existed in her everlasting *scrinium*. (In the chronicle materials in II. x and III. iii Elizabeth is both temporal goal and simultaneously present from the beginning and so indeed contains all of British-Faery history inside herself.) By implicitly twisting the formula into *in scrinio pectoris poesis*, Spenser makes it cooperate in the by now familiar paradox of the Faery Queen creating *The Faerie Queene*.

A similar paradox pervades the invocation of Cupid in the proem's third stanza, where Elizabeth again is subliminally present.

> And thou most dreaded impe of highest Ioue,
>   Faire Venus sonne, that with thy cruell dart
>   At that good knight so cunningly didst rove,
>   That glorious fire it kindled in his hart,
>   Lay now thy deadly Heben bow apart,
>   And with thy mother milde come to mine ayde:
>   Come both, and with you bring triumphant Mart,
>   In loves and gentle jollities arrayd,
> After his murdrous spoiles and bloudy rage allayd.

While Cupid impels the hero toward Gloriana, he is also the erotic force emanating from her. In fact, Spenser does not call him Eros or Cupid but "Faire Venus sonne." Together the two invocations of stanzas 2 and 3 express the Virgo-Venus paradox well-suited to the Virgin Queen who controlled great courtiers like Leicester and Hatton with amatory manipulations; who made marriage negotiations the successful instrument of a foreign policy designed to prevent alliance of the Catholic powers France and Spain; and who, even more, was a Virgin Queen mystically married (in the words of a broadsheet of 1571) to "My dear lover England."[20]

By uniting "triumphant Mart" with Venus "*After* his murdrous spoiles and bloudy rage allayd," Spenser may have incorporated into stanza 3 a timely allusion to the victory over the Armada. The national euphoria that followed the victory naturally found expression in increased adulation of Elizabeth: for instance, on 24 November 1588 she entered London formally in a triumph; and her Accession Day (17 November) became a major annual festival.[21] In a national poem in her praise an allegory of the Armada's defeat would be encomiastically invaluable. It would be particularly apt in Book I, because the English, with an eye to propaganda as well as piety, carefully attributed their delivery to a clearly Protestant God: "God breathed and they were scattered" was the motto of one of Elizabeth's Armada medals.[22] But the sixteen months between the victory and Ponsonby's entry of *The Faerie Queene* in the Stationers' Register on 1 December 1598 would scarcely have given Spenser time to redesign Book I so as to include such an episode. He could easily introduce an Armada allusion into the proem, however, without disturbing the poem's structure, as he may have done with the image of triumphant Mars led by Venus and Cupid. If so, the invocation of stanza 3 presents an anti-Spanish Venus, served by Mars, to complement the antipapal Virgin of stanza 2.[23]

In stanzas 2 and 3 we see Spenser managing his words to gain a secondary set of meanings that insinuate a sense of Elizabeth's immanence and anticipate an encomiastic technique in the poem at large. For, besides representing the queen through fictive *genus* and protagonists who befigure her by *res gestae* and *comparatio*, Spenser also often maneuvers otherwise apparently incidental details into connotative positions where they give off momentary reflections of the queen and imply that she is the principle informing the world as well as the poem.

Stanza 4: An Orphic Hymn

> And with them eke, O Goddesse heavenly bright,
> Mirrour of grace and Majestie divine,

Great Lady of the greatest Isle, whose light
Like Phoebus lampe throughout the world doth shine,
Shed thy faire beames into my feeble eyne,
And raise my thoughts too humble and too vile,
To thinke of that true glorious type of thine,
The argument of mine afflicted stile:
The which to heare, vouchsafe, O dearest dred a-while.

The last stanza of the proem follows the two-part structure of the hymns attributed in the Renaissance to Orpheus: praise by accumulated epithets, then petition, to which Spenser adds in the alexandrine a *votum*, or gesture of offering. There are three such epithets. The first, "O Goddesse heavenly bright," practices the strange veneration of Elizabeth as quasi-divine. The cult was not merely poetic. Roy Strong has pointed out that the queen's image was held to be genuinely sacral and mysteriously expressive of the monarch herself, even by Anglican apologists who otherwise rejected images as Romish superstition; and that people of all classes wore her image on medals and cameos for its beneficent effects.[24] The first epithet not only expresses the cult of *diva Elizabetha* but, through "heavenly bright," also especially associates her with Astraea stellified as Virgo (under which sign, almost too appropriately, Elizabeth was born) and with the Venus Coelestis of the Neoplatonists.

The three epithets progress from the deified to the more nearly human. The second, "Mirrour of grace and Majestie divine," establishes the divine empress's proper relation to God: she makes visible his two main attributes of grace and majesty (analogous to the more usual mercy and justice). The mirror image occurs in all three proems of 1590. The second and third declare that the poem provides mirrors of the queen's realm and person. But in the first, she is the mirror—a mediatrix who communicates the divine ineffability to human perception. This Christ-like role expresses the Protestant cult of Elizabeth as national savior.

The third epithet brings us from goddess and mirror to localized national "Lady": "Great Lady of the greatest Isle, whose light / Like Phoebus lampe throughout the world doth shine." Here, Spenser appropriates the motto of Philip II's impresa *Iam illustrabit omnia* ("Now he will illumine all things"), which depicted Apollo driving his sun-chariot over land and sea,[25] and so asserts that Philip's claim to world domination and championship of the true faith properly belong to Elizabeth. The allusion is apt as a post-Armada gesture, transparently promoting anti-Hispanic imperial ambitions, and turning the outdoing topos to propaganda.

Together these three epithets form a triad typical of Renaissance Neoplatonism, in which the middle term serves to mediate between the two otherwise potentially opposed terms. Here, Elizabeth contains all three elements of the triad in herself. While apotheosis as goddess allies her with God, her intermediate function as a mirror allows her divinity to become visible in the human queen of a real isle. Because she mirrors God's attributes of grace and majesty, to see her is, in some sense, to perceive God himself.[26] That Elizabeth bridges the potentially opposed realms of heaven and earth is an idealistic conception essential to Spenser's encomium as presented in 1590. By defining a real monarch, it avoids the traditional Augustinian dualism between the Cities of God and This World that would set heaven and England at odds and that would place a low valuation on human achievement in the service of the state. In fact, Spenser's poem of 1590 implies as enthusiastic an estimate of human capability at its best as can be found in Renaissance humanism. Because Elizabeth is a goddess, Gloriana's knights can pursue their quests in this world, secure in the knowledge that the good they achieve in her service will be recognized in heaven. And the poet can sing her praise, knowing that it will be in harmony with the angels' hymns. Thus, the triad whereby Elizabeth unites heaven and earth must necessarily begin the first overt piece of her encomium in *The Faerie Queene.*

The hymn of stanza 4 balances on its fifth line—"Shed thy faire beames into my feeble eyne"—which, like the stanza, is in one half devoted to the queen, in the other to the poet. This line marks the typical division of an Orphic hymn into praise and petition. In the stanza's second half, the poet petitions the goddess for inspiration to "raise my thoughts too humble and too vile, / To thinke of that true glorious type of thine." The inability topos is prominent here, and the adjectives applied to the poet—

"humble," "vile," "afflicted"—have their Latin senses of physical lowness. But the extremes of exaltation and abasement and the idea of a humble poet who may be raised to behold a celestial mirror recapitulate Piers's vision of Colin's ascent in *October*. The parallel reminds us that the poet's self-abasement effects advertisement. Indeed, the last two lines bring the paradox into the open, the eighth with its "argument of my afflicted style" still bespeaking inability and the passive poet's dependence on inspiration from the potentially creative goddess if the poem is to come into existence, while the alexandrine—"The which to heare, vouchsafe, O dearest dred a-while"—presents the poem as fait accompli and the poet as active creator, with the queen now the passive receptor. Because the queen is a goddess the poem is made possible, but the articulation of her true glorious type depends on the hymnic powers of the English Orpheus.

Epic as Hymn

As an Orphic hymn, the fourth stanza implies that the epic it prefaces is also in some sense a hymn. Indeed, at the beginning of Book I the poet confirms his identification with the hymnist Orpheus by a judiciously placed tree catalog. A. C. Hamilton has suggested that "contemporary readers would have responded" to this catalog "as an imitation by which the poet reveals his kinship with Orpheus who first moved trees with his song."[27] The main poets to make the tree catalog conventional are in fact precisely those antecedent to Colin in the *Calender:* Chaucer, from whose tree catalog in the *Parliament of Fowls* (176–82) Spenser borrows details; Virgil, in *Eclogues* 8. 61–68; and, most important, Orpheus himself, whose song Ovid describes as convoking a mixed grove of trees and making them dance (*Met.* 10. 90–104). As a result, the catalog appears as a signature of the poet who fulfills Orpheus's hymnic role. Prominent in the list of trees is "the Laurell, meed of mightie Conquerours / And Poets sage" (1. 9). Its epithets not only hint at an equivalence of heroes and poet as figures in the poem, but also pointedly imply that Spenser expects official recognition as national epicist; "meed" inevitably suggests pecuniary as well as honorific reward.

By making an Orphic hymn its immediate preface, Spenser imputes a hymnic cast to *The Faerie Queene*, its "argument" said to be the goddess's true glorious type. The imputation finds raison d'être in Renaissance literary theory, where the hymn was affirmed the oldest kind of poem and, in accordance with the principle of decorum, often declared the highest: gods supersede princes. The revival of the literary hymn by Pius II, Pontano, Marullo, Vida, Scaliger, Ronsard, and Spenser in *Fowre Hymnes* is in part a humanist response to the Homeric, Orphic, and Callimachan hymns and in part an effort to provide modern examples to fill a gap at the apex of the hierarchy of kinds.[28] But when the Virgilian career-model made epic the highest ambition of Renaissance poets, the theoretical supremacy of the hymn was rather awkward. In his *Poetices* (1. 3), for instance, Scaliger acknowledges this supremacy, but he repeatedly proclaims the *Aeneid* the greatest of poems. Similarly, Sidney agrees that the hymnic poets were "chiefe both in antiquitie and excellencie," yet asserts that among the genres "the Heroicall . . . is not onely a kinde, but the best and most accomplished kinde of Poetry."[29]

But the epideictic view of literature avoids the inconsistency by emphasizing that hymn and epic are similar: the fact that the Callimachan and longer Homeric hymns were mainly laudatory narratives of the god's deeds made them appear as divine equivalents to the epic conceived of as encomiastic biography of a hero. Puttenham, whose theory of literature is clearly epideictic, properly distinguishes hymn and epic according to decorum as highest and second-highest kinds but then somewhat blurs divine and princely matters by making them "all high subjects, and therefore are delivered over to the Poets Hymnick & historicall who be occupied either in divine laudes, or in heroicall reports." And he straddles the genres by using heroic terms to describe "all your Hymnes & Encomia of Pindarus & Callimachus, not very histories but a maner of historicall reportes."[30] If we note that the Orphic and shorter Homeric hymns apostrophize the god (usually by a series of epithets or attributes) and close with a prayer and that the Callimachan and longer Homeric hymns augment these two features with a long narrative, we begin to see that there is a spectrum of hymnic genres, moving from the paeanic Orphic hymn to the longer narrative hymn to the hymnic or encomiastically conceived epic. Because of the veneration of the *Aeneid*, the literary hymn, in spite of its position in theory, was in practical terms simply not credible as supreme genre and the epic was. But the epideictic theorist's approximation of hymn and epic bridges the impasse by allowing epic to take on a hymnic function (at least abstractly) and so assert its de facto supremacy without undue threat to the hierarchic scheme of the genres.

At this point, it is worth turning back to the first alexandrine of *The Faerie Queene:* "Fierce warres and faithfull loves shall moralize my song." The syntax here seems perverse: one expects the line should say that "fierce wars and faithful loves are moralized in my song"—that is, allegorized heroic and erotic narratives make up the poem. But Spenser instead insinuates that "my song" has priority over both narrative and allegory, that epic is subordinate to *carmen*. If we read "song" as meaning hymn or encomium, we can see that, given the theoretical concept of hymnic epic, Spenser has designed the line to say that his poem is essentially a hymn and secondarily an allegorical epic. And, in fact, a little less than a year after *The Faerie Queene* appeared, he describes it as a set of hymns to Eliza who "hath praises in all plenteousnesse" showered on her by "Colin her owne Shepherd. / That her with heavenly hymnes doth deifie" (*Daphnaida*, 227–30).

Thus, if we see in *The Faerie Queene* only an allegorized romantic epic, we resist Spenser's assertion that it is encomium. In the epideictic categorization of genres, the epic is by nature encomiastic. What Spenser's first proem tells us is that, in his epic, encomium takes precedence over events. It will be easier to see how the episodes of the poem are encomiastic if we realize that when Spenser associates his epic with Virgil's he assumes that the *Aeneid* is a panegyrical biography (the Fulgentian view, explained in chapter 1); that each of Aeneas's acts bespeaks his praiseworthy mastery of one of the virtues proper to a hero; and that praise of Aeneas implies praise of his supposed descendant, Augustus. Similarly, in *The Faerie Queene* each successful episode in a knight's quest redounds to Gloriana's praise, and each unsuccessful episode falls short of contributing to that praise, though it cannot detract from it. Thus, Elizabeth, through her fictional "true glorious type," not only originates the quests and receives their achievement as a sacrifice to her glory, so that the quests are ultimately hers; but she is also the criterion by which each knight's degree of success or failure is measured. For the demigoddesses who preside over the ideal forms of each virtue (like Caelia and Alma) are types of Elizabeth, as Spenser eventually tells us.[31] The knights' goals are consequently identical with the queen herself, just as the goal of the quest that coordinates the others, Arthur's, is the Faery Queen. Hence, her panegyrical biography is made up of their efforts to achieve the virtues which she embodies and which she inspires. Thus, in a broad sense, each book of the poem can be considered an act of encomium— one of the "heavenly hymnes" that "deifie" her.

But there are also passages, episodes, and especially figures in *The Faerie Queene* that express Elizabeth's praise in more specific ways. Spenser draws our attention to several of these in the proems to Books II and III. An investigation of some of these notably encomiastic features in the poem of 1590 is the subject of the next three chapters.

CHAPTER THREE

1590
One That
Inly Mournd

As one of the encomiastic strategies of *The Faerie Queene*, Spenser identifies various female figures in the poem with particular attributes of Elizabeth. He twice mentions Belphoebe and Gloriana in such terms, but from time to time Una, Britomart, Amoret, and Florimell also express a similar typology. Una, the Elizabeth figure who dominates Book I, is the subject of this chapter. Spenser pointedly makes her the first of Elizabeth's types in the poem, for Una's name not only implies in a Platonic sense the unity behind apparent multiplicity, but also the unity of the several subsequent encomiastic types in the unique, phoenixlike queen. What Spenser especially depicts in Una is the unity of Elizabeth's sacred and political roles. She betokens two main aspects of Elizabeth: in terms of religious allegory, she is the temporal head and genius of the English church (conceived of as an ancient church restored by Elizabeth); and, in terms of Tudor political myth, she is the rightful queen too long withheld from her own kingdom. According to the first sense, Una leading Redcrosse to her father's kingdom means that the True Church guides the wayfaring Christian to recover the spiritual state of Eden; according to the second, that Elizabeth brings England to realize its national destiny. But Spenser's identification of Elizabeth with the True Church conflates religious and political allegory to yield such readings as the following: true belief leads England to the accession of Elizabeth; or the queen guides the Christian believer to redeem a nation. In Redcrosse's quest, holiness is inextricably personal and national. In that quest, Una is both his guide and his goal.

The earliest known comments on Una are John Dixon's marginalia, presumably written in 1597.[1] Dixon was an enthusiastic Protestant and patriot who responded sympathetically to Book I and saw in Una a figure who simultaneously betokens the queen and the True Church. For instance, his gloss on the betrothal rite—"The Church and the Lambe Christe united by god himselfe. a happie knotte whereby peace hath beine Continewed 39 year"[2]—succinctly recognizes how Spenser has fused the church anagogically married to Christ and the queen mystically and historically married to her realm into one image aptly called Una. Dixon's reading probably expresses what every Elizabethan would recognize in Una: Elizabeth's role as at once savior of her realm and of true religion and legally head of both.

These fused political and ecclesiastical aspects of Una are most evident during static moments of suspended narrative that are characteristic of the poem and which I have called *icons*.[3] In these, Spenser pauses to examine a picture of a royal figure whose attributes expressed in encomiastic topoi bespeak the queen's praise. Such icons, indeed, are the device Spenser most often uses to set forth Elizabeth's encomium through her types. Their characteristic effect is revelation that excites wonder and desire: a lion comes upon the unveiled Una and is at once converted to fealty and erotic worship; a momentary apparition of Florimell automatically reorganizes the chivalry of male knights; the virgin-goddess Belphoebe breaks into a forest clearing and evokes base lust from the unworthy. Such icons both transform and inform the narrative contexts in which they appear and are thus akin in their effect to Joyce's epiphanies. But praise through a type can also occur without benefit of an icon. Later in this chapter I will discuss examples of such non-iconic and partially iconic encomium. Icons, however, furnish more immediately noticeable examples of encomium. More than any other encomiastic tactic in *The Faerie Queene*, they convey the sense that Elizabeth's "true glorious type" actually is the poet's "argument"—that she is the meaning underlying both the poem and the real world of which the poem is the fictive image. Three icons are prominent in Book I: the first, where Una appears in the initial tableau; the second, where Una removes her veil and is revealed to a lion; and, the third, where Redcrosse at last sees Una unveiled.

The First Icon: Una with Ass and Lamb

In the first icon Una appears accompanied by Redcrosse:

> A lovely Ladie rode him faire beside,
>   Upon a lowly Asse more white then snow,
>   Yet she much whiter, but the same did hide *comparatio*
>   Under a vele, that wimpled was full low,
>   And over all a black stole she did throw,
>   As one that inly mournd: so was she sad,
>   And heavie sat upon her palfrey slow:
>   Seemed in heart some hidden care she had,
> And by her in a line a milke white lambe she lad.

> So pure an innocent, as that same lambe,   *comparatio*
>   She was in life and every vertuous lore

[i. 4–5]

Here the white ass, stole, and lamb associate Una with the church. Both ass and lamb appear in terms of the typically encomiastic device *comparatio*. The ass image is complex in its suggestiveness. It inevitably recalls Christ's entry into Jerusalem, "meek, and sitting upon an ass" (Matt. 21:6), and so anticipates in plaintive form Una's triumphant entry in canto xii: like Christ, Una is about to enter upon a passion that will redeem a kingdom. Redcrosse, of course, is recognizably the wayfaring *miles christianus* who reenacts Christ's role; but when he defaults, Una herself assumes the identification with Christ that is already potential in the ass image.[4] As John M. Steadman has shown, the ass is also a traditional symbol of the clergy: in Alciati's emblem "Non tibi, sed religioni" an ignorant crowd worships an ass rather than the image of Isis it bears.[5] The parallel implies that Una is the proper object of veneration and so makes the queen identical with the True Church. What the ass bears and the clergy preach is thus Elizabeth herself. But Spenser also makes the ass "more white then snow," echoing Psalm 51:7, "Thou shalt wish me and I shall be whiter than snow"—in Tudor prayer books the psalm proper to the penitential office for Ash Wednesday.[6] These liturgical associations of penitence and purification make the ass symbolize specifically a chastened and reformed clergy. But, by managing the *comparatio* to make Una "much whiter" than her ass, Spenser

thus figures Elizabeth the True Church bearing the reformed sacraments. Spenser's counterpoising of Duessa to Una confirms this reading, for, as Douglas Waters has shown, Duessa expresses the Reformation tradition of Mistress Missa: the Roman mass polemically depicted as witch and harlot.[11] Second, Una and her Lamb offer an anagoge of the mystical marriage of the church to the Lamb which is a climax of the eschatological vision of Revelation (e.g. 19:17)—"the Lambe Christe" John Dixon saw figured in the betrothal—and thus expresses the adulatory cult of Elizabeth that converts the medieval pairing of Christ and the Virgin to Christ and the Virgin Queen.[12] Third, Una's lamb symbolizes her potential marriage to the English knight of Saint George. The lady leading a lamb is a feature of the Saint George story.[13] And the knight's red-cross device is a sign of Christ and Saint George that serves as the standard of England. These two signs come together in the Easter image (still common in church decoration) of the lamb holding a red-cross banner. Here at the beginning of the poem their combination is only potential. But in liturgical terms it looks toward the victory of cantos xi and xii where, after her knight's three-day fight with the dragon, Una as the church doffs her black stole and puts on the white vestment of Easter (xii. 22), reversing her initial Ash Wednesday associations. In terms of political myth, the potential combination of lamb and red cross augurs the union of England with its queen, who has first been seen leading a lamb that externalizes her own innocence.

After these largely ecclesiastical *comparationes*, Spenser caps the icon with a political realization of *genus* (descent): the Lady "by descent from Royall lynage came / Of ancient Kings and Queenes," who once ruled "all the world" "from East to Westerne shore" (i. 6). This kingdom is later identified as Eden, so that Una's parents are, in one sense, Adam and Eve, the parents of mankind, and her quest to deliver Eden from the dragon is the church's proper mission. But the encomiastic hyperbole declaring the whole world Una's legitimate empire also arises from the polemic of Elizabethan imperialists which was based on the medieval contest of pope and emperor.[14] Apologists for the queen as head of the church, such as Jewel and Foxe, cited the supremacy of the emperor at early church councils, a position eroded by the papacy but restored by Henry VIII. Spenser's specification of Una's *genus* betokens Elizabeth searching for restoration of the ancient supremacy of the emperors with her accession—an event that also, in some sense, restores England to an unfallen Edenic state. In contrast, Una's antithesis, Duessa, claims to be "sole daughter of an Emperour" who "the wide West under his rule has, / And high has set his throne, where Tiberis doth pas" (ii. 22). Her *genus* shows the other, antipapal side of the proimperial polemic. For the throne beside Tiber is clearly the pope's, who, by assuming the role of "Emperour," usurps the ancient imperium. The phrase "high hath set his throne" sardonically connotes self-appointment.

The last figure in Una's pageant (one too easily ignored) is the dwarf who bears her "needments" (i. 6). He is usually explained as an allegory of reason or prudence.[15] Insofar as Una is revealed faith, the dwarf is its ancillary, reason (just as, for Hooker as well as Aquinas, philosophy is theology's servant). Insofar as Una is Elizabeth, the dwarf is counsel, perhaps even an adversion to so shrewd and prudent a counsellor as Burghley. In both roles his usefulness is real but limited. As a dwarf he is no hero and "did lag" as if resisting the quest; and his advice in the woods of Errour, "Fly fly/ . . . this is no place for living men" (i. 13), is even feckless: Truth not Reason is the antidote to Errour. But he is a "wary Dwarfe" (v. 45), whose instinct for survival twice saves the impulsive and inherently suicidal Redcrosse from death in dungeons (v. 52; vii. 19–20). Without his humble service Una could not finally enter her redeemed kingdom.

The Second Icon: Una and Her Lion

The second icon occurs at the beginning of canto iii where a lion comes upon the unveiled Una. The first two stanzas of the canto condition our response to this icon. They provide the first instance of one of the poem's characteristic phenomena: the intrusion of the narrator-persona in the guise of a commentator who pretends to be helpful but is actually contradictory. The intrusive narrator in the *Orlando* no doubt stimulates Spenser's imitation. However, as Robert Durling points out, in Ariosto "the most

striking quality of the Poet's many comments on the conduct of
the narrative is their expression of an attitude of absolute control."[16] Because Ariosto's narrator expresses godlike if capricious
dominance, Spenser's takes on a predominantly passive posture,
yet another form of the encomiastic topos of inadequacy. At the
same time, Spenser's narrator-commentator paradoxically insinuates his role as creator and omniscient author. This receives
complex statement at the beginning of canto iii.

> Nought is there under heav'ns wide hollownesse,
>   That moves more deare compassion of mind,
>   Then beautie brought t'unworthy wretchednesse
>   Through envies snares or fortunes freakes unkind:
>   I, whether lately through her brightnesse blind,
>   Or through alleageance and fast fealtie,
>   Which I do owe unto all woman kind,
>   Feele my heart perst with so great agonie,
> When such I see, that all for pitie I could die.
>
> And now it is empassioned so deepe,
>   For fairest Unaes sake, of whom I sing,
>   That my fraile eyes these lines with teares do steepe
>   To thinke how she through guilefull handeling . . .
>   Is from her knight divorced in despaire
> And her due loves deriv'd to that vile witches share.

These lines contain a double paradox, for the speaker styles himself as both helpless lover and poet and he makes the poet both
passive receptor and active creator. Central to both postures is the
erotic image of the "heart perst," which is also one of Spenser's
favorite images to describe an orator's effect.[17]

The narrator's posture as lover progresses in stanza 1 from
generalized male reaction to beauty in distress, to the more personal "I" of mid-stanza, who then responds in stanza 2 to Una's
story in particular. But, before mention of Una, the line "I,
whether lately through her brightnesse blind," where "her" is
without referent as if a self-evident allusion, bespeaks the narrator-lover's obsession with the queen. The words "compassion,"
"die," "pitie," and "empassioned" have both erotic and pathetic
senses, voicing the feelings of Elizabeth's helpless lover England

for her sufferings before she becomes queen—a political myth allegorized by Una's wandering. Significantly, these stanzas come just after the misguided erotic pathos Redcrosse has shown Duessa and just before the lion's true erotic pathos toward Una. The narrator-lover is correlated with both, for his reaction corrects Redcrosse's betrayal and articulates the lion's right response. However, because of the limitations of his role, the narrator, unlike the poet's other creatures, cannot enter the narrative and translate his emotions into action.

The narrator-poet expresses the same passive posture as the narrator-lover. That posture takes two forms, both prominent in stanza 2. First, there is the sense that he is reader not creator, responding with pierced heart and tears to Una's story. Second, if he is the poet, he is merely repeating a familiar story (for example, "To thinke how she . . ."). But both stanzas also assert authorship. "I, whether lately through her brightnesse blind" may in fact insinuate an omniscient poet who has already been blinded by the sunlike vision of the unveiled Una, although the narration has not progressed quite this far. Certainly, at the beginning of stanza 2, the poet's passive and active roles interpenetrate intensely:

> And now it is empassioned so deepe,
>   For fairest Unaes sake, *of whom I sing*,
>   That my fraile eyes these lines with teares do steepe

Here the idea of the narrator as moved audience reaches its most extreme statement, only to be interrupted by "of whom I sing"—the Virgilian *cano* formula that conventionally asserts the epicist's authorship.

In these stanzas the narrator emerges as a playful enchanter captivated by his own effects—a benign opposite to the bad enchanter Archimago who can take "As many formes and shapes in seeming wise, / As ever Proteus to himselfe could make" (ii. 10). Educated to read the poem by the Protean narrator's trickiness in the first two cantos, the reader now openly deals with that narrator as one of the poem's mutable phenomena. From this point on, the narrator's intrusions (especially in the exordia often beginning cantos) remind us that the poem is a kind of dialogue with this devious voice in which our alertness and sense of proportion are continually being tested.[18]

But the posture of helpless author also realizes the inadequacy topos. Not surprisingly, part of stanza 2 develops into a plaintive encomium of Una which is organized by the Aphthonian disposition:

Though true as touch, though daughter of a king,	*qualitas rei, genus*
Though faire as ever living wight was faire,	*corporis bonum*
Though nor in word nor deede ill meriting	*res gestae*

Such praise by topoi prepares us for the encomiastic icon which is about to occur.

There is a polarity in *The Faerie Queene* between symbols of wandering, fortune, and process, on the one hand, and of permanence, epiphany, and even eternity, on the other—an opposition epitomized in the *Mutabilitie Cantos* as between "this state of life so tickle" and "the pillours of Eternity." Normally, the poem presents a hero's narrative passage through the shifting phenomena of experience. But this process is occasionally punctuated by informing revelations serenely unaffected by time. The ultimate among these is Redcrosse's anagogic vision of New Hierusalem "Wherein eternall peace and happinesse doth dwell" (x. 55). Each book contains a major example in what C. S. Lewis called its allegorical core, but which would more precisely be termed matrix (in the sense of a pattern from which examples are made). The House of Alma, for instance, illuminates Guyon's temperance by its permanent image of body serenely governed by soul, an image juxtaposed to Maleger's siege in the mutable world outside. Similarly, certain iconic revelations silhouetted against a context of narrative wandering offer informing images immune to time. The first icon of Una is of this sort but difficult to apprehend as such because it occurs so early that it lacks narrative context. With the second, however, Spenser manages the disjunction between static revelation and narrative flux with conspicuous precision.[19]

After the exordium, the third stanza of canto iii concentrates on Una's wandering "as in exile . . . / To seeke her knight" (a teleological wandering quite different from Redcrosse's impulsive wandering). Then, in stanza 4, the disjunction of wandering and epiphany becomes sharply apparent. "One day nigh wearie of the yrkesome way" she alighted and "laid her stole aside." Suddenly, iconic revelation occurs:

> Her angels face
> As the great eye of heaven shyned bright,
> And made a sunshine in the shadie place;
> Did never mortall eye behold such heavenly grace.

Technical encomium here embraces only the topos *corporis bonum* and a narrator's parenthesis expressing hyperbole. Immediately the fortune-ridden process of narrative takes over: "It fortuned out the thickest wood / A ramping Lyon rushed suddainly." But then the lion "with the sight amazed, forgat his furious force," and the icon is reinstated for three stanzas as he converts rage to kisses and fawning, the narrator expresses his amazement (st. 6), and Una utters her plaint (st. 7). "At last" toward the end of stanza 8 "Arose the virgin borne of heavenly brood" and wandering resumes. But in the meantime the lion and the narrator have beheld "heavenly grace." The encomiastic amplification here forces its way beyond comparisons to envision Una-Elizabeth as part of the fixed order of eternity that transcends mutable process but also grants it purport. To simplify the overlapping meanings generated by this icon, I will separate four motifs: Una as rightful queen, as True Church, as Venus-Virgo, and as poet herself.

In spite of our somewhat insecure grasp of topical allegory in Book I, we can discern in this episode an assertion of Elizabeth's lawful right, particularly as denied by the bull of 1570 excommunicating "the Pretended Queen of England and those heretics adhering to her."[20] According to the commonplace theory of correspondences, both sun and lion symbolize monarchy and hence justice: as Falstaff notes, "the lion will not touch the true prince."[21] Here, the revelation of Una-Elizabeth as the sun translates a hunting lion into a royal lion who mimes out confession of Una's rightful claim and yields her "his princely puissance" (st. 8). As "heavenly grace," Una automatically tempers the "furious force" of the lion of justice, expressing the imperial analogy to the divine virtues that Mercilla with her chained lion portrays in Book V.

Significantly, the lion enters "ramping," or rampant. This heraldic adjective alludes to the gold-crowned lion rampant which was the dexter (and so more honorable) supporter of Elizabeth's arms. The sinister supporter was a dragon gules, the red dragon of Cadwallader (through whom the Tudors claimed descent from Arthur) portrayed on Arthur's helmet (vii. 31). These had been the supporters of the arms of Elizabeth's father, Henry VIII, who had pointedly adopted the lion rampant from the arms of the hero-king Henry V. The lion rampant thus conveys a strong sense of aggressively independent Englishness. When she married Philip, Mary Tudor combined the arms of England and Spain to give Spain the superior position and relegated the lion rampant to the sinister side to honor the Hapsburg eagle. Obviously, the Tudors saw in heraldry a medium of propaganda. Hence, Elizabeth carefully restored the supporters of her father's arms as supporters of her own.[22] The lion rampant who literally supports Una thus recognizes her lawful right even in exile when she is replaced in Redcrosse-England's affections by Duessa. When in defense of "his soveraine Dame" the lion attacks Sansloy by "ramping on his shield" (iii. 41) inscribed "Sans loy," he rejects unlawful papal claims to authority in England as well as Philip's during the Marian period. Archimago's pretense not to understand "what the Lyon meant" (sts. 26, 32) expresses papal deceit in denial of Elizabeth's right.

As in the first icon, Una here betokens Elizabeth as the True Church, no longer, however, under the figure of Jerusalem exiled in Babylon but as the Woman Clothed with the Sun driven into the desert (Rev. 12). As Fowler following Hankins shows, this figure in Reformation exegesis meant "the sufferings of the true Church." Since the sun was a symbol of Christ as judge (*sol iustitiae*), being clothed with the sun comes to mean "the incorporation of the Church in the body of Christ."[23] And in fact for a moment in stanza 3 Una's identity merges with Christ's. For the "ramping Lyon" who "With gaping mouth at her ran greedily" unmistakably echoes Psalm 22:13, "They gape upon me with their mouths, as it were a ramping and roaring lion." Because of its opening words ("My God, my God, why hast thou forsaken me?"), the psalm is an inevitable part of the Holy Week liturgy. In the Prayer Book of 1549 it is set as a proper for the Good Friday eucharist. The allusion makes Una confronted by the lion of "avenging wrong" momentarily analogous to Christ facing his enemies.[24] But the lion is also a symbol of Christ, and the apocalypse of Una instantly converts him into her lover. As he "kist her wearie feet, / And lickt her lilly hands with fawning tong" (st. 6), there is an intimation of the church's erotic image as Christ's bride. As Hankins points out, the Woman Clothed with the Sun is identified in exegesis with the bride's search for her lover in the Song of Songs, traditionally allegorized as the church's search for her lover, Christ.[25] The love between Una and her lion thus adumbrates momentarily the union of Elizabeth the True Church with her lover Christ/justice/English royal power. Significantly, in the next episode the lion destroys an agent of ecclesiastical abuse, Kirkrapine, although superstition (Corceca) and episcopal absenteeism (Abessa) remain.

In this icon Spenser also uses again the paradoxical Venus-Virgo image for Elizabeth. The lion's response to her "sight" with protective eroticism and his own version of *Frauendienst* ("humble service to her will," st. 9) betokens her status as Venus, while the outdoing topos "Did never mortall eye behold such heavenly grace" suggests Gabriel's salutation to the Virgin as "full of grace." In fact, Augustine interprets the Woman Clothed with the Sun as the Virgin bearing Christ.[26] Una's plaint in stanza 7 contains two liturgical allusions to the Virgin. The lion who "mightie proud to humble weake does yield" echoes Mary's canticle, the Magnificat: "He hath put down the mighty from their seat: and hath exalted the humble and meek." And Una's accusation against "the God of my life" (Christ-Redcrosse), "why hath he me abhord?" recalls the Te Deum: "When thou tookest upon thee to deliver man, thou didst not abhor the virgin's womb." Finally, the first figure met by the "royall virgin" (st. 5) on her journey with the lion is Kirkrapine's whore, Abessa, who "a pot of water bore" (st. 10), perhaps a perversion of the water-carrying sieve of virginity which was one of Elizabeth's badges.[27]

Two variations on the encomiastic motif of the queen as the

creator of her own poem also appear here. First, Una's plaint "softly echoed from the neighbour wood" (st. 8), expressing the woods-resounding Orpheus formula. Second, Una's apparition brings a lion "Hunting full greedie after salvage blood" to an Edenic pax, just as Orpheus charms predators into a peacable kingdom. (The turning point is the prey/pray pun in "But to the *pray* when as he drew more ny" where predation turns to worship.) Thus, Una unconsciously preempts the poet's role, reducing him to an astonished spectator: "O how can beautie maister the most strong. / And simple truth subdue avenging wrong?" (st. 7). But the narrator's worshipful recessiveness also paradoxically draws attention to the poet as *vates* who can comment on the icon with omniscience: "Did never mortall eye behold such heavenly grace."

Third-Canto Encomium

It is important to note this icon's third-canto position, for the third canto of Book II contains another encomium, the icon of Belphoebe. Their parallel nature extends into several matters of detail. (1) Una, for instance, is a figure of Venus searching for Redcrosse-Mars, while Belphoebe is a figure of Diana. (2) In the Una episode a lion breaks in upon a lady in a wood; in the Belphoebe episode a lady looking for a beast in a wood breaks in upon a lout. (3) Una's beauty converts the lion's rage to erotic worship; Belphoebe's beauty first moves Trompart to worship but then moves Braggadochio to lust. From another point of view, Una's beauty excites ennobling feelings, Belphoebe's arouses destructive impulses—the two fundamental reactions to beauty in the poem at large. (4) Both cantos pit figures of *invidia* against subjects of praise. When Archimago disguised as Redcrosse accosts Una later in canto iii, he expresses the "envies snares" and "guilefull handeling" (I. iii. 1–2) that threaten her praise in the exordium to the icon. And Braggadochio, with his envy of a chivalric and courtly role and his "vaine of glory vaine" (II. iii. 4), allegorizes *invidia*.[28]

Given the well-known parallelism of Books I and II, encomium in matching third cantos is predictable. Such parallelism apparently does not extend to Book III, which is quite different in its organization of materials. Yet in the third canto of Book III we find still another unmistakable piece of encomium: a realization of *genus* that makes Elizabeth climax the line of Britomart and Artegall. Students of Spenser know that this episode imitates the one piece of sustained encomium in *Orlando furioso*: Merlin's prophecy that the offspring of Bradamante and Ruggiero will create the Este dynasty. Bradamante's vision occurs in Ariosto's third canto. This is exactly why Spenser situates Britomart's vision in the third canto of Book III. For Book III in some form was likely the earliest written part of *The Faerie Queene* as we have it,[29] a poem then closely modeled on the *Orlando* and like it organized by cantos only. Readers of Ariosto's poem still recognize familiar territory when they turn to Spenser's third book.

Whatever the true story of the poem's evolution may be, Spenser maintained third-canto encomium as a recurrent feature. In fact, the device becomes a touchstone of the poem's encomiastic design so that the declining thrust of praise in the books added in 1596 can be gauged by its management.

Una in the Narrative

It is important to recognize that recurrent figures in *The Faerie Queene* do not maintain the same allegorical senses at all points. After canto iii, for instance, the typology that associates Una with the Woman Clothed with the Sun is latent until canto xii. Nor does she consistently figure forth the queen. The contemporary reader John Dixon noted Una as a type of Elizabeth only at those moments I have called icons, although the typology certainly functions at many other points in the narrative. Such adumbrations are not necessarily encomiastic, however. Her death-wishes (vii. 22–25), for example, although they act out Elizabeth's role during the Marian persecutions, more readily evoke pathos than praise: Una herself censures Redcrosse for similar despair, and Arthur recognizes the danger in her resistance to reason (vii. 40–42). In other words, Una ranges in meaning from the encomiastic to the blameworthy, with various shades in between. In what follows I wish to comment on some partially encomiastic episodes in which she appears.

In their separate stories, Una's wandering contrasts with her knight's. His is impulsive and inherently suicidal, evincing through its imagery a descent from man to plant, rather like Fradubio's.[30] Una's wandering, however, is teleological: she not only searches for her knight but also ascends by gradations from the animal to the fully human. For the creatures who help her are, in order, the lion, the half-human satyrs, the beast-tamer Satyrane who is three-quarters human, her own human but grotesque dwarf, and finally the brilliant hero Arthur. To use the Aristotelian terms familiar in the Renaissance, Redcrosse's separate experience declines through the sensitive to the vegetative levels of the soul, while Una's rises by degrees to the intellective level expressed by Arthur's "goodly reason" (vii. 42). The pattern of her wandering intimates praise of Elizabeth as the principle impelling man to realize his proper rational nature.

The satyr episode presents an inchoate form of encomiastic stasis that nevertheless remains subordinated to the conditions of narrative, although its analogies to the lion icon suggest that another icon of Una is about to occur. In both episodes Una's veil is removed, first by herself and now by Sansloy. In the first a lion changes from aggressor to savior, and here Una is rescued from Sansloy's "Lyons claws" (vi. 7) by satyrs who, in a deliberately incongruous simile (st. 9), become a lion. And in both the authorial voice realizes the inadequacy topos by combining passivity and omniscience.

The potential icon falls short of realization, however, because the subhuman wood-dwellers cannot comprehend the implications of the images they focus on Una. They respond to her in three ways. (1) The satyrs and fauns, "singing all a shepheards ryme," make her the cult object of a spring fertility festival and "worship her, as Queene with olive girlond cround" (st. 13). But the veneration expressed by this charming idyl introduces the threat of immobility that pastoral usually imposes on narrative. (2) Old Sylvanus, however, gropes toward understanding Una by expressing the outdoing comparisons of actual encomiastic technique, once hitting directly on the cult of Venus-Diana (st. 16).

Unable to synthesize these in Elizabeth, however, he instead compares Una to his boy-lover Cyparisse whom he indirectly killed—an ominous recollection that dissipates the potential encomium. The sense of threat crystallizes (3) when the nymphs see Una's "heavenly grace" and "envie her in their malitious mind" (st. 18). As usual in Spenser, wherever good exists, the iconoclastic force of *invidia* is latent. In this frustrated encomium, with its attitudes ranging from wonder and bemusement to antagonism, it remains for the narrator to assume omniscience and articulate an accurate response to Una as royal type by interjecting epithets like "her beautie soveraine" (st. 12) and "that mirrhour rare" (st. 15).

At some other points in the narrative Una also implies encomium in non-iconic terms. While the satyrs make her "th'Image of Idolatryes" (st. 19), Satyrane "learnd her discipline of faith and veritie" (st. 31), thus responding to her as the True Church and also as a type of queen, for he first perceives her in encomiastic terms of *animi bonum* and *comparatio* ("He wondred at her wisedome heavenly rare, / Whose like in womens wit he never knew") and *res gestae* ("when her curteous deeds he did compare"—st. 31). Similarly, Arthur, attempting "to read aright / The course of heavenly cause" (ix. 6), wonders whether his succor of Una is analogous to his erotic quest for the Faery Queen of his vision (st. 7). Obviously, the analogy arises from their common typological relationship to Elizabeth. There is a similar case of overlapping types when Caelia, so named "as thought / From heaven to come or thither to arise" (x. 4), recognizes Una "to spring from heavenly race" (st. 8–9). The emphasis on celestial *genus* intimates, in a non-iconic way, the eternal beyond the narrative flux and implies that the queen is a celestial Idea that sheds meaning upon the milieu of experience and history.

Duessa as a Type of Blame

The main concerns of epideictic rhetoric, praise and blame, are related to each other like mirror images: in Aphthonius, *laus* and *vituperatio* use the same topoi. Just as the satirist focuses blame by specifying a praiseworthy norm, so the encomiast can introduce dispraise to silhouette praise. Spenser does this by creating in Duessa a figure of blame who is, in detail after detail, Una's opposite. If Una is unity, Duessa is duplicity. Topically, they betoken respectively the Anglican and Roman churches, and Elizabeth as against Mary Tudor (who brings Redcrosse-England to a dungeon altar "On which true Christians bloud was often spilt"—viii. 6) and Mary Stuart (who claims England in canto xii). Una as the Woman Clothed with the Sun is matched by Duessa as the scarlet-clad Whore of Babylon "with whom the kings of the earth committed fornication" (Rev. 17:1). Una's expression of Elizabeth's Venus-Virgo cult is parodied by Duessa's oxymoron of herself as "virgin widow" (ii. 24), a legally impossible state. And Una's ass betokening the reformed clergy negates Duessa's "wanton palfrey" (ii. 13), which probably means the lascivious Roman priesthood of Protestant polemic, later replaced by the obscene seven-headed beast of papal power. Similarly, Una's chaste wimple and stole (offering a glimpse of reformed episcopal vestments) matches Duessa's headgear "like a Persian mitre" (ii. 13)—(Jewel speaks of "the tyranny of the Bishops of Rome and their barbarous Persian-like pride")[31] which becomes a "triple crowne" (vii. 16) or "crowned mitre" (vii. 25), pointing to papal assumption of imperium, while her "gold and purple pall" (vii. 16) becomes a papal disguise for the scarlet dress of the Whore of Babylon. Further, the unveiling of Una has its demonic parody in the stripping of Duessa, ironically realized as dispraise of the body from head to toe, including a distorted inadequacy topos: "Her neather parts, the shame of all her kind, / My chaster Muse for shame doth blush to write" (viii. 48).

The polemical impetus that leads Spenser to invent such a figure appears, for example, in an official prayer for the queen in 1580: "Strengthen her hand, to strike the stroke of the ruin of all their superstition ["our enemies," "Antichrist"], to double into the bosom of that rose-coloured whore that which she hath poured out against thy Saints, that she may give the deadly wound not to one head, but to all the heads of that cruel beast."[32] Duessa's beast is not only the seven-headed beast of Revelation but also the Lernean hydra slain by Hercules (vii. 17). Another official prayer uses exactly this image for Spain and Rome:

74

"Break, O Lord, the Hydra his heads."[33] The hydra or a woman with a hydra was a standard emblem of *invidia*.[34] By making Duessa's beast a hydra, Spenser insinuates that the Hispano-papal response to Elizabeth is envy—the force that conventionally threatens the praiseworthy.

Finally, as Una overlaps Caelia as a royal type and shares her celestial *genus*, so Duessa overlaps Lucifera, riding beside her in the procession of sins and sharing that fake queen's *genus* from Pluto and Proserpina. Duessa's descent from Pluto insidiously underlies the description of Redcrosse after he has coupled with her and been surprised by Orgoglio: "Disarmd, disgrast, and inwardly dismayde" (vii. 11)—a line important enough to be soon redacted "disarmed, dissolute, dismaid" (vii. 51). Each of these verbs puns doubly or triply with the last suggesting Dis's (Pluto's) maid—an infernal version of the epithets "pure unspotted Maid" and "royall Mayd" applied to Una (vi. 46–47). Both versions of the line utter the name Dis three times in a demonic formula that reverses the conditions in which Redcrosse set out (1) wearing the ancient armor of the Christian virtues (but now "disarmd"), (2) aided by grace (now "disgust") and absolution (now "dissolute") through (3) the agency of a maid (now "dismaid"). While Una-Elizabeth-ecclesia guides Redcrosse-England to redeem Eden from its wasteland condition, Dis's maid plays the role of a female Pluto who ravishes a male Proserpina, Georgos, whose saintly name means earthworker or plowman and so connotes fertility (like Proserpina in her spring phase). She then delivers him to a destructive earthquake figure whose name *Ge*aunt *Org*oglio parodies Georgos and so represents negation of England's Edenic possibility.[35]

In fundamental terms, Duessa expresses envy of Una. In this role she overlaps Archimago, another sometime papal figure who "hated" Una "as the hissing snake, / And in her many troubles did most pleasure take" (ii. 9). Both of them lay "envies snares" (iii. 1) for her. As enemy to the good, the creative, and the praiseworthy, envy is an omnipresent threat in Renaissance culture, and Spenser is particularly sensitive to its capacity to harm. His canon begins with a charm against envy in the envoy that precedes the *Calender*, and it ends in total irony with the Triumph of

Envy in Book VI of *The Faerie Queene*. In the figure of Duessa, envy seeks to destroy or at least supplant Una as both rightful queen and True Church in the affections of Redcrosse-England. More broadly, she presents envy's assault on encomium and so on the poem itself. It is interesting—and disturbing—to observe the interaction of envy and praise as Spenser's encomium proceeds.

The Third Icon: Una in Her Realm

Canto xii centers on the icon of Una unveiled to Redcrosse, flanked by two other encomiastic events betokening Una's *genus*: her entry into her ancestral kingdom and her father's performance of the betrothal rite. With such phrases as "That aged Sire" (st. 3), "that ancient Lord and aged Queene, / Arayd in antique robes" (st. 5), "that hoarie king" (st. 12), "That auncient Lord" (st. 15), Spenser assiduously reaffirms the antiquity of Una's *genus* asserted at the beginning of the book and so voices the Anglican apologists' claim that the Elizabethan church restored the independent British church founded in the apostolic age and equal in antiquity to the church of Rome. The first Christian emperor, Constantine, of partly British descent, supposedly brought Christianity as a state religion from Britain to Rome and to the undivided empire—the "east to Westerne shore" ruled by Una's ancient parents.[36] Foxe asserts that Elizabeth not only inherits Constantine's role but also outdoes him in it.[37] In the 1563 edition of *Actes and Monuments* she even appears enthroned inside a decorated capital *C* beginning the word "Constantine."[38]

Una's entry into her ancient parents' realm acts out Elizabeth's restoration of the British church. Her father is a "royall Pere" (st. 17)—not only her *père* and peer (as Elizabeth equals Constantine) but also equal among the fathers of the British church ("sage and sober Peres," st. 5) as listed by Foxe. Further, "royall Pere" points to the British kings' ancient supremacy over the church, said to be confessed in a letter from Eleutherius, bishop of Rome, to Lucius, first Christian king of the Britons: "you be God's vicar in your kingdom."[39] Spenser extends this claim further by making Una's father a priest-king who, acting literally as God's vicar, himself performs the "sacred rites" of betrothal with "His owne two hands, for such a turne most fit," kindling "The housling fire" (the rite that begins the Easter feast) and sprinkling holy water (sts. 36–37). The ancient British king who subsumes sacerdotium in imperium accords with the Tudor reading of the papal-imperial controversy. And he affirms Elizabeth's inheritance of this role by acknowledging, with puns on her name, "The fairest Un' his *onely* daughter deare, / His *onely* daughter, and his *onely* heyre" (st. 21). Like Lucius, Elizabeth is God's vicar in her realm and, more ambitiously, from Constantine inherits the role of Christian empress of East and West.

Una's triumphal entry impinges on the iconic in stanza 8 where the procession stops and maidens "her ador'd by honorable name" but differs from the frustrated icon among the satyrs by its sense of recognition. Here, Spenser makes the deliberately false step of a *comparatio* to Diana (st. 7), too obdurately virginal for a betrothal, only to abandon the attempt because Una, once perceived as she is, makes comparison impertinent: "Who in her selfe-resemblance well beseene, / Did seeme such, as she was, a goodly maiden Queene." (In amplification of encomium, irrelevance of comparison is the ultimate tactic.) Coronation with a garland has venereal associations, for it redeems the garlanding attempts earlier in this book, all connected with lascivious Venuses, and is the typical act of a spring fertility festival. Together with the references to Diana and a maiden queen, it produces the Virgo-Venus paradox characteristic of Elizabeth's praise. The coronation "twixt earnest and twixt game" blurs the line between fiction and history, presenting at once a play-form and a typological anticipation of the queen's accession and coronation.

The apotheosis in the icon itself (sts. 21–24) is more anagogic. Technically, it amplifies *corporis bonum* (Una's "heavenly beautie" of st. 22) with a sun comparison. But Spenser arranges this icon so that the entry of Una unveiled mimes out the stages of an actual sunrise. At first (st. 21) Una comes forth not like the sun rising but rather like the morning star "To tell that dawning day is drawing neare." But instead of proceeding to the "long wished light" anticipated by the imagery, Spenser diverges during stanza 22 to dwell on Una's garment, "All lilly white, withoutten spot, or pride." Here the lilies of virginity fuse with the erotic allusion (noted by Upton)[40] to the beloved in the Song of Songs 4:9, "Thou art all faire, my love; there is no spot in thee," to create the Virgo-Venus paradox once more. At the same time, since Una has just "layd her mournefull stole aside, / And widow-like sad wimple throwne away" (the Lenten accouterments of "her wearie journey"), her mysterious white garment, "That seemd like silke and silver woven neare, / But neither silke nor silver therein did appeare," points to the church putting on the vestments of Easter. When the narrator returns in stanza 23 to the sun image to find it already risen in "The blazing brightnesse of her beauties beame, / And glorious light of her sunshiny face," he retreats, protesting incompetence: "My ragged rimes are all too rude and bace." The delaying tactic gives a sense of climax to this icon where Una fuses the royal sun-image with the ecclesiastical Woman Clothed with the Sun, as in the icon of canto iii; but there it is plaintive, here, triumphant. Once again, the polarity between Una's brightness and the poet's inadequacy is exactly that in the hymnic climax of the first proem.

Like the other icons of Una, this apotheosis of "Her heavenly lineaments" provides a moment of perceived eternity beyond the mutable world, a "celestiall sight" that is for Redcrosse the erotic analogy to his vision of New Hierusalem, now become the "new Jerusalem . . . prepared as a bride adorned for her husband" of Rev. 21:2. At such moments Spenser typically complicates visionary encomium by introducing comic or playful elements. Here, the solemn ceremony of betrothal, issuing from the mystery of the revealed Una, shatters as Archimago breaks in, characteristically overplaying his current role of "breathlesse" messenger: "falling flat" before the ancient king, "great humblesse he did make, / And kist the ground, *whereon his foot was pight*" (st. 25). If this last detail means the ground the king stands on, it is redundant but recalls the similar pleonasms of Archimago's first appearance in the poem.[41] If it means the actual ground under the foot itself, it is visually absurd, an attempt to exceed the excessively sycophantic gesture of kissing the royal foot. In either case, Archimago's obsequious punctilio burlesques ceremony itself and parodies the venerable dignity of Una's father, who is about to respond to her decorous entry ("that her right well became") with a formal oration. But the oration, reduced by metonymy to "thus," never takes place: the aged king *"Thus* gan to say. But eare he *thus* had said . . . "A moment later, "thus" betokens not the oration but the letter displacing it, "Which he disclosing, red *thus,* as the paper spake" (st. 25). The basic comic strategy of incongruous juxtaposition extends to the voice of the narrator who, in a moment of overconfident omniscience, anticipates the "great wisdome, and grave eloquence" of a speech that is not delivered. Since wisdom joined to eloquence is a commonplace among the goals of humanist rhetoric, the narrator is acclaiming the speech in advance as a model oration. Frequently the narrator offers us easy, approving platitudes only to turn and reexamine them with an instructive irony. Here, Spenser trips up his narrator with the same tactic.

Such playful variance is a typical strategy in the 1590 *Faerie Queene,* which continually demands that we perceive in more than one way.[42] The combination of apotheosis and burlesque brings about a multiple perspective that prevents us from seeing only the ideal. While it suggests how the queen makes eternity momentarily perceptible in time, it simultaneously asserts mutability. The attitude as a whole is ironic (and, like most irony, latently pessimistic).

Opposition of mutability and eternity is built into the fabric of the canto itself. For, as well as Archimago's comic yet sinister interruption and Duessa's continuing claim, there are other reminders of mutability like the "proud luxurious pompe . . . swollen up but late" in princes' courts (st. 14); the "Unhappie" "hard necessitie" (st. 19) that takes priority over the imagination's longing for "ease and everlasting rest" (st. 17); Archimago's escape despite "continuall watch" (st. 36); the "feare of evill fates" (st. 37) that threaten consummation of the marriage; "the dull Melancholy" (st. 38) that music merely restraints; and finally Una's being "left to mourne" (st. 41). But at the same time these typically Spenserian gestures of *lacrimae rerum* occur in a canto remarkable for its indications of structural symmetry which imply the permanence of the poetic monument and so offer a temporal adumbration of eternity. Just as the earthly "song of love" (st. 38) celebrating the union of England and its goddess is echoed by the "trinall triplicities" singing the divine love "on hye" (st. 39), so this epithalamic canto echoes, to a degree, the perfect order of the angelic music.

One obvious clue to its order is the similarity of the first and last stanzas. This stanza pairing hints at a larger mirror-image symmetry, beginning at either end and meeting in the middle. Hence, of the canto's forty-two stanzas, those of the first half (i.e. st. 1–21) match the corresponding stanzas of the second half beginning from the last stanza (i.e. sts. 42–22). Such a symmetry can be traced for several stanzas at either end, then becomes less pronounced. It appears in the form of complementary subjects, complementary phrases in corresponding lines, and even as identical words in corresponding lines:

stanza 1		stanza 42	
poem as ship		poem as ship	
l. 3	"land"	l. 3	"land"
l. 7	"her journeyes end"	l. 7	"And then againe abroad"

stanza 2		stanza 41	
l. 7	"that balefull Beast"	l. 7	"that monstruous beast"

stanza 3		stanza 40	
l. 1–2	"hastie joy" of "That aged Sire"	l. 1	"great Joy . . . of young and old"
l. 2	"all that land"	l. 2	"throughout the land"
l. 4	"understand"(rhyme words)	l. 4	"understand"
l. 7	"hand"	l. 7	"hand"

stanza 4	stanza 39
earthly music heard in heaven: "triumphant Trompets *sownd* on hye,/That sent to *heaven* the ecchoed report"	angelic music heard on earth: "a *heavenly* noise/Heard *sownd* through all the Palace"

stanza 5	stanza 38
processional entry of Una's parents	"great feast to solemnize" the betrothal
l. 7 "armes to sownd"	l. 7 "warbling notes to play"
l. 9 "signe of victorie and peace"	l. 9 "song of love and jollity"

the sixth stanza from the end (st. 37) the quasi-nuptial betrothal takes place. In that stanza, repetition of "ever" points to a permanence symbolized by the secret lamp. But six is also here the number of "hard necessity"—"the terme of those six yeares" (st. 19) that intrudes between the betrothal and the return of Redcrosse "The marriage to accomplish." That is, six as the number of marriage is subjected to the paradoxical meaning of seven ("hard necessity" versus "for ever") with their interaction implicit in their multiple, forty-two. The paradoxical meaning of seven is worked out nicely in the sequence of stanzas sixth and seventh from either end, when the stanza of youths and maidens (st. 6) is succeeded by the threateningly virginal figure of Diana (st. 7), while the threat from Archimago (st. 36) is succeeded by the betrothal (st. 37). At the same time, Diana betokens permanent virginity, and Archimago is a manipulator of changes, so that the paradoxical meaning of seven is complete in both stanzas.[44]

Finally, it is important to recognize that the poem-ship metaphors beginning and ending this canto's symmetry are part of its texture of water and marine imagery.[45] For Redcrosse, "swimming in that sea of blisfull joy" (st. 41), his betrothed is the sea-born Venus. For the narrator to tell Una's unveiled beauty would be "to strive against the streame" (st. 23). These images extend a larger marine metaphor for Redcrosse and Una's wanderings. The knight recounts "his voyage long" (st. 15) through a "sea of deadly daungers" (st. 17), and Una's adventures become a movement from sea to shore where she "Must landed be, now at her journeys end" (st. 1). Underlying both is an implicit analogy to Ulysses' voyage homeward. Earlier, in a playful *comparatio*, the narrator has described Una seeking her knight "With paines farre passing that long wandring Greeke" (iii. 21). Here, Redcrosse's tale of his wanderings told to the king of Eden recalls Ulysses' account of his marine adventures to Alcinous who rules a garden-paradise (*Od.* 9–12). The parallelism of episodes in Books I and II reinforces the Ulysses-typology, for Guyon's voyage (II. ii) overtly reenacts Ulysses', and its goal is unmistakably anti-Circean. That Una as well as Redcrosse should appear as Ulysses is of a piece with their interchangeability of associations. But she also has the role of Penelope, type of the faithful wife. The second-last stanza, where Redcrosse purposes "Unto his Faerie Queene backe to returne: / The which he shortly did, and Una left to mourne," strongly evokes Ulysses' telling Penelope of his new and fatal voyage (*Od.* 23. 250–85).[46] But here Spenser refocuses the motif of Redcrosse-Ulysses' second voyage to find its meaning in the queen. For at the end of this canto the hero's range of movement is circumscribed by two encomiastic types: he leaves Una-Elizabeth only to serve Gloriana-Elizabeth.

The bent of the marine imagery is to link Una's ancestral kingdom, Eden, with Elizabeth's island realm—"This other Eden, demi-paradise," "This precious stone set in the silver sea" eulogized in *Richard II* (act 2, scene 1). In this context the Ulysses analogy, with its sense of an exile returning to purge his homeland, agrees with the Elizabethan apology that, after ages of wandering and error, Britain had recovered its ancient pristine church and its traditional independence with Elizabeth's accession. In fact, the marine imagery implies that by entering her realm Elizabeth has restored Britain to its antique status among the Fortunate Isles of fabulous geography.[47]

Canto xii is multiply suggestive. In the betrothal of Una-Elizabeth-True Church-Diana-Venus-Penelope-truth to Redcrosse-England-Saint George-Christ-Hercules-Mars-Ulysses-soul, the planes of meaning intersect freely. Looking at this canto as the climax of Book I, we can see why Spenser made Una the first encomiastic type of Elizabeth in the poem. She stands, in broad terms, for the oneness behind multiplicity and, more precisely, for the unity that underlies the many facets of the queen's praise. As the encomiastic types of Elizabeth accumulate in the poem of 1590, her initial praise through Una gathers these into one.

CHAPTER FOUR

1590

Mirrours More
Then One

The image of the mirror occurs in all three proems of 1590, each time with a different sense. In the first, Elizabeth is herself "Mirrour of grace and Majestie divine," reflecting God's attributes to human eyes. In the third, the "mirrours more then one" are her encomiastic types expressed through the poem's heroines like Una (in fact, a possible sense of "more then one" is "in addition to Una"). The most important of these are the subject of the present chapter: Belphoebe, Amoret, and Florimell. Since Gloriana is the goal of the Tudor ancestor-figure Arthur and Britomart the queen's fictive progenitrix, I will discuss them in the following chapter on Elizabeth's *genus*. Like Una, these figures mime out in the narrative the various *res gestae* of Elizabeth and so help realize in *The Faerie Queene* an encomiastic epic like the Fulgentian *Aeneid*. Indeed, Spenser manages the mirror image of the proem to Book II, which makes the poem itself a "faire mirrhour," to draw attention to the queen's *res gestae* and *genus* in that book. Through "certaine signes here set in sundry place," the queen may view her own "face," "realmes," and "great auncestry" (st. 4). Spenser thus overtly points out the two encomiastic set pieces of Book II: the third-canto exercise in *corporis bona* where the icon of Belphoebe mirrors the Virgin Queen's beauty (four stanzas are literally devoted to her face); and the tenth-canto exercise in *genus*—her history as read by Arthur and Guyon. Further, by including her "realmes in lond of Faery" in the same list as "face" and "auncestry," he draws attention to signs, in Book II, of Elizabeth's praise as ruler of a potential empire—a feature I will discuss in the second section of this chapter.

These indications of the nature of encomium in Book II emerge from a playful process earlier in the proem where the poet-commentator attempts to answer the perversely literal question "Where is that happy land of Faery?" with an equally perverse geographical speculation that, since now "dayly" "Many great Regions are discovered," the location of Faeryland may be too.[1] From this pseudonaive defence against the ancient charge that poets tell lies, the poet suddenly takes on a prophetic role: "later times" may even find worlds "within the Moones faire shining spheare," and indeed "such to *some* appeare." From the obdurately literal geographer emerges the visionary geographer, the *vates* who discerns in Faeryland the Idea of the Elizabethan state. The false geographical problem that the poet poses only to rescue us allows Spenser to introduce a list of American discoveries:

> Who ever heard of th'Indian Peru?
> Or who in venturous vessell measured
> The Amazons huge river now found trew?
> Or fruitfullest Virginia who did ever vew?
>
> [st. 2]

He deploys these references in a scheme of amplification called auxesis or *incrementum*, realized "by making the latter word always exceed the former, in force of signifycation,"[2] and here culminating in the oxymoron "fruitfullest Virginia" that expresses the Venus-Diana paradox of the queen herself. These American references praising Elizabeth initiate a recurrent New World motif in Book II. In 1584 Raleigh had named the vague area north from Spanish Florida "Virginia," a grand gesture extending the cult of the Virgin Queen to an anticipated American empire.[3] That Spenser incorporates American allusions including "frutifullest Virginia" in a book where the queen's encomiastic icon is the virgin Belphoebe points to a connection between Belphoebe and the New World. In what follows, I shall describe the icon of Belphoebe and then explore some of the American context of Book II of which that icon is the cultic center.

The Icon of Belphoebe

Unlike the matching third-canto icon of Una, the apparition of
Belphoebe is so sharply disjunctive from context that Harry Berger has discussed it in terms of "conspicuous irrelevance."[4] While
Una's icon evokes erotic and pathetic feelings, Belphoebe's aloof
icon corresponds to her magisterially competent and detached
virginity. Both realize the topos *corporis bona*, with Belphoebe's by
far the more elaborate. It doubles the form of blazon or catalogue
raisonné of the body from head to foot, each part compared to
something conventionally beautiful, by adding a subsequent
catalog from foot to head.

A swiftly escalated scheme of auxesis introduces the blazon:

> Eftsoone there stepped forth
> A goodly Ladie clad in hunters weed,
> That seemd to be a woman of great worth,
> And by her stately portance, borne of heavenly birth.
>
> [iii.21]

Berger notes that these images in reversed order furnish the disposition for the blazon, which progresses from the divine nature
of Belphoebe's face to the figure she cuts in her hunting costume.[5]
This arrangement juxtaposes hyperbole with realism and so is
inherently comic. In fact, the introductory auxesis itself is comic,
breathlessly reassessing Belphoebe in each successive line, and so
rapidly reaching a genetic of "heavenly birth" based, astonishingly, on observation of the lady's physical posture ("portance")
that the act of exaltation and the effect of playfulness unite.

The first four stanzas (22–25) show the queen's "face" as promised in the proem and are epitomized as "So glorious mirrhour of
celestial grace, / And soveraine moniment of mortall vowes" (st.
25). These two lines sum up the *krasis* (Greek, blend) or "goodly
mixture" which Berger has shown to be a concept of temperance
intrinsic to this book and one embodied by Belphoebe. At the
same time, the encomiastic need for hyperbole works against the
temperate idea of goodly mixture, producing instead a jostling of
opposites, as in the first stanza of the blazon:

> Her face so faire as flesh it seemed not
> But heavenly pourtraict of bright Angels hew,

> Cleare as the skie, withouten blame or blot,
> Through goodly mixture of complexions dew;
> And in her cheekes the vermeil red did shew
> Like roses in a bed of lillies shed,
> The which ambrosiall odours from them threw,
> And gazers sense with double pleasure fed,
> Hable to heale the sicke, and to revive the ded.

In the first three lines the face transcends the quality of "flesh" to become "heavenly." But "withouten blame or blot" more nearly approximates human than angelic nature in its allusion to the Virgin Mary (*immaculata*, without spot). And "goodly mixture of complexions" by a surprising reduction ascribes the angelic clarity of Belphoebe's face to the commonplace physical theory of the humors. In the stanza's second half this angelic face acquires intensely sensual cheeks. Here the roses of passion and lilies of chastity, are, by an internal rhyme, made sharply erotic ("roses in a *bed* of lillies *shed*"), but with the further sense of desire contained by chastity. For a moment a goodly mixture of Venus and Diana seems achieved. But at once the surprising addition of the flowers' "ambrosiall odours" creates a new and totally sensual mixture, protracting the simile beyond its referent so that the "gazers sense" of "double pleasure" in seeing and smelling ("ambrosiall" and "fed" suggest eating as well) derives from the flowers rather than the now forgotten cheeks. The startling final line, the capping of another auxesis, in which the odors not only feed the gazers' sense but "heale the sicke" and "revive the ded," suddenly brings us, without even grammatical transition, from deep sensuality to the sacred and miraculous: from smelling flowers to the English monarch's traditional gift of healing to the miracles of Christ himself. It is hard to realize that the line is part of a description of a lady's cheeks begun just four lines earlier. This dizzyingly versatile stanza does not effect a goodly mixture so much as express the classical Renaissance tension between mean and transcendence as expressed in the double emblem of the July eclogue: *In medio virtus—in summo felicitas*.[6] It also insinuates the sexual tensions inherent in the cult of the Virgin Queen. These are clearly evident in the further stanzas on Belphoebe's face. For instance, the Graces usually associated with Venus each "with meekenesse to her bowes," but at the same they time signal "amorous retrate" (st. 25).[7]

Spenser's sense of fun in this delightful description appears in his placement of the inability topos *after* the nearly four stanzas relentlessly anatomizing Belphoebe's face: "How shall fraile pen descrive her heavenly face, / For feare through want of skill her beautie to disgrace?" Its location calls attention to the straining after brilliant, extreme effects up to this point and separates it from the noticeably more relaxed manner of the rest. In the transition at the beginning of stanza 26—

> So faire, and thousand thousand times more faire
> She seemd, when she presented was to sight,
> And was yclad, for heat of scorching aire,
> All in a silken Camus lylly whight

—the parenthetical clause "when she presented was to sight," with its suggestion of revelation by as well as to the narrator, confutes the inadequacy topos with simultaneous authorial assertion. Spenser interposes it brilliantly between a summation of extreme hyperbole ("So faire, and thousand thousand times more faire / She seemd") and a down-to-earth recognition of Belphoebe's need to dress for the weather ("And was yclad, for heat of scorching aire, / All in a silken Camus lylly whight"). He thus imparts a comic picture of the would-be temperate poet who, if he cannot rightly articulate Belphoebe's goodly mixture, can at least, like Medina, struggle to hold opposites in balance.

The details of Belphoebe's dress which follow (sts. 25–26) are straightforward, largely unmetaphorical description. Given the previous "perles and rubins," the line "Below her ham her weed did somewhat traine" is cool and prosaic, and the word "ham" (meaning the calf) strikingly banal. This juxtaposition of modes develops into self-parody in stanza 28, on Belphoebe's legs, which returns to the earlier manner of overelaborated simile as the blazon begins to reascend the body:

> Like two faire marble pillours they were seene,
> Which doe the temple of the Gods support,
> Whom all the people decke with girlands greene,
> And honour in their festivall resort.

Here the delightful euphemism whereby we ascend the lady's legs to "the temple of the Gods" brings us to an almost totally playful celebration of the Virgin cult. Circumlocution to avoid indelicacy collides with zealous amplification that insists on prolonging the simile into the idea of a popular religious festival.[8] But the simile has a simultaneously serious dimension: for the leg-pillars supporting the temple of the body catch at the Pauline image, especially apt in this book, of the body as the temple of the Holy Ghost (1 Cor. 6:19). Yet the comic incongruity which immobilizes a huntress into a piece of sacred architecture is pursued with perverse consistency as the narrator takes pains to describe how Belphoebe manages to move upon her pillars: "Those same with stately grace, and princely port / She taught to tread, when she her selfe would grace." And "when the flying Libbard she did chace, / She could them nimbly move, and after fly apace"—a virgin without spot hunting a spotted beast. But the syntax of "after fly apace" readily suggests that, when her leg-pillars began to move, the rest of Belphoebe soon followed.

As the blazon ends, the narrator finally stumbles with happy irony on three images that articluate the *krasis* or temperate goodly mixture that has so far eluded him. (1) "Her daintie paps . . . like young fruit in May" (st. 29) catches in a natural way the sense of venereal Diana and fruitfullest Virginia. (2) And when he finally adds her hair (wittily distanced from the four stanzas of face beginning the blazon), it is at once artfully "crisped, like golden wyre," and blowing freely in the wind "like a penon" (st. 30). (3) Nor can he tell "whether art it were, or heedlesse hap" that adorned that hair with flowers.

Camden records that Edward VI called the Lady Elizabeth "by no other name, then his sweet sister Temperance."[9] If Belphoebe here serves to praise the queen as exemplar of temperance, such a sense emerges easily and gracefully at the end of the icon, where art and nature blend beyond possibility of distinction—in obvious contradiction to art mocking nature in Acrasia's perverted Bower (xii. 61).

Rather than attempting to undermine or satirize the encomium to which he is committed, Spenser produces, in the icon of Belphoebe, a piece of witty but true praise in which the solemn, moral, and emblematic are interfused with the playful and parodic. This sort of passage gives the lie to the hoary cliché that makes Spenser the sober and earnest English counterpart of the witty and capricious Ariosto. For Spenser, high seriousness and Ariostan sportiveness interact, often projecting dazzlingly multiple effects.

Two comparisons, to Diana and Penthesilea (st. 31), close the icon and so agree with the Aphthonian disposition of *laus* which ends with *comparatio*. The lines on Diana so nearly translate *Aeneid* 1. 497–502 on Dido dressed as a hunting nymph as to bring its context into play: the stories of the fall of Troy and Aeneas's mission to found New Troy.

> Such as Diana by the sandie shore
>   Of swift Eurotes, or on Cynthus greene,
>   Where all the Nymphes have her unwares forlore,
>   Wandreth alone with bow and arrowes keene,
>   To seeke her game; Or as that famous Queene
>   Of Amazons, whom Pyrrhus did destroy,
>   The day that first of Priame she was seene,
>   Did shew her selfe in great triumphant joy,
> To succour the weake state of sad afflicted Troy.
>
> [st. 31]

The comparison of Belphoebe to the "Queene / Of Amazons" who came "To succour . . . sad afflicted Troy" brings the Trojan allusion into the open. This pair of virgin-similes with Trojan-Roman associations invites an analogous alignment of Belphoebe-Elizabeth and Troynovant or, to use the language of the proem, the Virgin Queen and fruitfullest Virginia. In fact, "the Amazons huge river now found trew" of the proem has already laid the ground for an American fulfillment of Belphoebe's precursor, the Queen of Amazons. That the icon devoted to celebrating the virginity of Elizabeth should occur in the encomiastically strategic third canto of a book containing a texture of allusions to the New World is not coincidence. For Spenser makes Belphoebe, who preaches the pursuit of "honor" by "painfull toile" "In woods, in waves, in warres" (sts. 40–41), the moral incitement behind a potential imperial realization of Troynovant, which the Virgin Queen had allowed Raleigh to name Virginia. Indeed, the paradox of fruitfullest Virginia is a geographical and grammatical equivalent to the partly venereal icon of Belphoebe as fruitful virgin. To respond to the provocative "conspicuous irrelevance" of her icon, we must understand something of the late-Elizabethan political myth of American empire. Below I wish to examine two allusions to that myth, the garden in the Bower of Bliss and the Cave of Mammon.[10]

Fruitfullest Virginia Who Did Ever Vew?

In the Bower of Bliss episode which climaxes Book II, Spenser unmistakably imitates Tasso's Armida episode.[11] Tasso locates Armida's palace among the Fortunate Isles, far west of the Pillars of Hercules.[12] The virgin-prophetess who conducts Carlo and Ubaldo there compares their voyage to Ulysses', who perished in the Atlantic, and (by epic prophecy) to Columbus's, characterized as a civilizer greater than Bacchus or Hercules. She describes the lands he will discover in terms applied in the Renaissance to the New World: its fertility, temperate climate, cannibalistic natives, and their need of Catholic faith and European civility (*Ger. lib.*, XV. 25–32). She even refuses to let Carlo explore an island because heavenly decree has fixed the date of the voyage of discovery (sts. 38–40). Obviously, Tasso introduces these American details to glorify Columbus and a Catholic empire in the New World, an emphasis Spenser must avoid. But he does borrow the distinctive American coloration of Tasso's episode and adds to it two New World allusions of his own: a catalog of sea monsters and an arrangement of real and artificial plants of the same species.

Guyon's three-day voyage to Acrasia's island, with its obvious Odysseyan features, expands Tasso's introduction of Ulysses' fatal voyage (derived in turn from *Inferno*, XXVI). In the pattern of imitation, Guyon thus replaces Tasso's Columbus who completes Ulysses' failed voyage by reaching the New World. The encyclopedic list of sea monsters that Guyon and his palmer encounter, however, is Spenser's addition. That intimidating monsters were to be expected on the voyage to the New World is only one of several features from medieval travelers' lore (especially Mandeville) incorporated in the sixteenth-century fantasies about America, a process begun by Columbus himself.[13]

Another such fantasy located in America the lost terrestrial paradise which Columbus actually claimed to have discovered.[14] For instance, Tasso's Carlo and Ubaldo pass islands where the earth yields food without tillage and there are no seasons (XV. 35–36); it is always spring on top of Armida's mountain (sts. 53–54); and grapes of all seasons grow there together, some green, some yellowing, some purple (XVI. 11). Spenser picks up this image of the temperate earthly paradise (e.g. xii. 51), particularly developing Tasso's grapes that know no season:

> Some deepe empurpled as the Hyacint,
> Some as the Rubine, laughing sweetly red,
> Some like faire Emeraudes, not yet well ripened.

> And them amongst, some were of burnisht gold,
> So made by art, to beautifie the rest,
> Which did themselves emongst the leaves enfold,
> As lurking from the vew of covetous guest
>
> [sts. 54–55]

The gem imagery Spenser adds, especially the climactically placed emeralds, as well as the covetous guest, hint at the conquistadors in Peru. The emeralds "not yet well ripened" is, in fact, a doubly apt image, applicable to both emeralds and grapes, for Peruvian emeralds were said to ripen chemically in their lode, like fruit, until they attained perfect color throughout.[15] But Spenser goes much further to combine actual metal goldsmith's grapes with the jewellike real ones. By so doing he associates this garden with reports of wonderful Inca gardens full of realistic plants made entirely of gold and silver. Raleigh, for instance, in his *Discoverie of Guiana* (1596) quotes in both Spanish and English the account in the official historian Francisco Lopez de Gomara's *General History of the Indies* (1550) of such a garden, sited like the Bower on an island: "They say, the Ingas had a garden of pleasure in an Iland . . . which had all kind of garden hearbes, flowers and trees of Gold and Silver, an invention, & magnificence til then never seen."[16] Such gardens were apparently well-known among American wonders, to judge from Montaigne's description of the "amazement-breeding magnificence of the never-like seen Cities of Cusco and Mexico" where the first item noted is "the admirable Garden of that King where all the trees, the fruits, the Hearbes and Plants, according to the order and greatness they have in a Garden, were most artificially framed in gold."[17]

In early Spanish accounts, these metal plants always figure as the ne plus ultra of the Incas' seemingly casual use of gold. The context of such passages, of course, is always an assertion of the riches to be had in Peru. Raleigh's quotation from Gomara comes from just such a passage, and Raleigh uses it to argue for the existence of El Dorado. The golden grapes in Acrasia's garden may derive from Spenser's association with Raleigh, but he focuses the image differently to indicate a perverted and seductive art. In fact, in the Bower, Spenser picks up from Tasso the myth of the American terrestrial paradise and subjects it to an ironic treatment not in his original. For instance, he adapts Tasso's prelapsarian weather (XV. 53–54)—"Gently attempred, and disposed so well, / That still it breathed forth sweet spirit and holesome smell" (st. 51)—only to elaborate it in outdoing comparisons qualified by sinister nuances, like "Thessalian Tempe, where of yore / Faire Daphne Phoebus hart with love did gore," that climax in an attempt to outdo "Eden selfe, if ought with Eden mote compaire" (st. 52). Comparison to Tempe is a standard feature of praise of place.[18] But the speculation that this garden may be "More sweet and holesome, then" Eden casts doubt not only on the Bower's "Gently attempred" nature but also on the myth of America as terrestrial paradise that is one of its allusions. Significantly, Spenser twice translates the term *terrestrial paradise* as "Paradise on ground" in the case of the Bower (xii. 58, 70) but as "earthly Paradize" in the case of Belphoebe's *locus amoenus* (III. v. 40). Just as Acrasia's name means no *krasis* and thus negates Belphoebe's goodly mixture, so her island with its American coloration is a vicious parody of the Virgin Queen's potential American dominion, fruitfullest Virginia. As the example of Verdant shows (II. xii. 79–80), the myth of America as a sensual paradise poses a threat to the young hero's temperance (his face still shows "amiable grace, / *Mixed* with manly sternnesse"), his Martian *virtù* (his arms are hung on a tree), the Belphoebean ideal of honor won by sweat ("ne for honour cared hee"), and, of course, his life (his name in its negative phase is Mordant).

Along with sensual indolence, Spenser presents greed—the lure of easy gold—as the other great pitfall for the Virgin Queen's adventurers attempting to realize fruitfullest Virginia. If the Bower hints at the dangers to empire inherent in the myth of the New World as terrestrial paradise, the Mammon episode of canto vii poses the threat from the most alluring item in American mythology, the fantasy of El Dorado. Most of its New World coloration occurs toward the beginning as Guyon comes upon Mammon among

> Great heapes of gold, that never could be spent:
> Of which some were rude owre, not purifide
> Of Mulcibers devouring element;
> Some others were new driven, and distent
> Into great Ingoes, and to wedges square;
> Some in round plates withouten moniment;
> But most were stampt, and in their metall bare
> The antique shapes of kings and kesars straunge and rare.
>
> [st. 5]

In one of its senses, the discovery of Mammon appears to depict the conquistadors' experience when they came upon the gold of the New World. The "new driven . . . Ingoes"[19] recall the conquistadors' habit of reducing to manageable bars the huge treasuries in wrought gold found in Mexico and Cuzco. The repeated image of Mammon's gold as "Those precious hils" (sts. 6, 7, 9) reflects the vastness of the American treasure, which staggered the European imagination. The "round plates withouten moniment" recall the gold plates lining the interior of Incan temples, which were among the first forms of gold Pizarro's men could lay hands on.[20] The "antique shapes of kings and kesars straunge and rare" marking some pieces make them products of an exotic culture, like Mammon himself, his gold coat covered with "antickes and wild Imagery" (st. 3), who first appears as something foreign to expectation—"An uncouth, salvage, and uncivile wight" (st. 4). Mammon's claim to godhead (st. 8) may bear some reference to the kind of incident relished by Elizabethan propagandists and recounted by Bartolomé de las

Casas, who tells of an Indian chief displaying a small chest of gold as the Spaniards' god and source of their cruelties.[21] More important, when Mammon pours his hills of gold "through an hole full wide" to hide them "from straungers envious sight" while Guyon tries to stop him, he possibly recreates the Cuzcans' attempt to hide their treasures from Spanish avarice, while Guyon's reaction interestingly puts him for a moment in a conquistador's role. All chroniclers of the Conquista speculate on how much treasure the Indians concealed. Raleigh, for example, quotes Gomara to the effect that the Inca Huayna Capa "had an infinite quantitie of silver and gold unwrought in Cuzco which was lost by the death of Guascar, for the Indians hid it, seeing that the Spaniards took it, and sent it to Spayne." Raleigh fanatically believes Spanish tales that a son of the said Inca escaped the Pizarros to found a richer "Empyre of Guiana," which "hath more abundance of Golde then any part of Peru, and as many or more great Cities then ever Peru had when it florished most." Its hypothetical ruler he confidently calls "Inga the Emperour," and its imperial city, Manoa, is El Dorado. Even though his expedition of 1595 failed to discover it, Raleigh can promise with extraordinary confidence that "those commanders and Chieftaines, that shoot at honour, and abundance, shal find there more rich and bewtifull cities, more temples adorned with golden Images, more sepulchres filled with treasure then either Cortez found in Mexico, or Pazzaro in Peru: and the shining glorie of this conquest will eclipse all those so farre extended beames of the Spanish nation."[22] In short, here is an English associate of Spenser's obsessed with the phantasm that led so many Spanish adventurers to grief.

Alerted by the American allusions, we may view Guyon's descent to Mammon's House of Richesse, where "dead mens bones" lie instructively around barred coffers (st. 30), and to the central gold refinery, "the fountaine of the worldes good" (st. 38), as in one of its senses an enactment of the pursuit of El Dorado or some similar fantasy of easy American wealth. Two further details strengthen this assumption. First, Guyon finds Mammon in "desert wildernesse" (st. 2) which he has reached under the metaphor of a pilot guiding his ship (st. 1). Second, Guyon has also just passed "beyond that Idle lake" (st. 2). Raleigh believed that El Dorado lay on a huge salt-water lake "like unto *mare caspium*".[23] In any case, Guyon's willing response to Mammon's act of hiding gold and his invitation "Come thou . . . and see" (st. 20) corresponds nicely to Raleigh's obsession and to the pull of El Dorado on the imagination of the adventurous. The timing of this allegory is instructive, since in the 1580s the sea-dogs' energy is just beginning to turn toward ideas of feasible empire.

Raleigh is prominent in the 1590 installment. The Letter to him follows the dedication to the queen, and there is the dedicatory sonnet to him, his own two splendid sonnets praising the poem, a handsome compliment to his *Cynthia* (III. pro. 4), and a topical allusion through Timias (III. v). That Raleigh's obsession with empire should also find a place is not surprising. The late date of his Orinoco voyage (1595) as defended in the *Discoverie* (1596) offers no problem for Spenser's possible association of El Dorado and Raleigh in the episode, for Raleigh's account basically embroiders the already existing myth. His vision of another Incan empire reserved for British exploitation complements the anti-Hispanism of the 1580s—the decade when English translators saw fit to offer several chronicles of the Conquista, as well as the period of Raleigh's association with Spenser.[24] But it is odd that, given his flattering attitude toward Raleigh in the poem of 1590, Spenser should make allusion to El Dorado a topical aspect of the hero's main temptation—one from which he does not emerge unscathed. One infers that the topical relevance of the episode must be of somewhat monitory character.

Guyon's name has been derived from the romance figures Huon of Bordeaux and Guy of Warwick, and more recently from the etymology for George in the *Legenda aurea* (thus giving both Books I and II Georgos heroes), and from the river of Eden called Gehon (Guyon enters Mammon's golden temple at II. vii. 43 and Una speaks of "Gehons golden waves" at I. vii. 43—an exact piece of correspondence).[25] But the American allusions may stimulate an additional meaning: knight of Guiana. Both Guiana and Virginia were Raleigh's projects. And in the poem Raleigh is especially associated with the honor of the fruitful virgin Belphoebe. In fact, in the Letter Spenser ingratiatingly asserts that the name

Belphoebe imitates "your owne excellent conceipt of Cynthia." It
is to Belphoebe's virginity that Timias (whose name means honor)
must accommodate himself and so vindicate "her honour" (III. v.
45, 51). With the Mammon episode Spenser seems to be saying
that Guyon-Raleigh, knight of Guiana and prototype of the
Elizabethan imperialist, must manage such lures as El Dorado
with temperance and self-discipline like Belphoebe's. Otherwise,
the gold of Guiana and fruitfulness of Virginia become destruc-
tively opposed goals. Only the knight who expresses Belphoebe's
goodly mixture in the New World can, like Georgos, safeguard
fertility (as Guyon does for Verdant) so that sensuality is not
lethal but paradisal and manage the gold of Guiana so that it
approximates the Edenic gold of Gehon.

Although Guyon successfully parries Mammon's temptations
to easy wealth and bought dignities, he does enter this *katabasis*
through curiosity about gold; and, no matter how we may read
the cause of his fainting at its end, he emerges as vulnerable as
Redcrosse after the corresponding adventure of I. vii, even
though that knight's culpability is evident, while Guyon's is
obscure. The result makes it clear, however, that instant American wealth is the great test of the temperate hero, that it is intensely difficult to respond to El Dorado with a Belphoebean
goodly mixture. Guyon begins by confronting Mammon with
such an attitude to wealth—"right usaunce" (II. vii. 7)—but in the
ensuing debate distorts it. Reacting to Mammon's claim to divinity (and hinting at the old allegorical etymology "Dis quasi
dives"—"Pluto means wealth"),[26] Guyon rejects any goodly
mixture of honor and gold: "Regard of worldly muck doth *fowly
blend*, / And low abase the high heroicke spright" (st. 10). Even
though Mammon riddles this assertion by noting the economic
meaning of knightly accouterments, Guyon is soon expounding
pairs of concepts construed to highlight their opposition: "purest
streame" versus "mucky filth" (st. 15) or the "Angels life" of the
Golden Age and the unmitigated avarice of the age of gold (sts.
16–17). He is, in fact, expressing not Belphoebe's goodly mixture
but Acrasia's *a-krasis*, or no blend. Ironically, only after seeing
Mammon's smelter does Guyon return to a temperate attitude
based on right use: "All that I need I have; what needeth mee / To

covet more, then I have cause to use?" (st. 39). But his foul blend of attitudes toward Mammon, simultaneous curiosity and rejection, undermines his temperance at a rudimentary physical level and leads to the outbreak of the passions (Pyrochles and Cymochles) in a new malevolent phase. That they enter as "sonnes of Acrates old" (viii. 9) denotes their etymological connection with Acrasia and so pinpoints the contradictory Acrasian character of Guyon's response to Mammon. In his *Discoverie* Raleigh's response to El Dorado expresses analogous contradictions: on the one hand, insistence on civility toward the Indians; on the other, feverish, neoconquistadorial promises of a richer Cuzco meant to be exploited.

In terms of topical allegory, Spenser insinuates that an intemperate British attitude to American wealth invites Spanish pillage of Gloriana's potential empire. From this point of view Guyon becomes literally Guiana, passive before the conquistadors' "greedy hunger" for spoil of "armour bright" (st. 15). In fact, Pyrochles and Cymochles have strong Catholic associations if we remember the sense of paynim and Saracen in Book I: here they are seven times called "Paynim" or "Pagan," swear by "Termagaunt" (st. 30) and "Mahoune" (st. 33), and come with Archimago—altogether, a satiric image of Catholic exploitation of New World peoples egged on by papal sanctions. Pyrochles and Cymochles may perhaps represent Portugal and Spain between which the pope had divided the New World. Interestingly, Cymochles' image for Guyon echoes the gold associations of both Gehon and Guiana ("gold all is not, that doth golden seeme"—st. 14) as well as American adventurers' experiences with fools' gold.

Significantly, it is Arthur who rescues Guyon. For the polymath, magus, and visionary proponent of empire, John Dee, when asked to advise about the queen's title to North America, had traced her claim there to Arthur's colonization.[27] In 1580 Dee presented Elizabeth with a map of America and an outline of her claims based on ancient British voyages. "He concluded that Elizabeth had a right to much of Atlantis, or America, because of the trip made by 'the Lord Madoc' . . . who, Dee believed, led 'a Colonie and inhabited in Terra Florida, or thereabouts.'"[28] While in Leicester's service Spenser knew Dee as a fellow member of the

Areopagus, a speculative academy centered on Sidney. Dee's enthusiasm for the project of an Elizabethan colonial empire based on ancient Arthurian claims would certainly appeal to Spenser. In Eumnestes' library Guyon reads in the history of Gloriana that the first Faery emperor, Elfin, "all India obayd, / And all that men America now call" (II.x. 72)—a clear allusion to Dee's claim that Elizabeth's ancient progenitor Arthur held dominion in America. Notably, it is Elfin's successors who build Cleopolis, making the American empire antedate Gloriana's city itself. When Arthur rescues the Knight of Guiana from paynim exploitation, then, he assumes the role of American protoemperor as propounded by Dee.

Arthur's other main exploit in Book II also has American touches, for Maleger attacks him with arrows "Headed with flint, and feathers bloodie dide, / Such as the Indians in their quivers hide" (xi. 21). Their wounds are incurable, "so inly they did tine," like the Carib arrows poisoned with curare reported by Peter Martyr.[29] Maleger's attack portrays sickness entering the body through sin: his twelve troops comprize the seven sins and attacks on the five senses. Touch is attacked by the troop "most horrible to vew, / And fierce of force" with "stings of carnall lust" (xi. 13). Nothing fits the idea of disease entering the body through lust better than the sixteenth-century horror, syphilis, which Spenser earlier cites as Lechery's "fowle evil, that all men reprove, / That rots the marrow, and consumes the braine" (I. iv. 26) and which was notorious for its American origin.[30] Maleger's name (*mal* and *aeger* both mean "sick") and the Indian image for his attack readily associate him with syphilis. Arthur's appropriately difficult victory over him removes an American threat to fruitfullest Virginia. (Note that Maleger first attacks Alma, "a virgin bright"—II. ix. 18.)

Finally, we may note two features of the Mammon episode that oppose the apparition of the queen as Belphoebe. These are Philotime and Proserpina's garden. Mammon's daughter Philotime (love of honors) perverts Belphoebe's criterion of honor, and her "great gold chaine" reaching to heaven from hell perverts a familiar image of rational cosmic order into an upward scrambling.[31] Guyon refuses Philotime's hand on the grounds of "trouth yplight, / And love avowd to other Lady late" (vii. 50). This lady is pictured in the "faire image of that heavenly Mayd" (i. 28) on his shield, i.e. the Virgin Queen as Virgo-Diana-Astraea. At Medina's castle, Guyon has already praised her in terms whereby her virtues put wealth in its proper perspective, transfiguring Mammon's image of "great heapes of gold" into spiritual terms: "In her the richesse of all heavenly grace / In chiefe degree are heaped up on hye" (ii. 41). The goods Mammon offers find their true use in their subordination to her, for everything "great or glorious in mortall age, / Adorns the person of her Majestie" (ii. 41). The British Virgo thus affirms the hierarchy of values that Mammon and Philotime pervert. It is worth noting that Guyon's paean of the "most glorious Virgin Queene alive" echoes Raleigh's naming of Virginia in her praise and his encomium *The Ocean to Cynthia*: "In widest Ocean she her throne does reare, / That over all the earth it may bee seene" (ii. 40).

The black garden of Proserpina is fruitfullest Virginia's demonic opposite (just as Philotime's meretricious court is the demonic opposite of the Virgin Queen's). Though the garden's features are of Graeco-Latin derivation, its tree of golden apples also suggests the metallic Incan gardens. Certainly the allusion to Hercules' quest for the golden apple of the Hesperides ("great Atlas daughters") and to "swift Atalanta" (vii. 54) have western connotations, while Hippomenes' achievement of Atalanta and Acontius's of Cydippe with the aid of golden apples offer types of Eve's loss of chastity by eating an apple and hence the loss of a paradise through gold. The wordplay on "golden fruit" that gains Acontius's "fruitlesse suite" draws attention to the contrast with fruitfullest Virginia. In fact, in this anthology of golden apples in mythical history, the reiteration of "goodly" accumulates irony and hints that "goodly golden fruit" (st. 55) is another aspect of perverted art's mimicry of nature's fruitfulness and so is at odds with the effortless synthesis of art and nature in Belphoebe. The final allusion—Paris's award of a golden apple to Venus that eventuates in Troy's fall—connects this garden and tree with empire lost. Its golden apples threaten Troynovant's realization of fruitfullest Virginia. At the end of this subepisode the tree's fruit becomes simply "rich fee" (st. 56). The walled garden and great tree are traditional accouterments of the terrestrial paradise, the paradise Columbus claimed to have come upon, but here become an infernal paradise made deadly by mismanaged gold.[32]

Part of the far reaching complementary nature of Books I and II lies in their broad political meanings. Together they portray two senses of Britain as empire: in the first, a sovereign state; in the second, colonial empire like Spain's. The national myth of Book I focuses on the recovered independence of Britain-Eden and has a basis in the achievements of Elizabeth's reign. But in Book II the corresponding political myth of Britain's imperial destiny overseas points to something almost totally contingent. The brilliant new name Virginia represents a claim. Hence, the texture of American allusions tends to negative expression, with more anti-Hispanic than pro-Virginian nuances. Our closest glimpse of its positive aspect is the appropriately elusive apparition of Belphoebe.

Amoret

As Belphoebe's twin, Amoret should present a complementary type of the queen, but her encomiastic role is imperfectly realized. Notably lacking is an icon to match Belphoebe's and so to carry through the expression of the royal Venus-Virgo cult begun in the myth of their birth, a fanciful piece of encomium through *genus*. Their begetting by the sun upon Chrysogone blends unmistakable analogies to the virgin birth of Christ and the immaculate conception of Mary ("Pure and unspotted from all loathly crime, / That is ingenerate in fleshly slime"—III. vi. 3). As Roche shows, Spenser even inserts a psalm verse (110:3) associated with the Christmas liturgy and so with Christ's birth and Mary: "Her berth was of the wombe of Morning dew."[33] This extravagant *genus* makes the queen's double nature as Venus-Virgo a cosmic feminine principle: "These two were twinnes, and twixt them two did share / The heritage of all celestiall grace" (vi. 4). Their polarity is reflected narratively in Venus and Diana's flyting (vi. 11ff.) and structurally in the placement of the birth story between Belphoebe's paradise at the end of canto v and Amoret's foster home in the Garden of Adonis at the end of canto

vi. Each is proposed for ladies' emulation, Belphoebe as "faire ensample" of "perfect love, and spotlesse fame / Of chastitie" (v. 54) and Amoret as "th'ensample of true love alone, / And Lodestarre of all chaste affection" (vi. 52). In fact, Spenser goes to considerable lengths to make a parallel construction of these two cantos which are of nearly the same length (fifty-five stanzas in canto v, fifty-four in canto vi), and there are many instances of matching lines in matching stanzas: e.g. "Belphoebe was her name" (v. 27. 9) and "her Amoretta cald" (vi. 28. 9); "Dy rather dye, then ever from her service swerve" (v. 26. 9) and "Therefore needs mote he live, that living gives to all" (vi. 27. 9). Many similar bits of line-to-line parallelism express the complementary nature of Diana and Venus as types of Elizabeth.

In spite of this elaborate balancing, Spenser depreciates Amoret slightly in favor of Belphoebe. Of the twins she was born "in the second place" (vi. 4), "The younger daughter of Chrysogonee" (vi. 51). And, in the canto parallelism, Belphoebe's fifth canto is significantly one stanza longer than Amoret's sixth (six is a Pythagorean number of marriage, but five is the number of sovereignty).[34] When we recall that there is no icon of Amoret to match her twin's and that in the proem to this book (and in the Letter) Belphoebe is singled out as a type of the queen with no mention of Amoret, it appears that some shift of emphasis during the poem's evolution has played down Amoret's encomiastic role. If we assume, as seems safe, that the basic material of Book III dates from an early period of composition, the twins' complementary roles in the present III. v–vi would nicely reflect the situation of the self-proclaimed Virgin Queen, whose marriage negotiations with Alençon were in controversial progress when Harvey was reading some part of the poem in 1580. But the question grew irrelevant as the decade progressed (Elizabeth was fifty-seven in 1590), making desirable the attenuation of Amoret as a type of the married queen. In the installment of 1596, at least, Spenser has so far dissociated Amoret from the queen that he can press her into the service of topical allegory as the unfortunate Elizabeth Throckmorton (IV. iv. 7). Spenser could easily have invented one more disposable female like Aemylia and Poeana for this incidental purpose. By using Amoret, he deliberately (though

retrospectively) undermines her twinship with Belphoebe as encomiastic strategy.

To demand consistent allusion in individual figures, however,
is to read against the plasticity and imaginative freedom of this
poem which allows Amoret at one point to mirror the queen, at
another a lady permanently banished from her court. While the
Throckmorton allusion plays down encomium through the twins
at least in Book IV, it simultaneously reaffirms the conceptual
and narrative relevance of their twinship. For the situation of
Timias, caught between the alternatives Belphoebe and Amoret,
expresses their effectiveness as feminine polarities, just as it parallels the goddesses' debate over Cupid in Book III.

In the final episode of the 1590 installment, however, Amoret
at the House of Busyrane still bears topical, though perhaps not
strictly encomiastic, reference to Elizabeth. The name Busyrane
is said to be adapted from Busiris, a legendary Egyptian tyrant
who sacrificed strangers, tried to rape Atlas's chaste daughters,
and was deposed by Hercules.[35] This etymology is appropriate to
the chaste Amoret's torture by the sexual sadist Busyrane and
rescue by Britomart, who outdoes Hercules in surviving flames of
passion. But Busyrane's name can also be divided Busy-rane to
suggest "busy *rana*" (frog), an etymology which accounts for the
whole name. Once elsewhere in the poem Spenser creates a similar name, by prefixing an English adjective to a Latin noun: Rud-
dymane (II. ii. 2) explicitly derives his unhappy name from
"ruddy *manus*" (hand). The busy-frog etymology alludes, I think,
to the queen's proposed French marriage of a decade earlier. According to her habit of nicknaming courtiers, she had dubbed
Alençon her "Grenouille" (frog).[36] Her jewels at the time included a gold flower supporting a frog with Alençon's physiog-
nomy. The conceit of the Frog Prince who did a-wooing go
caught on sufficiently for Drake at his knighting to present the
queen with a timely frog of diamonds.[37] The Stationers' licensing
of "A moste Strange weddinge of the frogge and the mowse" on
21 November 1580 shows that the negotiations had imbued this
ancient rhyme with a new pertinence (it should be remembered
that the frog is not successful).[38]

From our vantage point, the on-again-off-again French marriage appears as a subtle piece of diplomatic brinkmanship. To many Elizabethans, however, it seemed to betray the emotionally profound marriage of England to the Virgin Queen, which corresponded (as Book I shows) to Christ's mystical marriage to the church. Sidney may have been rusticated from court for his letter against the match. And Spenser's satirical *Mother Hubberds Tale*, which styles Burghley and Alençon's agent Simier as Fox and Ape, may have cost him his place with Leicester.[39] If the busy-frog etymology is valid, Spenser in this episode presents in Amoret an image of the queen already half-married to Scudamour (England, and perhaps Leicester as well), who is being sacrificed to a tyrannous Cupid by Busyrane—either the Frog Prince, the marriage scheme itself, or its proponents, of whom the principal was Burghley.[40]

Encomium of Elizabeth in this episode appears less through Amoret than Britomart. That is, Spenser brings in a mythical ancestress and militant type of the queen to effect the rescue of another type of the queen and thereby compliments Elizabeth on extricating herself from the wicked enchantment of the French marriage. Hence, Burghley's supposed censure of the poem—"a mighty Peres displeasure" (VI. xii. 41)—may have been reaction to travesty of a central concern of his career. The pragmatic lord treasurer did not much applaud works of imaginative literature,[41] but Spenser's defensive references to him at the beginning and end of the books added in 1596 indicate specific objection to the earlier poem. It is often assumed that Burghley saw pornography in the passage where Scudamour and Amoret consummate their marriage.[42] The busy-frog explanation seems to me more likely. Certainly it is consistent with the lines of defence in the fourth proem which audaciously set England's love for the queen against Burghley's failure to "feele kindly flame."

Defense of the poet's erotic role is implicit in the Busyrane episode. In fact, the spectacle of Amoret's "trembling hart" drawn from her breast and "Quite through transfixed with a deadly dart" (III. xii. 21) perverts one of Spenser's favorite images for oratorical effect, the pierced heart. The suffering lover's heart pierced by the chaste lady's arrows is a sonnet cliché, here twisted by reversal of sexes. Its commonplace version can be seen in

Figure 7. The triumph of Cruel Chastity. From a fifteenth-century majolica plate, by courtesy of the Victoria and Albert Museum.

figure 7, where a fifteenth-century Italian majolica plate shows a male lover depicted as St. Sebastian and bound to an extravagantly pruned tree (suggesting repression of nature) while a determined lady shoots arrows at him. Between them a chalice (suggesting sacrifice) contains his heart twice transfixed. The man's banner "O qanta crudelta," the triumphal car, and the border of lilies indicate a Triumph of Cruel Chastity seen from a male perspective. In Amoret's case the somewhat paranoid pleonasm "Quite through transfixed" and its reprise "Seeming transfixed" (xii. 31) hint that Cupid's triumph and her torture externalize her image of herself as a sexual sacrifice to a husband named from his armed-Cupid shield. What Spenser is suggesting, though in negative terms, is the lover's dependence on the poet's art. The symbiosis of the erotic and verbal appears in positive form when Scudamour and Amoret's coupling depicts "that faire Hermaphrodite" (xii. 46 in 1590 ed.) Not only is the hermaphrodite an emblematic *typus matrimoniae* but, as child of Mercury and Venus, fuses rhetoric and desire. Boccaccio says Hermaphroditus was conceived when Mercury seduced Venus by his eloquence and that the child was part female as an effect of his copious terms of endearment.[43] As Scudamour's courtship of Amoret in the Temple of Venus shows, his failure as a lover derives from a defect of eloquence. (Significantly, Britomart comes upon him while pursuing Ollyphant, a giant of indiscriminate lust.)

Florimell

Like Belphoebe and Amoret, Florimell probably dates from the poem's early Ariostan phase, for she is based on the peregrine beauty Angelica for whose love Orlando goes mad. By transforming Ariosto's bitchy coquette into a royal type, Spenser performs a characteristic piece of overgoing. He makes Florimell's identification with Elizabeth explicit in Arthur's "wish, that Lady faire mote bee / His Faery Queene," "Or that his Faery Queene were such, as shee" (III. iv. 54). But in Florimell we find a figure distinct in kind from the other encomiastic types. In fact, the Florimell-Marinell story constitutes a national fertility myth, so heavy with reference that its effect is, in Roche's word, "passive."[44] For in spite of Florimell's remarkable velocity, she belongs less to the poem's action than to its symbolism. There are icons of Una; there is also Una as protagonist. But Florimell is almost continually iconic, inviting wonder and desire wherever she appears: three times in a single stanza she is admiringly underidentified as "wight" (III. v. 5).

Marinell is, if anything, more passive—the object of Florimell's search. He has one moment of activity as he tries to defend his Rich Strond. But he falls like "the sacred Oxe" (III. iv. 16) and later reacts to Florimell like a plant after "cruell winters tine" that "gins to spread his leafe before the faire sunshine" (IV. xii. 34). Both similes indicate his passive, ritual nature and his role in the fertility myth. His name and parentage (III. iv. 19–20) and his proprietorship of the Rich Strond "Of pearles and pretious stones of great assay, / And all the gravell mixt with golden owre" (III. iv. 18) makes it plain that Marinell denotes the sea and its wealth. Florimell is a land figure. Her name means flowers and honey, recollecting the biblical Promised Land of milk and honey as well as the flower-gathering and flower-bringing fertility figure Proserpina, an allusion furthered by her descent to Proteus's wintry grotto while the snowy Florimell replaces her above.[45] But Florimell also insinuates Psyche searching for her lost lover Cupid (III. v. 9), the chaste phase of Helen,[46] the life-giving, sea-born Venus (IV. xii. 1–2), Venus reviving Adonis, and even the Virgin Mary, intimated by the spotted beast sent to attack her chastity (III. vii. 22). It is for this broadly mythical reason that the consummation of marriage, otherwise avoided in the poem, takes place in the case of Florimell and Marinell. In terms of national myth, it figures the marriage of the British Virgo-Venus-Proserpina to the Sea. Significantly, Florimell and Marinell meet in the context of the vast marine metaphor celebrating the Thames-Medway nuptials, for the Medway was home base for the royal fleet.[47]

For both Platonic and encomiastic reasons all good ladies in *The Faerie Queene* must be beautiful. But "Florimell the faire, / Faire Florimell" (III. v. 8) is the Elizabeth-type whose beauty is most insisted on. In a topos of outdoing that mixes encomium and playfulness, Florimell's dwarf tells Arthur her superlative beauty is her identifying feature: "The surest sign, whereby ye may her know, / Is, that she is the fairest wight alive, I trow" (III. v. 5)—a charming piece of tautology, elevating praise by *corporis bonum* beyond possibility of comparison. Several epithets here associate Florimell with the queen, for example, "a noble mayd," who is "Royally clad . . . in cloth of gold," for Elizabeth wore cloth-of-gold at her recognition procession and coronation.[48] Florimell's face, whiter than her palfrey "more white then snow," compliments the queen's striking and nurtured pallor,[49] and appears as well in the first icon of Una: though moving at different speeds, both white-faced ladies are riding on missions connected with Britain's destiny.

Curiously, Florimell's apparition only releases its encomiastic significance later in her dwarf's explanation. Occurring simply as an apparition, it is precipitated with comic suddenness into an already comic context where the narrator's admiration of the "goodly usage of those antique times" (III. i. 13) fulsomely glosses over the ironic situation in which Guyon, the patron of temperance, just flattened by an aggressively chaste Britomart, can only with difficulty be restored to a temperate state of mind by his Palmer and Arthur. The forest the reconciled knights enter is itself described in terms of comic *correctio* or *epanorthosis:* "Yet tract of living creatures none they found, / Save Beares, Lions, and Buls, which romed them around" (st. 14). In this woods of the passions and to these knights whose concord depends on sophistry, Florimell appears: "All suddenly out of the thickest brush . . . / A goodly Ladie did foreby them rush" who "scarse them leasure gave, here passing to behold" (st. 15). The crystal face, at once undercut by the proverbial simile "white as whales bone," [50] offers a comic touch, as does the perverse omniscience of "scarse them leasure gave, her passing to behold" which comes after the lady has been described in some detail. And the simile of Florimell as a comet in the next stanza is extended into terms that leave the lady far behind. These features typify the witty admixture that often complicates encomium in *The Faerie Queene*. Although in this case the encomium is not made explicit until four cantos later when the dwarf explains what we have seen, there is already implicit compliment to the queen as the ordering and informing center of existence. For Florimell's apparition at once reorganizes the knights. A glimpse of her beauty incites erotic effects, Guyon, and especially Arthur, being drawn after her by honorable emotions of protection but also by sexual curiosity (st. 18), while the foster has followed her with intentions of rape: "beauties chace" (st. 19) can mean either adoration or iconoclasm. Timias pursues the foster, while Britomart remains aloof because she follows another destiny, but also, from the perspective of encomium, because she is herself a type of the queen.

The comic episode where Florimell resists Proteus's attempts to seduce her (viii. 30–48) ends in the narrator's celebration of her chastity in an Orphic hymn of the short type:

Most vertuous virgin, glory be thy meed,
And crowne of heavenly praise with Saints above,
Where most sweet hymmes of this thy famous deed
Are still emongst them song, that far my rymes exceed.

Fit songs of Angels caroled to bee;
But yet what so my feeble Muse can frame,
Shall be t'advance thy goodly chastitee,
And to enroll thy memorable name,
In th'heart of every honourable Dame,
That they thy vertuous deedes may imitate,
And be partakers of thy endlesse fame.

[sts. 42–43]

As usual, Spenser here handles inadequacy paradoxically: the
angels' hymns are set against "my feeble Muse" which nevertheless can effect "thy endlesse fame." This paradox gives a special
twist to the Renaissance commonplace of the poet's power to
grant eternity of fame. For the angels have always ("still") sung of
Florimell's "deedes," although the poet is just now inventing
them. He is thus both the mere chronicler of Florimell's eternal
fame and the cause of it. In terms of the epideictic view of epic, it
is notable how the ideas of hymn and heroic narrative fuse here.

The inadequacy topos concluding stanza 43—"It yrkes me,
leave thee in this wofull state, / To tell of Satyrane, where I him
left of late"—exemplifies a typical Spenserian persona, the passive poet merely recording reality. How much this voice is a
reaction to Ariosto's typical persona of dominating author can be
seen by comparing "Ma non dirò d'Angelica or più inante; / che
molte cose ho da narravi prima" (XII. 66)—"But I will say no
more of Angelica right now, because I have many things to tell
you of first." Ariosto's persona toys with the simple fact that the
poet is writing his poem but won't reveal his plan. Spenser's,
perversely implying that the poet is not creating the poem but
merely recording it, is deliberately more subtle. Like the inadequacy topos of which it is an extension, it facilitates the elevation essential to encomium. An example of this voice at its most
extreme and comic occurs when Florimell, struggling with a sexually excited old fisherman, cries to heaven for help and is sec-
onded by the passive author:

O ye brave knights, that boast this Ladies love,
Where be ye now, when she is nigh defild
Of filthy wretch? well may shee you reprove
Of falshood or of slouth, when most it may behove.

But if that thou, Sir Satyran, didst weete,
   Or thou, Sir Peridure, her sorie state,
   How soone would yee assemble many a fleete,
   To fetch from sea that ye at land lost late;
   Townes, Cities, Kingdomes ye would ruinate,
   In your avengement and dispiteous rage,
   Nor ought your burning fury mote abate;
   But if Sir Calidore could it presage,
No living creature could his cruelty asswage.

                          [III, viii. 27–28]

Then the posture of author as helpless Homer comically alters, since "none of all her knights is nye," into *vates:* "See how the heavens of voluntary grace . . . / Doe succour send to her distressed cace" (st. 29). This passage shows to what superb comic ends Spenser takes his reversal of Ariosto's persona. It does not mean, of course, that Florimell's chastity is being mocked but that the moral and the witty fuse in mercurial ambivalence. As with the Belphoebe icon, but in Florimell's case more continuously, Spenser demonstrates that the cult of the Virgin Queen can be celebrated with levity and even parody. While their moral and national significance is paramount, yet it is this strain of gaiety in the portrayal of royal icons that most affectingly characterizes Elizabeth's encomium through her "mirrours more then one" in Books II and III.

1590

Destined
Descents

In one sense the whole *Faerie Queene* is an expansion of the en-comiastic topos *genus*, or praise through descent. For its allegorical time scheme makes events in a mythical Arthurian past simultaneously figure the Elizabethan age. But *genus* also appears in more precise terms. In addition to Britomart as Elizabeth's fictive ancestor, I will comment below on Arthur as a Tudor ancestor-figure and on Gloriana, who is not only the object of his quest but also the focus of a piece of ideal *genus* in Book II.

Gloriana

Every student of *The Faerie Queene* has some sense of what Gloriana is supposed to be. We learn at the beginning of the poem that she is "That greatest Glorious Queene of Faerie lond." Her "grace" is for Redcrosse "of all earthly things" the highest goal (I. i. 3). Gloriana is the glory of Elizabeth's imperial office; the desire to win glory that she inspires in the hero's breast, and which, when won, is identical with her; and the divine glory she reflects and participates in.[1] She is the first type of Elizabeth mentioned in the poem—just before Una appears. The quests in Books I, II V, and VI originate at her will and are heroic extensions of her glory.

But Gloriana does not appear in the poem, except by allusion, vision (in Arthur's dream, I. xi. 13–15), or picture (on Guyon's shield, II. i. 28). The third proem, like the Letter to Raleigh, makes Gloriana and Belphoebe examples of royal "mirrours more then one," figuring "In th'one her rule, in th'other her rare chastitee." But nothing in the poem is recognizable as a mirror of Gloriana. There is obviously a disparity between her near absence and the importance Spenser attributes to her. Josephine Waters Bennett argues from the paucity of references to Gloriana that, as a name for the Faery Queen, she was a late idea.[2] This is likely. Yet the fact that she is mentioned a mere five times in 1590 but only four additional times in 1596 shows that Spenser meant to limit the use of her name.

As Bennett, following Courthope, points out, deletion of Gloriana would not disturb the poem's framework.[3] But, while to remove the Faery Queen, whether or not called Gloriana, would do little violence to the narrative, it would deny one of the poem's most subtle encomiastic strategies, what Angus Fletcher calls the "taboo of the ruler." For Gloriana epitomizes the various meanings of the other royal types while herself remaining "unapproachable yet infinitely desirable."[4] She is made even more desirable when we see detailed images of what she is not in the fake queens Lucifera and Philotime. From an epideictic point of view, such figures express *vituperatio*, the dispraise realized by reversing the topoi of *laus*. In fact, at least one detail of design insists on opposing Philotime to the unseen Gloriana: for the stanza where Una speaks "Of Gloriane great Queene of glory bright" (I. vii. 46) exactly parallels that in which Philotime sits with her great gold chain "in glistering glory" (II. vii. 46). By keeping us aware of Gloriana in allusion yet denying us her image, Spenser carries through a special tactic of inadequacy that implicates the reader in deifying the empress by agreeing to her inaccessible nature. As a remote figure of veneration, always just beyond the bounds of narrative experience, Gloriana serves to compensate for the liability to fortune and mutability which complicates the roles of the other royal types who, in spite of iconic moments, are subject to the accidents of wandering. The Faery Queen is not. They betoken Elizabeth at some moments but not at others. Gloriana always figures the queen.

Two episodes contributing to the assertion of Gloriana are Redcrosse's comparison of her city, Cleopolis, with New

Hierusalem and the account of her descent read by Guyon in the House of Alma. Because Spenser places them in parallel tenth cantos as part of the visions of future and past associated, respectively, with the Houses of Holiness and Alma, these episodes build the idea of Gloriana into the complementary structure of Books I and II.

Spenser may have acquired the name Cleopolis from an encomium of Paris by one Quintianus Stoa (1514).[5] Its meaning, "city of glory," makes it an urban extension of Gloriana. But Redcrosse describes "great Cleopolis, where I have beene, / In which that fairest Faerie Queene doth dwell" in unencomiastic terms that make it inferior to New Hierusalem: "But now by proofe all otherwise I weene; / For this great Citie that does far surpas . . ." (I. v. 58). The marked dualism here approximates the Augustinian opposition between profane worldly glory and the glory of the City of God. But Spenser is too much the Christian humanist (at least at this stage of the poem) to leave dualisms unqualified. Here Contemplation turns away from the mystic's focus to correct the knight's pejorative view of Cleopolis, just as, a little later, he mitigates Redcrosse's extreme polarization of active and contemplative lives:

> Yet is Cleopolis for earthly frame,
> The fairest piece, that eye beholden can:
> And well beseemes all knights of noble name,
> That covet in th'immortall booke of fame
> To be eternized, that same to haunt,
> And doen their service to that soveraigne Dame,
> That glorie does to them for guerdon graunt:
> For she is heavenly borne, and heaven may justly vaunt.
>
> [st. 59]

Cleopolis thus has heroic value as the city of earthly fame, but it is more than that. Because of her own heavenly *genus*, the "glorie" Gloriana rewards her knights with also partakes of the heavenly glory. For her birth is a Platonic fiction implying her celestial existence as an Idea that not only makes Cleopolis analogous to the apocalyptic Jerusalem, but also actually links them. Gloriana makes it possible to transcend the basic opposition of heaven and earth. Contemplation's pronouncement is thus of a piece with the deification of the queen in the first proem. There she mediates heavenly grace, here heavenly glory.[6]

"Antiquitie of Faery lond," the history of Gloriana read by Guyon in the House of Alma, contrasts in every way with "Briton moniments," the history of British kings read simultaneously by Arthur. "Briton moniments" is chronicle history, drawn from Geoffrey of Monmouth and others and organized by relentless chronology. But the materials of "Antiquitie of Faery lond" are Spenser's invention, offering a myth of ideal Tudor history and organized by the need to proceed from glory to glory. Following the sixty-four dispiriting stanzas of British history, the seven stanzas of Gloriana's are lighthearted and breathtakingly concise.[7]

From an encomiastic point of view, both histories are exercises in *genus*. Gloriana's Faery history, however, is actually organized by the four subdivisions of *genus* in their Aphthonian disposition: *gens* (race), *patria* (country), *maiores* (ancestors), and *patres* (immediate forebears and parents). Gloriana's *gens* begins sweepingly with Prometheus's creation of man, a myth Spenser adapts from Natalis Comes,[8] because, unlike the biblical myth, it skirts the idea of a human fall, relegating guilt and punishment to Prometheus himself. The double nature of Prometheus's man, whom he made "of many partes from beasts derived, / And then stole fire from heaven, to animate / His worke" (II. x. 70), appears in the typical Renaissance device of the bilingual pun which requires awareness of Latin equivalents—hence "beasts" (*animalia*) / "animate." In stanza 71 the Faery race begins. Elfe, the man Prometheus created, mates with "no earthly wight, but either Spright, / Or Angell" whom he calls a Fay. The seemingly unfallen Faery *gens* that descends from this union is thereby half-superhuman like the semidivine heroes of primitive epic. Stanza 72 expands the topos *patria* to accommodate the Tudor claim through Constantine to ancient worldwide imperium, for the Faeries "all Nations did subdew" from India to America (a notable diversion from the usual topos of extent of fame, from India to ultima Thule). The capital built for this empire is Gloriana's Cleopolis. The stanzas of *maiores* (73–74) record the consistent successes of her ancestors, not without levity. These boggle the mind when we learn of "seven hundred Princes, which main-

taynd / With mightie deedes their sundry governments." Even
Spenser's powers quail at the prospect of inventing 700 more
names beginning Elf–: "That were too long their infinite contents
/ Here to record, ne much materiall." So in lieu of giving any
information about them, the narrator with comically perverse
didacticism simply insists that their "famous moniments, / And
brave ensample" be followed, whatever they were, by "kings and
states imperiall." Once again gaiety complicates encomium.

The final two stanzas on *patres* incorporate the Tudors in this
Faery myth. Spenser omits the awkward cases of Edward VI and
Mary to clear the line of success from Henry VII through Henry
VIII to Elizabeth. But he includes Henry VIII's elder son, Arthur (Elferon), by way of salute to the dynastic myth of descent
from Arthur. The climax, of course, comes in Gloriana herself:
"Fairer and nobler liveth none this howre," "Therefore they Glorian call that glorious flowre" (st. 76). Unlike Arthur's British
chronicle, the Faery myth of history makes events ancillary to
meaning: the teleology informing time's process is Gloriana. The
Elfin line of master-rulers and the Promethean creation of man
himself have her as their end. The final line of this encomium by
genus—"Long mayst thou Glorian live"—is the *votum* that closes
the Aphthonian disposition of praise. But it also insinuates the
disturbing irony that Gloriana brings the Elfin line to both climax
and close. Like Elferon's untimely death, this suggestion of the
nagging problem of the succession infects the culmination of
praise with a little of the wearisome reality of "Briton moniments."[9]

Arthur

While the history Guyon reads is an overt exercise in *genus*,
Spenser insists that the depressing history Arthur reads also expresses praise by the same topos:

> Thy name, O soveraine Queene, thy realme and race
>   From this renowned Prince derived arre,
>   Who mightily upheld that royall mace,
>   Which now thou bear'st, to thee descended farre,
>   From mightie kings and conquerours in warre,

Thy fathers and great grandfathers of old,
Whose noble deedes above the Northerne starre
Immortall fame for ever hath enrold

[II. x. 4]

Of the stanzas preceding this, the first two imitate line by line the
opening of Ariosto's third-canto celebration of the Este *genus* and
its need for "More ample spirit, then hitherto was wount" to
record "the famous auncestries / Of my most dreaded Soveraigne"
(st. 1). But when Ariosto begins to speak in a confident authorial
persona ("s'in me no erra / quel profetice lume che m'inspiri"—"if
the prophetic light inspiring me does not err"), Spenser diverges
into an inadequacy topos typical of him:

A labour huge, exceeding farre my might:
How shall fraile pen, with feare disparaged,
Conceive such soveraine glory, and great bountihed?

[st. 2]

The fourth stanza, quoted at the beginning of this paragraph,
departs totally from Ariosto to claim that the aim of the history
Arthur reads is praise of the queen by *genus*. This strategy of
imitation would nicely introduce the Faery history read by
Guyon. But, as the fourth stanza makes clear, what is being
introduced is the pessimistic chronicle read by Arthur. It tells his
own *genus*, which, according to Tudor myth, is also the queen's.
As we read that tedious account, the introduction's claim that it
testifies to the "Immortall fame" of its subjects may seem perverse. Spenser's emphasis, however, is not so much on the degree
to which the claimed Arthurian pedigree dignifies Elizabeth as on
the glory and significance she reflects back upon the historically
murky and morally perplexing British chronicle from which her
line emerges.

The claim to descent from Arthur was useful propaganda for
Henry VII. If his elder son had survived him, England's second
Tudor king would have been Arthur II. But the Arthurian claim
gradually became embarrassing to dispassionate historians and of
diminished value for the now established dynasty. As the brilliant
success of Elizabeth's regime became apparent and its colonial
ambitions emergent, however, Arthur acquired new relevance as

a national symbolic figure,[10] a role recognized by such disparate voices as Foxe's and Ronsard's. Foxe accepts the historicity of Arthur as a Briton king, is sceptical about legends of his conquests, yet sees their epic potential as "worthy to be joined with the Iliads of Homer."[11] And Ronsard's hymn to Elizabeth (1567) "sketched the Arthurian legend as the basis of English glory and suggested an epic poem in honor of Arthur."[12] Even shrewd Burghley, with his interest in objective history, felt it proper to defend the myth of Arthur.[13]

It is this Elizabethan stage of the Arthurian myth of descent that Spenser uses, but with the encomiastically invaluable insinuation that it is Elizabeth that glorifies Arthur. Just as minutiae adumbrating the queen permeate the texture of the poem, so in a lesser way do details hinting at Arthur as a Tudor. In his fight with Cymochles, for instance, Arthur's wound flows "Red as the Rose" (II. viii. 39). And he describes his upbringing (the topos *educatio*) as "Tutours nourriture" (I. ix. 5), meaning both tutor's teaching and teaching of the Tudor. More important, the qualities of Arthur's image when he first appears, "arrayed meet" (I. vii. 29), foreshadow Elizabeth in tangential but compelling ways. His armor shining "Like glauncing light of Phoebus brightest ray" (st. 29) obviously allies him with the royal sun-symbol. The "one pretious stone" on his baldric which, "Shapt like a Ladies head, exceeding shone, / Like Hesperus emongst the lesser lights" (st. 30), suggests the queen, especially by the encomiastic hyperbole. "In the chronicles," Isabel Rathborne notes, "Arthur is represented as particularly devoted to the Virgin whose picture he bears on his shield,"[14] but here she has been replaced by the Virgin Queen. The winged dragon on Arthur's helmet has a literary history proceeding from Turnus's helmet (*Aeneid* 7.785) to Tasso's Soldan's (*Ger. lib.*, IX. 25). But here it principally connotes one of the two supporters of the royal arms, the dragon of Cadwallader (a key figure in the Tudor claim to descent from Arthur). The shield "all of Diamond perfect pure and cleene," so inviolable "That point of speare it never percen could, / Ne dint of direfull sword divide the substance would" (st. 33), points particularly to the cult of the queen's virginity. Its clairvoyant capacity derives from Tasso (XIV. 77, XVI. 29–31), but its sense of impregnable chastity is Spenser's addition. In fact, its excision from "Adamant" puns on Greek *adamantos*, unconquerable, and *adamatos*, unmarried. (A further pun, suggesting Eve's excision from Adam, again parallels the Virgin Queen with the Virgin who repairs the fault of Eve.) Further, the effect of the shield's light uses the same outdoing topos of sun and moon outshone (st. 34) which are part of Eliza's praise in *Aprill*. In Arthur's fight with Orgoglio the fortuitous unveiling of "that sunshiny shield," "The light whereof, that heavens light did pas" (viii. 19–20), blinds Duessa's seven-headed beast and fatally paralyzes the giant. John Hankins notes the recollection here of Psalm 84:11, "For the Lord God is a sun and shield,"[15] which accords with the usual reading of Arthur in this episode as a special emissary of divine grace. And Martha Craig suggests that, by making the shield of diamond, Spenser is punning on "deus-mundus" (God in the world).[16] But "*dea*-mundi" would be closer to diamond, betokening the queen as deified empress and vehicle of divine will. This incident offers a type of the Faery Queen's ultimate triumph over the Paynim King and celebrates the virgin cult of Elizabeth: the apotheosis of her virginity unveiled not only succors her British champion but exposes the obscenity of Spain's whoredom with Rome, as well as confounding, in a broader sense, the pride of the flesh.

This image of Arthur carried over nine stanzas (29–37) is a kind of encomiastic icon of Elizabeth by *genus*. While the Tudor myth of descent enables his appearance here, Arthur's accouterments hint that his relevance lies in prefiguration of his descendant. In fact, both the chronicle Arthur reads and his erotic quest for the Faery Queen reflect his role as British Hercules laboring to realize Elizabeth.

The chronicle-history "Briton moniments" pulls in three interpretative directions. (1) On its surface, it implies absence of moral design in history: time seems intransigent to value. In the case of the first Christian king, Lucius, "This good king shortly without issew dide, / Whereof great trouble in the kingdome grew" (II. x. 54). In spite of heroism, Bunduca (Boadicea) triumphs only "whiles good fortune favoured her might" (st. 56). Even if fortune were not indifferent to virtue, human perfidy is competent to thwart permanent accomplishment: "Nought else, but treason, from the first this land did foyle" (st. 48). (2) There is at the same time a sense of repeating pattern in history that somewhat intimates design. British history begins with "Brutus anciently deriv'd / From royall stocke of old Assaracs line" (st. 9). Descent from the founder of the Trojan dynasty sets up parallels between Britain and Troy, while the "fatall error" that drives Brutus to Britain matches Aeneas's impulsion by fate ("fato profugus," *Aen.* 1. 2) from Troy to Latium. As the chronicle progresses, hints of typology link ancient British and early Roman kings. Donwallo, founder of the dynasty after Brutus, is a lawgiver whose success makes him "The gracious Numa of great Britannie" (st. 39). And Guitheline's wise queen, Mertia, is like "Aegerie, that Numa taught" (st. 42). But, as the *October* and *November* eclogues imply, repetition (like patterned wallpaper) is a trap which the imagination seeks to escape by a gesture of transcendence. (3) Finally, here and there in the chronicle, queens and heroines appear who foreshadow Elizabeth and, by typology, intimate escape from frustration and recurrence. For instance, Guendolene, who defeated her unfaithful husband, Locrine, and ruled in her son's place till his coming of age, manifested "Through all this realme, the glorie of her sex, / And first taught men a woman to obay" (st. 20). Bunduca, who tried valiantly to free Britain from Rome, inevitably adumbrates Elizabeth, a typology strengthened by encomiastic *comparatio:* "O famous moniment of womens prays, / Matchable" to heroines "Whom antique history so high doth raise" (st. 56). And Spenser extols Constantine's British mother, "faire Helena, the fairest living wight," who "in all godly thewes, and goodly prayse / Did far excell" (st. 59), in the encomiastic language used of Elizabeth's types in the poem, particularly Florimell. The dim light shed by these remote types of Elizabeth allows the British chronicle to participate a little in the contrast between British and Faery histories, which in turn reflects the poem's fundamental opposition between wandering and stasis.

Arthur's patriotic outburst when the chronicle breaks off with "untimely breach" (st. 68) seems unwarranted by its dispiriting nature unless we understand the exclamation as an intuition of Elizabeth.[17] His "delight, to heare / The royall Ofspring of his native land" (st. 65) not only expresses the subtopos *patria* but anticipates his descendant. Angus Fletcher points out that "the interaction of the two modes of heroic existence, faery and Briton, is an interaction of two aspects of time, its recurrent forms and its linear, evolutionary forms."[18] This interaction occurs in the pairing of the two histories. As Arthur's response to "Briton moniments" shows, it is also implicit within that chronicle. In erotic terms, it appears in the British knight's search for the Faery Queen. Like "Briton Moniments," Arthur's quest articulates an energy running through British history that drives it toward the advent of Elizabeth in linear time.

One name for this energy is Prays-desire, who functions, in the Jungian sense, as Arthur's (and, more broadly, Britain's) *anima*. On the one hand, she externalizes the royal goal of his erotic quest and his meaning as a figure of *genus*, as her dress of purple and gold suggests (ix. 36, 37). In this sense, Prays-desire means "praying for one's desire." On the other, the poplar branch she extends emblematizes Arthur's Herculean role as a hero whose labors aim at honor. In this sense, Prays-desire means "desiring praise" or, as the lady puts it, "great desire of glory and of fame" (st. 38). But to desire glory is ipso facto to desire Gloriana, the poem's object of praise. Alciati says the poplar is a sign of Hercules because its leaves, dark on the upper, light on the lower side, stand for the night and day Hercules upheld Atlas's burden.[19] Black and white were also the queen's personal colors, worn by her champions at ceremonial tournaments.[20] Prays-desire's poplar makes Arthur Gloriana's special champion. In her self-transcendence she contrasts with Guyon's corresponding *anima* figure, Shamefastnesse, whose withdrawn nature shuns the self-exposure implicit in the public pursuit of honor. Shamefastnesse means more than Plautus's *pudor*, the ability of a well-bred young man to blush, although that is part of her meaning (cf. sts. 43, 44). For the bird she holds "which shonneth vew, / And keeps in coverts close from living wight" seems to be the nightingale, who once lost a singing contest to Pan's pipes and so does "sit, as yet ashamed, how rude Pan did her dight" (st. 40). Although scholars have not agreed on the bird's identification, Spenser's lines echo the Homeric *Hymn to Pan* (16–18), where a bird that is certainly the nightingale has lost a singing contest with that god: "not even she could excel him in melody—that bird who in flower-laden spring pouring forth her lament utters honey-voiced song amid the leaves."[21] Shamefastnesse's bird suggests the modesty that shrinks from the public competition inherent in the social pursuit of glory (perverted in Braggadochio's self-promoting vaingloriousness) and which expresses *verecundia*, or sexual modesty (perverted in Braggadochio's incompetent, Pan-like rapist inclinations). Shamefastnesse allies Guyon with the queen's private Belphoebean type (her bird and Belphoebe are both denizens of the woods), while Prays-desire externalizes the impetus that makes Arthur and British history seek the Faery Queen.

Spenser builds Arthur's evanescent goal into the parallelism of Books I and II by making it an early feature of each ninth canto. In Book I, canto ix, Arthur's explanation of his quest is erotic—a "fervent fury" (st. 8) that transcends his training "Those creeping flames by reason to subdew" (st. 9) and which is the erotic correspondent to the *furor poeticus* said to elevate Colin in *October*. The Idea of the Faery Queen goes beyond the basic moral scheme whereby reason orders the passions and generates a "forced fury" (st. 7) or historical causality which fuses God's "fatall deepe foresight" with love's "fresh bleeding wound" (st. 7) that impels Arthur's erotic quest. The dreamed-of "royall Mayd" (st. 13) who leaves tangible "pressed gras, where she had lyen" (st. 15) has a paradoxical nature, embracing both the elusive Idea of the Faery Queen and the Tudor Elizabeth who will historically fulfill Arthur's quest. The contrasting ideas of British and Faery time thus interpenetrate in this passage. For, according to the dreamed-of "Queene of Faeries," Arthur will know her love "As when just time expired should appear" (st. 14). Meanwhile the knight voices his characteristic strain of *lacrimae rerum*, "Nothing is sure, that grows on earthly ground" (st. 11). The tension between realization of an elusive lady at the end of just time and heroic acceptance of mutability typifies Arthur's paradoxical role as both progenitor of Elizabeth and frustrated quester after her Faery type.

At the beginning of the parallel ninth canto of Book II, however, Arthur's search is more heroic than erotic. His inquiry about the lady's head imaged on Guyon's shield evokes an outburst of encomium by *corporis* and *animi bonum*, in which the lady's "most glorious visage" outdoes her "picture dead" and "the beautie of her mind . . . / That is her bountie, and imperiall powre" is "Thousand times fairer then her mortall hew" (st. 3). Arthur's response articulates Prays-desire: "My whole desire hath beene, and yet is now, / To serve that Queene" (st. 7). But both Arthur and Guyon agree that "Fortune, foe of famous chevisaunce," frustrates that quest, leaving the British knight no course but to "constant keepe the way, in which ye stand" (st. 8). The block that makes the Faery Queen available to Guyon's experience but not to Arthur's is a law of the poem, an extension of the double British-Faery time scheme. We automatically respect this law by not asking why Guyon or Una can't put Arthur on the road to Cleopolis. Underlying it is the conflict between Arthur's roles as progenitor and as lover. Each role partially frustrates the other. It is often assumed that Spenser meant to unite Arthur and Gloriana as lovers, possibly in a twelfth book. But such an episode would violate the carrot-and-donkey nature of Arthur's quest, in which Gloriana's elusiveness is essential to her omnipresence as Idea, as well as to Arthur's role as ancestor. The first proem represents Arthur's quest for "fairest Tanaquill" as frustrated by nature. Arthur's failure to discover Gloriana allies him with us and our inability to find her image in the poem.

Britomart

As martial heroine and fictive ancestor of Elizabeth, Britomart expresses encomium through both type and *genus*. The mythological figures underlying her role as type include Diana, Venus, Psyche, and, especially, Minerva.[22] Spenser probably knew of a Cretan Diana called Britomartis; according to Elizabethan antiquarians, Diana was anciently worshipped in Britain under that name.[23] Britomart obviously means "British Mars," a sense present narratively in such displaced forms as Britomart-Mars rescuing Amoret-Venus from Mulciber's fire (III. xi. 26) or, comically, as Britomart without armor defending herself against Venus-Malecasta and, unsuccessfully, the bow of Cupid-Guardante. More broadly, Britomart's connection with Mars allows Spenser to present a type of the queen as Britain's champion, the "maid Martiall" Glauce speaks of (III. iii. 53). One problem posed by a panegyrical epic honoring Elizabeth is that she cannot readily be presented as central militant hero like Aeneas. The device of patron-knights who act as the Faery Queen's heroic agents and the use of Elizabeth's ancestor Arthur as coordinating hero circumvent the problem. But in Britomart, Spenser confronts it.[24]

Britomart dominates the first three cantos of Book III. Canto iii contains the prophecy of Elizabeth's *genus* from her, and in the parallel three-stanza exordia of cantos ii and iv the narrator progresses from playful Amazon fantasy to encomium that overtly identifies her as a royal type. In the exordium to canto ii a wittily omniscient and antiquarian author examining the "record of antique times" (st. 2) finds that "envious Men" have suppressed the tradition of female supremacy in "prowesse martiall" (st. 1). By devising "streight lawes to curb their liberty" they have forced women to reveal their superiority as politicians, "That now we foolish men that prayse gin eke t'envy" (st. 2). In the third stanza Britomart offers "precedent" for the earlier martial stage of feminine history, while her Minervan role is diverted to the queen whose "wisedome" is "precedent" for women's recent political success. Here the management of the inability topos makes clear the subordination of Britomart "whose prayse I write" to Elizabeth "whose prayse I *would* endite." Britomart's Amazon role can be depicted. The queen's wisdom (like Gloriana's image) is beyond representation: "Thy selfe thy prayses tell, and make them knowen farre."

In the similar exordium to canto iv the playful complaint, according to the topos *ubi sunt*, of the loss of women's "Antique glory"—"That matter made for famous Poets verse"—hints at the rebirth of martial heroines in Elizabeth: "doen they onely sleepe, and shall againe reverse?" (st. 1). Then the commentator ignores his own suggestion and misleadingly develops a typical encomiastic comparison by less in which the Amazon Penthesilea (earlier compared to Belphoebe), the Old Testament heroine Deborah (a favorite Protestant cult-name for Elizabeth), and Virgil's "aspera virgo" Camilla "Cannot with noble Britomart compare" (sts. 2–3). By reacting with "envy sore" and "proud disdaine" (in its root sense from Latin *disdignari*, to be unworthy) to the stories of these old heroines, he suggests a bemused author unaware of his own encomiastic subject, then abruptly reverses the posture:

> Well worthy stock, from which the branches sprong,
> That in late yeares so faire a blossome bare,
> As thee, O Queene, the matter of my song,
> Whose lignage from this Lady I derive along.

These lines affirm the relationship between Elizabeth and Britomart through *genus*. The idea of the blossom that validates the stock rearranges categories of importance so that Britomart now derives her meaning from her offspring, an arrangement of values that descends in order of worth from Elizabeth to Britomart to Penthesilea, Deborah, and Camilla.

Britomart expresses praise through *genus* both by her erotic search for Artegall and by her line, which climaxes in Elizabeth. As a feature of panegyrical epic, praise of a ruler through a fabulous ancestor begins with the *Aeneid*, but, as the contrasted roles of Dido and Lavinia show, Virgil's ancestor myth is almost antierotic. In Bradamante's search for Ruggiero, whose line will be the Este dynasty, Ariosto gives Virgil's device an erotic motive. Britomart's search for Artegall imitates Ariosto's story. But Spenser magnifies the erotic component to make Cupid the force that impels history to realize Elizabeth. Although Book III, canto iii conspicuously imitates Ariosto, Spenser replaces Ariosto's invocation (which he transfers to the chronicle canto of Book II) with his own three-stanza apostrophe to the celestial Cupid. In its first stanza, Cupid is a divine cosmic principle which, in its human manifestation, produces "noble deeds and never dying fame." In the second, it orders time by expressing "divine foresight" in "destined descents." And, in the third, Britomart's quest becomes its great example. Her response to Cupid's darts manifests "noble deeds and never dying fame" and fulfills God's "fatall purpose" that gives history its meaning. Britomart and Cupid thus become the human and celestial agents in time's search for Elizabeth through "dew degrees and long protense" (st. 4).

At least two other national epics of the Renaissance echo Ariosto by locating or beginning dynastic history or prophecy in the third section. The third canto of the *Lusiads* begins da Gama's account of Portuguese history from its origins. And in the third book of the *Franciade* Leucothoe prophecies that Francus will father the line of French kings (III. 269ff). But Spenser's is the closest imitation of Ariosto's third canto, both progressing from invocation based on *genus* to Merlin's dynastic vision addressed to an Amazon ancestor. The four stanzas (III. iii. 21–24) in which Merlin tells Britomart that "from thy wombe a famous Progenie / Shall spring, out of the auncient Troyan blood" (st. 22) to include "Renowned kings, and sacred Emperours" (st. 23) parallel Merlin's announcement to Bradamante (*Or. fur.*, III. 16–19) line for line. But in one detail Spenser departs from Ariosto to avoid, as he habitually does, the Virgilian encomiastic motif of the Golden Age returned. While, through the government of Bradamante's descendants, "ritorneran la prima etá de l'oro" (st. 18), Britomart's British descendants, once "broken with long warre," will successfully defend themselves "Against their forrein foe, that comes from farre, / Till universal peace compound all civil jarre" (st. 23). This salutes the armed peace celebrated by Elizabeth's subjects and hints at triumph over Spain and an imperial pax Britannica corresponding to the Augustan peace. But the Golden Age returned was a particularly common theme in Elizabethan panegyric. The care Spenser takes to avoid it in an otherwise extremely close piece of imitation seems to anticipate its ironic use in Book V.[25]

From Ariosto's third canto Spenser also derives the encomiastically invaluable strategy of inserting into the chronicle a fictive ancestor whose adventures may thus be freely improvised. Though Bradamante and Ruggiero are fictive, their descendants are historical. The line from Britomart and Artegall is likewise genuine chronicle. But it also continues the chronicle from Brutus to Uther in "Briton moniments." By transferring Ariosto's third-canto invocation to the canto containing "Briton moniments," Spenser uses imitation structurally to fuse the two chronicle stages—one history, one prophecy—into a single act of *genus* which is also a stroke of overgoing: the Este descend from fictive Carolingian ancestors, but Elizabeth fulfills a complete national chronicle that goes back to the foundation legend of Brutus, who clears the island of giants to found Troynovant (cf.II. x. 7–13). "Briton moniments" breaks off abruptly at Uther, making Elizabeth's ancestor Arthur its next potential event. But it is also during Uther's reign (III. iii. 52, 55) that Britomart learns of her line, when Merlin continues the Galfridian chronicle begun in "Briton moniments." One of the obvious meanings of the name Artegall (sometimes Arthegall) is "Arthur's equal." Just as Arthur's armor foreshadows his descendant, so Artegall has for device "a crowned little Ermilin" (III. ii. 25). An emblem of virginity, the ermine inevitably suggests the Virgin Queen.[26] Carrie A. Harper, in her still valuable study of Spenser's use of British chronicles, remarks that "Arthegall takes Arthur's place in the chronicle" and that Artegall, as "brother unto Cador Cornish king" (III. iii. 27), "stands in the same relation to Cador that Arthur does" in two minor chronicles Spenser consulted, where Arthur is Cador's half-brother.[27] As ancestors, Britomart and Artegall are fictive equivalents to Arthur, and so their placement in the otherwise authentic chronicle overlaps his.[28] This double *genus*, historical and fictive, may be represented thus:

"Briton moniments" (II. x)   Merlin's prophecy (III. iii)

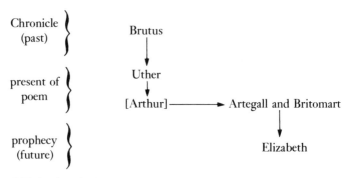

While Merlin's prophecy completes Arthur's chronicle, Spenser manages its materials differently to bring them to a mid-point between the relentless realism of "Briton moniments" and the ideal dynastic myth "Antiquitie of Faery lond." As in "Briton moniments," time and fortune here often appear indifferent to virtue. The worthy Vortipore is "at the last to th'importunity / Of froward fortune . . . forst to yield" (st. 31); and Artegall himself is "Too rathe cut off" (st. 28) even before his son's birth. But, unlike the mere temporal sequence of "Briton moniments," the events in the prophecy imply an Augustinian view of history organized behind the scenes by heavenly justice which rewards virtue, punishes vice, and guides destiny. Angels appear at Hevenfield to succour "good king Oswald" (st. 38)—apparently Spenser's invention.[29] British rule ends with Cadwallader because "th'heavens have decreed, to displace / The Britons for their sinnes dew punishment" (st. 41). But Merlin's lament for the "The royall seed, the antique Troyan blood, / Whose Empire lenger here, then ever any stood" (st. 42), subsides into a larger providential context when he foresees "the just revolution measured, / That they as Straungers shalbe notified" (st. 44). The mere fact that this chronicle material is prophecy pulls it, like "Antiquitie of Faery lond," toward a climax of meaning in Elizabeth. Like Faery history, where five stanzas cover the history of the world from man's creation and two the Tudor dynasty, Merlin's chronicle-prophecy is drastically foreshortened by "twise foure hundreth yeares" (st. 44) to increase the proximity of the British line and the Tudors. The only king mentioned between Cadwallader and Henry VII is William the Conqueror (st. 47). At the same time, the Saxon conquerors are themselves not without virtue, like the martyr "godly Oswald" (st. 39). In fact, the complement of Saxon tradition and British-Tudor dynasty appears in Britomart herself, who wears the armor of the Saxon warrior-queen Angela (from whom England was said to be named)[30] and tries to match her with "equall courage" (st. 56). She thus presents the melding in Elizabeth of royal Saxon and rekindled British tradition. (It is worth remembering that Redcrosse, in his role of Saint George the patron of England, is a Saxon prince—I. x. 65).

Spenser manages the chronicle materials of Merlin's prophecy to focus on the Tudor regime crowned by "a royall virgin" (III. iii. 49); and by foreshortening he expresses the Tudor myth of a revived British dynasty. Even during the Britons' period of "most obscuritee," signs of their latent virtue and potential return occur: figures like Griffyth Conan "the old sparkes renew / Of native courage" (st. 45). Fulfilling the promise in this imagery, the first Tudor appears as "a sparke of fire, which hath long-while / Bene in his ashes raked up, and hid" (st. 48).[31] But the "sacred Peace" he brings to the island's factions will be outdone by the international exploit of Elizabeth:

> Then shall a royall virgin raine, which shall
> Stretch her white rod over the Belgicke shore,
> And the great Castle smite so sore with all,
> That it shall make him shake and shortly learne to fall.
>
> [st. 49]

This prophecy within a prophecy, envisioning Elizabeth's triumph over Philip ("the great Castle" meaning Castile), appears in a flourish of bilingual punning. The "virgin" (*casta*) is set against the "Castle"; the "virgin" (*virgo*) extends a "rod" (*virga*); and the "white rod" (*virga alba*) hints at the chastisement of Alva, sometime Spanish commander in the Lowlands. "But yet the end is not." The movement into the future founders with Merlin's perturbed vision ("ghastly spectacle," st. 50) of the time beyond Elizabeth. This is encomiastic outdoing: the future without the queen cannot be contemplated. But it also articulates the ominous problem of the succession and retrospectively overcasts the whole prophecy, as if the depressing course of "Briton moniments" were to be reasserted.

Because prophecy establishes the purpose of Britomart's quest for Artegall, their meeting, delayed by Spenser until the poem's 1596 installment, can be exploited in other terms. Artegall's first sight of Britomart, in the sixth canto of Book IV, takes the familiar form of an encomiastic icon comically qualified by the narrator's voice. Here, the sexual determinism of Book III, canto iii becomes a parody of the passions, beginning with Britomart's unceremonious reception of Scudamour and his horse, "Whence neither greatly hasted to arise, / But on their common harmes together did devise" (IV. vi. 10). Like Scudamour's, Artegall's attack on Britomart begins in "dispiteous ire" (st. 11), discernible as an antierotic passion when considered in the light of Artegall's first appearance, at the Tournament of the Girdle, disguised as a "salvage" knight: his moss-covered armor and his automatic attack on Sangliere (French *sanglier*, boar) inevitably ally him with the sylvan, boar-hunting phase of Adonis (IV. 4. 39–40). He is soon defeated by a "stranger knight," later identified as Britomart, "Whence litle lust he had to rise againe" (st. 44); the pun on "lust" indicates the subliminal sexual action. In canto vi, as soon as Artegall fights on foot with "his direfull deadly blade" (st. 12) against a mounted Britomart, his wrath picks up unmistakable sexual innuendos, especially the blow that strikes "behind her crest," and "glaunst / Adowne her backe," "Till on her horses hinder parts it fell" (st. 13). The effect of the blow is amplified in an epic simile of lightning striking a steeple, where Artegall's stroke becomes Jove's lightning, Britomart's crest the steeple, and the horse's hind parts the church's fabric. While symbolic undertones hint at Jove's supremacy over Minerva and (by a remote anagoge) Christ's marriage to the church, the more immediate effect is comedy by disproportion.

As Artegall begins to win the hand-to-hand fight, the narrator protests in a set of such witty self-contradictions as "Ah cruell hand, and thrise more cruell hart, / That workst such wrecke on her, to whom thou dearest art" (st. 16). Here, the narrator is at once simpleminded, in his attitude of the sympathetic but helpless spectator, and perversely omniscient, insisting that Artegall recognize he is attacking the lady "to whom thou dearest art." This confusion of naiveté and omniscience eventuates in a fully naive speculation that ignores Merlin's revelation:

> Certes some hellish furie, or some feend
> This mischiefe framd, for their first loves defeature,
> To bath their hands in bloud of dearest freend,
> Thereby to make their lives beginning, their lives end.
>
> [st. 17]

The implicit mock horror at the mime of the sexual act and the relentless overlapping of contrary attitudes make this passage one of the most delightful authorial interpolations in the poem.

When Artegall shears away Britomart's ventail, her face appears in a moment of encomiastic comparison where realistic explanation undercuts the idealizing effect of the icon:

> her angels face, unseene afore,
> Like to the ruddie morne appeard in sight,
> Deawed with silver drops, through sweating sore,
> But somewhat redder, then beseem'd aright,
> Through toylsome heate and labour of her weary fight.
>
> [st. 19]

This comic apparition begins a potential blazon, like Belphoebe's, but frustrated because so little of the lady is visible. Exploring the incongruity inherent in a lady-knight, Spenser works on a golden-wire simile for Britomart's hair but it fritters away into pleonasm (st. 20). As a final comic touch, Artegall responds less quickly than do his sword and hand, as if "both of them did thinke, obedience / To do to so divine a beauties excellence" (st. 21). But when his mind catches up, he kneels "And of his wonder made religion, / Weening some heavenly goddesse he did see" (st. 22). Here the sonneteering language of love's religion blends with the need to restore Britomart's primacy over Artegall in whom he intuitively recognizes a type of the queen.

While this little encomiastic icon in its playful setting occurs in the 1596 installment of the poem, the incident arises from materials of the earlier installment. The meeting of Britomart and Artegall almost ends praise through "destined descents." The last touch of genetic encomium occurs with Britomart's vision of her impregnation by a crocodile at Isis Church (V. vii. 16); when this vision is interpreted (st. 23), it only restates Merlin's prophecy. In fact, as we come to the books added to *The Faerie Queene* in 1596, encomium itself begins to fall away, a phenomenon discussed in the following chapters.

CHAPTER SIX

1596
State of
Present Time

In 1917 Herbert Cory proposed that a decline in the poet's commitment overtakes *The Faerie Queene* in its later books. Edwin Greenlaw recognized this notion as unorthodox and squelched it in his review.[1] Recently, however, more and more readers have remarked on the disappointment and pessimism that darken the books added in 1596, especially Books V and VI. One proponent of this view entitles a chapter "What Happened to *The Faerie Queene?*"[2] Our own culture, of course, predisposes us to doubt idealism and detect feet of clay. But it is also true that new and perturbing ironies are demonstrable in Books V and VI. In fact, signs of tension in encomium are already apparent in *Colin Clouts Come Home Againe* (1591), where excited and vatic praises of Cynthia conflict with a stubbornly satirical picture of her court.

Given the inseparability of epic and encomium in the epideictic theory of literature, and of heroic action and royal praise in *The Faerie Queene*, any attitude that insinuates pessimism or moral doubt into the poem must affect the encomium. In the poem of 1590, the queen's encomiastic types stimulate the heroes' moral actions. A vision of the Faery Queen (real enough to imprint the grass) impels Arthur to the pursuit of an earthly glory which participates in heavenly glory. For, as Contemplation assures Redcrosse, Gloriana bridges Cleopolis and New Hierusalem. By transcending in her deified phase the dualisms earth/heaven and time/eternity, she makes public achievement and British heroism aspects of heavenly glory—a view which is only an amplification of the Protestant nationalism focused upon Elizabeth. ("Serve

God by serving the Queen," Burghley wrote his son at the end of his own long service.)[3] But in Books V and VI, where doubt taints the possibility of the hero's success, the strategy of royal encomium also become problematic. Although there is at least one clear instance of high encomium (Britomart's vision at Isis Church), the strain of praise in Books IV–VI is more characteristically muted or queried or ironic or even silent. Remarkably, Spenser invents no new major encomiastic types of the queen in the last three books except Mercilla, whose icon he perversely undermines. He also diminishes third-canto encomium, an important element of the poem's design in 1590. A survey of Spenser's altered use of this feature will serve as index to the attenuated encomium in the new books of 1596, which is my subject in this and the following chapter.

The Decline of Third-Canto Encomium

In the third canto of Book IV the nonce-figure Cambina is problematic as a vehicle of royal praise. Her precipitate arrival has the character of a triumph that implies encomium: the exotic lion-drawn chariot, decorated "After the Persian Monarchs antique guize" and bearing a lady who holds symbolic objects, reflects the woodcuts developed for Petrarch's *Trionfi*.[4] Her brief portrait (IV. iii. 39–40) touches on *corporis* and *animi bona* ("with her beautie bountie did compare"), adding a dash of outdoing ("passing faire") and a pinch of *genus* ("seemed borne of Angels Brood") that hints at Elizabeth through the venerable Angles/Angels pun. And her skill as a white magician expresses the topos *educatio* ("Well instructed by the Fay her mother, / That in the same she farre exceld all other"). But it is her symbols of concord—the caduceus, or "rod of peace" (st. 42), and cup of nepenthe—that particularly associate her with Elizabeth. To the pair of snakes usually entwined on Mercury's caduceus, Spenser adds an olive wreath which compliments Elizabeth's celebrated role as peace giver, while the peaceful enclosure of two serpents with one crown hints at the Tudor union of the Roses.[5]

But praise through Cambina is muted. Spenser does not drive the topoi toward the hyperbole that decorum requires of royal encomium and to which the poem has previously risen. Cambina's other role, as one of a quartet expressing concord among lovers, siblings, and friends, diminishes her encomiastic function. In this canto of concord she is particularly balanced with Canacee, whose learning "in everie science that mote bee" (ii. 35) matches Cambina's magic lore; and her magic ring, Cambina's caduceus and cup. The ring makes possible the equality of Cambell and Triamond, while the rod and the cup turn equality into friendship. But the Aristotelian idea that friendship requires equality applies as well to the "true friendship" (iii. 50) Canacee professes to Cambina, and when they ride off in one chariot, both of them "Admir'd of all the people, and much glorifide" (st. 51), the uniqueness demanded by encomium yields to the equilibrium required by these cantos about friendship.

The third canto of Book V has three episodes: the tournament celebrating Florimell's nuptials; the beauty contest between her and False Florimell; and the unmasking of Braggadochio. The first two try to prove an explicitly encomiastic proposition about Florimell: "that she all others did excell" (V. iii. 4). Outdoing in terms of *corporis bona* has been Florimell's hallmark and is even the means of identifying her (III. v. 5). But Marinell's vigorous attempt to blaze Florimell's supremacy by tournament instead brings it into jeopardy. Each day his success diminishes and on the third he is taken captive in what the commentator half-mockingly dismisses as a freak of fortune: "But what on earth can alwayes happie stand?" (V. iii. 9). His rescue from this "evill hap" is equally fortuitous: "It fortun'd" that Artegall arrives. There is no indication here of fortune disguising providential design, as when Arthur comes on Una "by good hap," but instead simply a sense of fortune's arbitrariness which controls recognition of Florimell's excellence.[6]

Florimell's indignity in the beauty contest results from her comic assumption that Braggadochio has established her supremacy, "And thousand thankes him yeeld, that had so well / Approv'd that day, that she all others did excell" (st. 15). Braggadochio instead diverts the now beleaguered formula of outdoing to False Florimell, whom "he did undertake, / Both her and eke all others to excell" (st. 16). Popular opinion agrees that hyperbole better fits Braggadochio's candidate, and, though the commentator sardonically puts this down to general failure of taste ("So feeble skill of perfect things the vulgar has"), Marinell himself opts for the truth of False Florimell. The confusion diverts the sun/monarch image into "two sunnes" in one sky (st. 19). The problem of which sun is regal is complicated by Artegall's having established Florimell's excellence with the aid of Braggadochio's shield "Which bore the Sunne broad blazed in a golden field" (st. 14). It is typical of a *gloriosus* to bear a pretentious device of bad heraldry (gold on gold).[7] But the temporary complicity of Artegall and Braggadochio embroils Florimell in an embarrassing confusion with such overbright and Phaeton-like fake queens as Lucifera; she and False Florimell both appear "Mounted in Phoebus charet fierie bright." The confusion, of, course is temporary. When the true Florimell melts the False, she appears as the sun in its seasonal aspect bringing spring, while her roses-and-lilies face, in this context (st. 23), connects her with Proserpina's vernal return. Three times in this canto False Florimell is "snowy" (sts. 10, 18, 24), and it begins by associating Florimell with cyclical "tourne" and "retourne" after "many moneths." But this seasonal version of the royal sun-symbolism makes Florimell distinct from the eternal perception of the sun afforded when Una lifts her veil and instead a natural, temporal principle like the gods in *Mutabilitie*. It is, of course, tempting to overstate the case. It seems safe to say, however, that in this third canto not only is a royal type qualified in her sun symbolism, but also that the encomiast's essential assertion—the supremacy of his subject—has come under scrutiny.

As part of the design matching Books II and V, Spenser has developed a set of situational and verbal correspondences that link Florimell (in V. iii) to Belphoebe (in II. iii). Braggadochio, for instance, enters the poem in Book II canto iii and leaves it in Book V canto iii. In both cases he attacks a royal type: in Book II his assault on Belphoebe's virginity is easily repulsed; in Book V his assault on Florimell's supremacy is put down with difficulty. Though the two cantos are of unequal length, correspondences are discernible if the stanzas are compared from the end of each canto, and one is noteworthy here.[8] The simile beginning "Such as Diana by the sandy shore" (II. iii. 31), which completes the icon of Belphoebe, matches precisely a simile on Iris beginning "As when the daughter of Thaumantes faire" (V. iii. 25). The Iris simile applies, however, not to Florimell but to False Florimell as an evanescent rainbow. Admittedly, her evaporation attests to the truth of Florimell. But Spenser's design of correspondences between these two cantos and his pairing of these two stanzas anticipates an encomiastically significant balancing of Belphoebe and Florimell which he then sidesteps. This curious behavior hints that the encomiastic drive of the poem is either weakening or being subtly deflected.

Book VI apparently contains no Elizabeth figures, old or new. Instead, in the third-canto position Spenser presents Serena. In the psychomachia or internal allegory she stands, as Hankins suggests, for Calepine's peace of mind.[9] In herself, however, she is a delightfully self-contradictory figure whose two moments of serenity are imprudent and lead to disaster. In the eighth canto, after wrongly blaming "The good Sir Calepine, her owne true Knight, / As th'onely author of her wofull tine," she feels much better and goes to sleep "Feareless of ought, that mote her peace molest" (sts. 23, 24). Cannibals arrive at once—changing Serena's self-pity into a paranoid fantasy of ritual dismembering or *sparagmos*[10] from which she is most reluctant to be rescued. In the third canto, after Calidore surprises her and Calepine as they "solace" "In covert shade" (st. 20), Serena feels serene enough to wander like Proserpina in fields of flowers. At once the Blatant Beast attacks. Not only is the meaning of Serena's name realized by parody, but instead of the expected third-canto revelation of a royal type, there is discovery of a sexual rendezvous. That Calepine "His warlike armes . . . had from him undight" invokes the Venus and Mars archetype, with its potentially pejorative connotations which taint with irony the narrator's easy approval of the lady as "courteous withall, becoming her degree" (st. 20). In fact, as part of the larger system of correspondences that link Book VI to Book I, the incident where Serena is snatched up by the Blatant Beast carefully echoes details of the parallel incident of Una and the lion.[11] But the apotheosis of Una transforms the royal lion's rage to noble eros, while Serena's casually displayed charms elicit the Beast's desire "For to have spoyled her" (st. 25). Serena thus becomes an ironic displacement of Una, delightful as Calepine's imprudently serene mistress, but clearly not a royal type. In fact, as Walter Oakeshott suggests, Spenser may have borrowed the name from Raleigh, whose carpe diem lyric "To His Love When He Had Obtained Her" begins "Now Serena be not coy." But Raleigh's Serena is certainly not the queen, whom he addresses in verse of intensely elevated decorum, but some other lady.[12] The failure to realize a third-canto type of Elizabeth here is of a piece with Spenser's seeming retreat in Book VI from the poem's encomiastic program.

One other feature distinguishes this canto from all previous third cantos which associate the royal lion with each encomiastic type. The most prominent is Una and her lion. In Book III (iii. 30) Britomart and Artegall's son defends his country "as a Lyon." In Book IV (iii. 39) lions draw Cambina's car, and in Book V (iii. 8) Marinell fighting "like a Lyon" defends Florimell's excellence. In Book II (iii. 28) the lion reference is submerged in Belphoebe's hierarchic and leonine pursuit of "the flying Libbard." In these cases, the lion plays a role of defense or succor. Book VI canto iii, however, not only lacks an encomiastic type, but the royal lion has been displaced by the obscene and iconoclastic Blatant Beast. So decisive a violation of pattern indicates a fundamental disturbance of the poem's earlier assumptions.

The Icon of Mercilla

Mercilla is the only major encomiastic type added in 1596. In her, Spenser figures Elizabeth as empress, seated in state and administering justice tempered with mercy. As such, she is the poem's closest approximation of the Faery Queen, gesturing toward Elizabeth enthroned while observing the encomiastically invaluable taboo against presenting an image of Gloriana. Mercilla's diplomatic servant Samient praises her international and pacific role as "A Princesse of great powre and majestie, / Famous through all the world, and honord'd far and nie," who does "even to her foes her mercies multiply" (V. viii. 16–17). But the next stanzas acknowledge the intractable "malice of her foes": "a mighty man" is attempting to "subvert her Crowne and dignity," destroy or bribe her knights, and plot her assassination. Samient's introduction of Mercilla thus counterpoises encomium and harsh political reality.

As Hankins points out, Samient's name means "togetherness," which he derives from Dutch *samen*, although Spenser twice uses "sam" to mean "together" in contexts implying concord.[13] The ending "-ent" gives "sam" the appearance of a Latin participle, so that "Samient" comes to mean bringing together. As Hankins notes, it is Samient who brings Arthur and Artegall to "faire accordaunce." In fact, stanza 14 is composed entirely of such expressions of mutuality as "Either embracing other lovingly." Such peace making becomes more difficult, however, as the episode begins to impinge upon intransigent contemporary realities. In spite of her name, Samient fails to bring to success Mercilla's attempted concordat "by mutual consent" (st. 20) with the Souldan's wife Adicia (Greek *adikia*, unrighteousness, i.e. Rome). Between Samient's encomium of Mercilla and the knights' arrival at her court, a rash of politically allusive allegories occurs. Adicia's repulse of Samient hints at the bull of 1570 that undermined Elizabeth's toleration of English Catholics. Arthur's defeat of the Souldan points to the Armada victory. And the protean Malengin apparently betokens the elusive Jesuit and missionary priests in England and Ireland. This cluster of allegories that separate Samient's encomium of Mercilla from her presentation points up the intractability of realpolitik to the policy of "faire accordaunce." The tension between the ideal of Mercilla and the practical difficulties of her clemency emerges in the juxtaposition in canto ix of an icon of the queen in majesty set against the thorny political and judicial problem of Duessa's trial.

The icon of Mercilla is an ideal portrait but without the playfulness of earlier icons. In fact, the narrator's voice, often the playful agent, is muted (although audible a moment before Mercilla appears in his interpretation of Malfont's name). Spenser instead elevates encomium to the hymnic level that, in epideictic theory, crowns the scheme of genres. It is the iconic counterpart of the Orphic hymn to the quasi-deified empress in the first proem. Spenser even observes the taboo against making an image of Gloriana: Mercilla organizes the setting but is not herself physically described. Unlike Una or Belphoebe or Britomart, she has no face, nor is there any attempt at blazon or praise of the body part by part. Instead, Mercilla is like a deity, apprehended indirectly through ritual objects. After Artegall and Arthur have "entred at the Scriene" (ix. 25), presumably like the ecclesiastical rood-screen separating nave from sanctuary, they come into the presence of a queen who is "set on high, that all men she might see, / And might of all men royally be seene" (st. 27). But Mercilla is not seen. Instead, the rest of the stanza describes her throne, and the next two describe the cloth of state upheld by angels. Allusions abound to the tabernacle furniture made by the lawgiver Moses and enshrined in a temple by the wise royal judge Solomon. Mercilla's "throne of gold full bright and sheene" recalls the "mercy seat of pure gold" from which God gave laws to Israel: "I will commune with thee from above the mercy seat, from between the two cherubims which are upon the ark of the testimony" (Exodus 25:17, 22). Mercilla in presence seated on a golden mercy seat is thus allusively related to God judging mercifully. There are cherubim on Moses' mercy seat, on the tabernacle curtains (26:6), and on the veil hiding the holy of holies where the mercy seat rests on the ark of the law (26:31–34). When Solomon's temple was finished, the ark was brought "into the most holy place" and "the cherubims spread forth their wings over the place of the ark" (2 Chronicles 5:7–8). While the musicians "praised the Lord, saying, . . . his mercy endureth for ever: . . . the house was filled with a cloud. . . . So that the priests could not stand to minister . . . for the glory of the Lord had filled the house of God" (13–14). (Cf. Hebrews 9:4–5.) The angels enfolding the ark and the mercy seat, the hymn to the divine mercy, the cloud identified with the glory that cannot be looked on, all appear allusively in the most intense part of the Mercilla icon.

> All over her a cloth of state was spred,
>> Not of rich tissew, nor of cloth of gold,
>> Nor of ought else, that may be richest red,
>> But like a cloud, as likest may be told,
>> That her brode spreading wings did wyde unfold;

Whose skirts were bordred with bright sunny beams,
Glistring like gold, amongst the plights enrold,
And here and there shooting forth silver streames,
Mongst which crept little Angels through the glittering gleames.

Seemed those little Angels did uphold
    The cloth of state and on their purpled wings
    Did bear the pendants, through their nimblesse bold:
    Besides a thousand more of such, as sings
    Hymnes to high God, and carols heavenly things,
    Encompassed the throne, on which she sate:
    She Angel-like, the heyre of ancient kings
    And mightie Conquerors, in royall state,
Whylest kings and kesars at her feet did them prostrate.

                                        [sts. 28–29]

Here "She Angel-like, the heyre of ancient kings" touches on
comparatio and *genus*. Otherwise, topical encomium yields to a
peculiar synthesizing in which the cloth of state, the cloud, the
angels, and the "Angel-like" queen seem momentarily to fuse or
be superimposed so that Mercilla is neither visible nor invisible,
but partly defined by the phenomena surrounding her, partly
identical with them. At first "All over her a cloth of state was
spred," but it rapidly evaporates to become "like a cloud"—a
simile depreciated by the commentator in an inadequacy topos
("as likest may be told"). In the following line ("That *her* brode
spreading wings did wyde unfold"), "her" stimulates several
readings. If Spenser means simply the cloud, then "its" would be
normal. He seems instead to be relying on feminine Latin *nubes*
(cloud) to set up syntactical ambivalence between the cloud and
an apparently winged Mercilla, whereby the cloud unfolds its
wings around Mercilla, who simultaneously either unfolds the
cloud with her wings or else has her wings unfolded by the cloud.
Thus, the angels sheltering the ark and mercy seat, the cloud of
the divine presence, and Mercilla herself merge. Similarly,
"Whose skirts were bordred with bright sunny beams" may mean
the edges of the cloudlike canopy or the actual skirts "with
plights" of Mercilla's dress; in either case, skirts suggest discrete
distance maintained in the presence of divinity, as in the hymn of
Milton's angels before the Father: "Dark with excessive bright thy

skirts appear" *(Paradise Lost, III. 380)*. But in the next stanza the angels that "crept" "through the glittering gleames" of these luminous skirts are found upholding the cloth of state, others surround Mercilla's throne, the overlapping ceases and the picture clears, only to have the synthesizing tendency recapitulated in "She Angel-like," which again momentarily conflates Mercilla and the angels surrounding her and activates the ancient pun "Non Angli sed angeli." The recollection of the presence in one tabernacle of the ark of the law and the mercy seat appears also in the "sunny beams" and "silver streames" mingled in the skirts of Mercilla or the cloth of state or both, which, in their sun and moon imagery, fuse justice and mercy as in the vision at Isis Church: that is, justice-sun-Osiris complementing equity (clemency)-moon-Isis. Like the Old Testament allusions and the sun-moon mixture, the momentary blending of Mercilla and the angels and the cloth of state associates her with the ideal harmony of justice and mercy proper to God himself.

In the rest of the icon, however, this ecstatic synthesizing vision yields to a more visually accessible arrangement in which Mercilla displays various emblems of mercy and justice. But these appear in alternating sequence without any attempt at fusion. Mercilla holds a scepter, "The sacred pledge of peace and clemencie." But the rusty sword at her feet which she can "sternely draw" betokens the force needed to destroy enemies and keep order, an image used by Elizabeth herself in this sense.[14] Then the Litae reassert mercy, only to be followed by the chained lion, which has many meanings, all of them violent: justice controlling enemies; rebellion suppressed; royal power held in restraint; the lion couchant, a royal emblem; the potentiality for anger (the lion responds to "salvage choler"); and the passions tamed, especially restraint of anger in judgment.[15] When Mercilla finally sees Arthur and Artegall, she puts on a "cheerfull countenance," "Yet tempred with some majestie imperiall" (st. 34), a pattern repeated in the next stanza when "Majestie and awe" yield to "more myld aspect." To understand the construction Spenser puts upon Mercilla's role in Duessa's trial, it is important to notice that mercy and justice are now no longer fused but instead alternate.

Before discussing the trial, it is worth noting that the only other court in the poem, Lucifera's, is, in political terms, the demonic opposite of Mercilla's. Both are types, negative and positive, of the unseen court of Gloriana. There are many contrasting features, for instance, Mercilla's royal lion versus Lucifera's papal dragon;[16] Mercilla's moderated sun symbol versus Lucifera's burning Phaeton; and the openness of both palaces to all, with the difference that Awe screens entrants to Mercilla's "To keepe out guyle, and malice, and despite" (V. ix. 22) which correspond to Malegin, the Souldan, and Adicia, the political enemies the knights must overcome before approaching Mercilla.[17]

Further, a piece of closely worked parallelism affecting Book V cantos ix and x opposes Mercilla and Geryoneo's Idol and climaxes in stanzas 27–29 of both cantos, where Mercilla on her mercy seat matches the Idol with its altar and victims, and her hymn-singing angels oppose the monster lying in darkness under the altar to receive its sacrifices. The pattern sets Mercilla's mercy and peace keeping against the Inquisition and Spanish imperialism. Significantly, with the beginning of Duessa's trial the parallelism ceases.

The Judgment of Mercilla

Juxtaposition of a static ideal vision against mutability, fortune, and heroic struggle is one of Spenser's most used strategies, realized here in the sharply marked shift from encomium to narrative when we move from the Mercilla icon to a problematic event of very recent history. The transition in stanzas 34 and 35 calls attention to the contrast. In stanza 34, where Mercilla, "sitting high in dreaded soverayntie," notices the knights, the words describing her denote descent (e.g. "stoupe") and affect the royal sun-image (a *comparatio* at the end of encomium as in the Aphthonian disposition): as the westering sun "Gins to abate the brightnesse of his beme . . . So did this mightie Ladie." An example of Spenser's habit of using an image in contrary senses, the sun *comparatio* denotes majesty accommodating itself to human perception but also makes the sun the creature of time and so recalls the real queen's advanced age.[18] The transition effected, expressions of subjection to time take over at once ("Now, at that instant, as occasion fell," st. 36), and temporal words organize the ensuing trial: "But after," "Then," "First." Nowhere in the poem is the contrast of eternal and mutable made so plain.

In the trial, justice and mercy become fixed alternatives, the prosecution arguing for justice, the defense for not innocence but mercy (st. 45). As Dunseath points out, "Spenser balances five reasons against Duessa and five in her favour";[19] these culminate in the pleas of Justice and Griefe. The alternatives are schematized around Mercilla when she places Artegall and Arthur on either side of her "and neare them none" (st. 37). As Fowler notes, Mercilla "is in effect balancing their virtues (of justice and clemency). She has assumed the posture of Virgo, and the scales of justice are in her hand."[20]

Dunseath remarks that "Mercilla condemns Duessa only after it is clear that Duessa has condemned herself."[21] This glosses over the curious fact that we never see Mercilla's judgment. Instead, when Duessa is "guiltie deemed of them all," Mercilla

> whose Princely breast was touched nere
> With piteous ruth of her so wretched plight,
> Though plaine she saw by all, that she did heare,
> That she of death was guiltie found by right,
> Yet would not let just vengeance on her light;
> But rather let in stead thereof to fall
> Few perling drops from her faire lampes of light;
> The which she covering with her purple pall
> Would have the passion hid, and up arose withall.
>
> [st. 50]

This stanza flaunts its oddities. Its poles of choice are the pleonasm "piteous ruth" (usually in this poem a figure alerting suspicion) and the seeming contradiction "just vengeance." The pronominal ambivalence of "her so wretched plight" hints that Mercilla's emotion is partly pity for her own role in a situation where mercy and justice are incompatible. Self-pity may indeed be the "passion" expressed when, without pronouncing judgment, Mercilla precipitately leaves the court, muffled in her purple pall. This image parodies the emblem of Iustitia blindfolded to show impartiality. (Earlier, Mercilla administers "Justice with indifferent grace," st. 36.) The ambivalence in the stanza reflects

Elizabeth's evasions during 1586–87 when parliament after Mary's trial unanimously petitioned for immediate execution; she asked them to find some means of sparing Mary and, when the petition was renewed, returned an "answer answerless."[22] Spenser depicts these vacillations not as a compassionate judge's tempering of justice with mercy but as an emotional impasse that obfuscates justice. René Graziani notes that parliament found in Elizabeth's policy "crudelis misericordia": "cruel pity" in that mercy to Mary was cruelty to the nation and the queen herself.[23] "Crudelis misericordia" is a paradox consistent with the contradictions of stanza 50. But it fits so oddly with the name Mercilla as to suggest criticism utterly foreign to the encomiastic stance.

If the authorial persona is muted in the icon, the five opening stanzas of canto x allow it full scope. From the first occurrence of this voice as commentator, we have learned to suspect its reliability. Here, hard upon Mercilla's perplexing withdrawal, the commentator introduces the theoretical question of whether or not mercy can be considered separate from justice. As Nelson rightly notes, Spenser "raises and avoids the question."[24] Dunseath smooths over the commentator's shiftiness by asserting that Spenser "has already demonstrated the exact relationship of mercy to justice through temperance in Mercilla's just action" and "now slyly apprises the reader of its true effect."[25] But this is what Spenser has *not* demonstrated. That he poses the question at all necessarily reflects back upon the Mercilla icon where the imagistic strategy presents justice and mercy, first, as conjunctive, then as complementary, but always as inseparable.

The commentator's argument in the first two stanzas of canto x may be clarified somewhat by paraphrase. The first stanza says that, whether or not God made mercy inseparable from justice, it equals justice in importance and (like justice) originates in heaven. The second qualifies both justice and mercy with the aim of showing mercy more significant: if justice can exercise equity (in the old sense, i.e. judicial conscience) while adhering to "just verdict," then mercy must be greater since it tries to save and reform the condemned while upholding "doome of right." But such praise of mercy seems contradictory. To mitigate judgment with equity is feasible. To attempt to save the condemned while upholding "doome of right" (in Duessa's case, a verdict of guilty and a death sentence) is merely a benevolent but feckless gesture. (I take "doome of right" to mean both judgment and sentence; they are used synonymously in ix. 49).

The suspicion of sophistry sharpens when in stanza 3 the commentator shifts all too easily to praise of Mercilla's mercy. Here the typically encomiastic topoi of outdoing and *res gestae* appear in the context of two seemingly rhetorical questions. These may be regarded as inadequacy topoi and so a device of amplification. But they also function as genuine questions. In the first, "Who then can thee, Mercilla, throughly prayse, / That herein doest all earthly Princess pas?," "herein" apparently refers to the effort to save and reform while still rendering a judgment—something Mercilla has not been shown to accomplish. Thus, the question of who can "throughly prayse" her "herein" may have an ironic literal sense that punctures fulsome gesture. In the second question, "What heavenly Muse shall thy great honour rayse / Up to the skies," a curious detail appears. The topos of extent of fame, conventionally from India to Thule, is updated: "From th'utmost brinke of the Armericke shore, / Unto the margent of the Molucas." "Armericke" is a nonce-word hybridizing America and Armorica. (Spenser has used "Armoricke," meaning Brittany, at II. x. 64 and III. iii. 41.) To confuse America and Armorica is to obfuscate the point of the topos.[26] Hence, we do not quite know where to look for "Those Nations farre" who adore her justice.[27]

The fourth stanza reports almost as an aside Mercilla's judgment of Duessa, while insisting on her mercy, praised by Arthur and Artegall

> When they had seene and heard her doome a rights
> Against Duessa, damned by them all;
> But by her tempred without griefe or gall,
> Till strong constraint did her thereto enforce.
> And yet even then ruing her wilfull fall,
> With more than needfull naturall remorse,
> And yeelding the last honour to her wretched corse.

It is hard to see how judgment could be "tempred *without* griefe or gall," since these are the poles of compassion or anger between which a judge might modify judgment according to conscience. In any case, at the end of canto ix Mercilla clearly reacts to the call for judgment with grief. (Griefe is the last spokesman for Duessa, temporarily bringing Arthur to a state of compassion.) The placement of the sixth line creates ambiguity. Did "strong constraint" at last force Mercilla to "doome a rights"? Or did it force her to temper judgment? Finally, the ambivalent "more then needfull natural remorse" is almost an oxymoron.

In the fifth stanza, Arthur and Artegall remain at Mercilla's court, observing "Royall examples of her mercies rare, / And worthie paterns of her clemencies." This comfortable generalization adroitly idealizes the chop-logic preceding it: for it is not possible for Mercilla to show significant mercy to Duessa. The end of the stanza implicitly admits this difficulty in the political allegory by suddenly divorcing Mercilla and Duessa from Elizabeth and Mary and asserting the antiquity of Mercilla's mercies: "Which till this day mongst many living are, / Who them to their posterities doe still declare." More than any other part of the poem, the second half of Book V insists on its political allusions. But these two lines hamper the political allegory by relegating Mercilla's mercy to a remote past and so undermine encomium by implying that the real queen can be more aptly praised through antique fiction than political fact. The polarity is analogous to that between Faery and British earlier in the poem. In Book II, however, the Faery and British chronicles complement each other. Here, ideal fictional antiquity and current allusion are set at odds.

It would be wrong to look for satire here and sentimental to feel that Mercilla has wronged Duessa. From the perspective of the poem's encomiastic program, the point is rather that the harmony of justice and mercy praised in the icon cannot be realized in political action, unless we ignore the clustered ambiguities of ix. 50–x. 5 and accept the salesmanship of the commentator, thereby abandoning the canny and inquisitive attitude toward reading the poem that Spenser has inculcated in us from the beginning. The attempt to gloss over the disparity between icon and action prompts disturbing but seemingly unanswerable questions: Why does Spenser in this Legend of Justice embody its correlative mercy in so unsatisfactory a way? Why name the queen's type Mercilla only to infect the name with ambiguity? And why choose as Mercilla's area of action an event about which Elizabeth behaved so uncertainly? There is also a related structural question which admits of discussion: What is the core canto of Book V?

Critics sometimes speak of the Mercilla episode as a core canto or (to use my term) matrix, probably because Spenser conditions us to expect this in the tenth canto.[28] The ninth-canto Mercilla episode, however, violates the expectation, and its five stanzas in canto x accentuate the displacement. If we consider the Mercilla episode the matrix, then we see for the first time a model itself examined in practice, with the result that the ideal is diminished in exemplary effect (cf. Book I where Redcrosse, not Caelia, must convert holiness into narrative). The episode at Isis Church actually is more like a matrix: that is, an idealized allegorical temple in which a heroine learns of her arcane role through an interpreted vision. This corresponds exactly to Redcrosse's experience in the House of Holiness and Arthur's and Guyon's in the House of Alma. As matrix, however, Isis Church in canto vii stands further from the tenth-canto position than does Mercilla's court. And the figure undergoing the experience is not the book's titular knight but Britomart. What Book V presents is two matrices, neither satisfactory in itself. If these reflect the image of justice's scales, they are noticeably not in perfect balance. As Kathleen Williams notes, "Mercilla's palace is a lesser companion piece to Isis Church."[29] For, as an allegory of the rigor of justice mitigated by equity or clemency, Isis Church has the serene success we expect at a matrix, while the relation of justice and mercy in the Mercilla icon becomes problematic. In fact, the Isis and Mercilla episodes together express the disparity between ideal and action, fiction and history, that, as we have seen, also occur in the Mercilla episode itself.

The Proem to Book V

The same disparity appears in sharp outline in the proem to Book V. By emphasizing in its first stanza the "oddes" that set "The image of the antique world" in opposition to the "state of present time," Spenser borrows a strategy common in satire (as when Juvenal measures the mores of his culture against the republican past). The difference is that Spenser does not claim truth for the normative past: it is an "image" or fiction distinct from the present—an admission not made in 1590 when Faery myth and purportedly factual British chronicle are paired. By so prefacing Book V, Spenser puts, in advance, a construction on those episodes in the second half of the book which allegorize in ideal terms certain events drawn from "state of present time." There any Elizabethan would recognize familiar events depicted as they had not occurred and in that discrepancy would sense political comment. A. B. Gough notes that "as an idealized version of history a great part of Cantos X and XI would be ridiculous"; in reality, "Prince Arthur retired with dishonour from the fight with the Seneschal, and Belge was glad to get rid of him, . . . Gerioneo and Grantorto were scotched, not killed."[30] This is true, with the important qualification that most of these events were for the reader of 1596 not "history" but recent occurrences: Burbon's rejection of his shield (V. 11. 53–4) brings us right up to Henri IV's conversion, 25 July 1593.

The disparity between present state and antique image gives the proem its intellectual design. Its first four stanzas construe the present as a stone age, Spenser's pessimistic addition to the Hesiodic Four Ages of decline from an ideal golden age: men were "backward bred" from their beginning; all their values are now reversed so that "Right now is wrong, and wrong that was is right." But its final stanza, an encomium of Elizabeth as deified empress administering justice, closely parallels the Orphic hymn in the first proem:

> Dread Soverayne Goddesse, that doest highest sit
>> In seate of judgement, in th' Almighties stead,
>> And with magnificke might and wondrous wit
>> Doest to thy people righteous doome aread,
>> That furthest Nations filles with awfull dread,
>> Pardon the boldnesse of thy basest thrall,
>> That dare discourse of so divine a read,
>> As thy great justice praysed over all:
> The instrument whereof loe here thy Artegall.

These two attitudes are curiously bridged by the sardonic claim that cosmic disorder is to blame for the reversal of values (st. 4). Fowler notes that Spenser's examples of heavenly disorder actually describe equinoctial precession which, though it "appeared to alter the heavens irreversibly, . . . was known in reality to be a cyclical phenomenon with a very long period. Spenser therefore implies that behind the seeming mutability of the cosmos there is an underlying order."[31] But Spenser actually does not go so far. Although no doubt aware of the cyclical nature of precession, he presents the celestial disorder that causes earthly decline as a movement of both toward their "last ruinous decay" (st. 6). It is hard to know whether to take the idea that the cosmos causes moral degeneration as mannered pessimism (as it is in Donne's *Anniversaries*) or a satirical stratagem. Spenser's choice of examples of planetary miscarriage suggests the latter. In particular, "that same glorious lampe of light, / That doth illumine all these lesser fyres," now "miscaried with the other Spheres" (st. 7), inevitably brings the sun-monarch analogy into play. Mars, most "amisse of all the rest" (st. 8), suggests martial failure, and the crab's intrusion "Into the great Nemean lions grove" (st. 6) implies the erosion of the Herculean role by envy.

The crux in the transition from cosmic decadence to royal praise occurs with the planet "old Saturne, that was wont be best" (st. 8), that is, most regular. But in the next stanza "Saturnes ancient raigne" refers instead to the ethical supremacy of the Golden Age when "All loved vertue," and "Justice sat high ador'd." The pretense that the meaning of Saturn and of "best" has not shifted is transparent sophistry. In stanza 10 we move from Justice in the Golden Age to justice as God's "imperiall" virtue and in stanza 11 to praise of the queen, who exercises this role "in th'Almighties stead." Here we find encomium rising arbitrarily from sleight-of-hand: the Golden Age and modern decay remain in opposition, while we hear the praise of the present monarch. But how does praise of Elizabeth affect a decadent age? Spenser invites this question by the organization of his proem but refuses the familiar steps that would allow encomium to transcend the polarity he has set up. A well-worn encomiastic device is praise of a ruler for restoring the Golden Age. Behind it is Virgil's famous "iam redit et virgo, redeunt Saturnia regna" (*Ec.* 4.6). But

Spenser refuses this easy connection. In fact, he habitually avoids the idea of the Golden Age returned, treating it either as a lost state or with mockery. Fowler notes it as odd that, given the Virgin Queen's Astraea cult, there is no allusion to her as Virgo in V. i. 5–11 where Astraea gives Artegall his sword.[32] No allusion would be more apposite to encomium. Nor is the analogy made at the end of the proem where, given eulogy of Justice in Saturn's reign, it would be natural now to associate the queen with Justice-Astraea-Virgo. The failure to make such connections leaves the encomium high and dry, isolated from the context Spenser sets up.

One clue to understanding this tactic may lie in the encomiastic stanza where Artegall is presented as the queen's "instrument" of divine justice. Astraea herself has prepared Artegall as an agent of justice before she abandons "wicked men" to become stellified as Virgo (i. 11). But the Faery Queen assigns Artegall his quest to deliver Irena from Grantorto (i. 4). That is, at the beginning of Artegall's quest Astraea and the Faery Queen are kept distinct. At its end, the Faery Queen's mind has changed: orders from "Faerie Court" recall Artegall, frustrating "His course of Justice" in Irena's kingdom and revoking Talus "from the right way" (xii. 27). In the commentator's terse aside assigning Artegall's recall to *invidia*—"But envies cloud *still* dimmeth vertues ray"—"still" has its old meaning "always." Envy, Detraction, and soon the Blatant Beast appear to malign Artegall. The episode depicts the end of Grey's career in Ireland. It is unique among the political allegories of Book V because there is no idealization whatever—as Judson notes, "no departure from fact."[33] As a result, the Legend of Justice closes on a surprisingly sour note, with justice not translated from ideal to reality but undone in practice by the agency ordained to administer it. The incident leaves Astraea and the Faery Queen far apart and suggests why Spenser sidesteps identification of Elizabeth and Virgo. To glance back at the last line of the proem: from the perspective of canto xii "instrument" takes on the ironic sense of a tool misused.

Intriguingly, the inadequacy topos at the end of the proem, where the poet craves pardon for "the boldnesse" of broaching "so divine a read, / As thy great justice praysed over all," echoes the description of the poet Malfont—once Bonfont—with his tongue nailed to Mercilla's screen: Malfont has "blazed" "bold speaches" and assumed "the bold title of a Poet bad" (ix. 25). The narrator pretends to be uncertain whether his name means "th'evill, which he did therein" or "a welhed / Of evill words, and wicked sclaunders" (st. 26). But this is "plainely to be red" when compared with the ambiguity enveloping "the purport of his sin" written "In cyphers strange, that few could rightly read, / BON FONT."[34] It is the crime or the name that few could rightly read? Or is the crime synonymous with being Bonfont? That is, must a responsible poet sometimes utter criticisms adjudged criminal by the regime? Certainly these lines effect one of Spenser's favorite strategies, the retroactive casting of doubt upon a simplistic assertion. Here, the ambiguity perturbs the judgment that Bonfont "falsely did revyle / And foule blaspheme that Queene for forged guyle." The two pleonasms "foule blaspheme" and "forged guyle" augment suspicion that political criticism or satire has been silenced under judgment of calumny. Puttenham's slip of the lip—"the Poets being in deede the trumpetters of all praise and also of slaunder (not slaunder, but well deserved reproch)"[35]—reminds us that blame is the negative side of the epideictic category and that the difference between blame and slander may depend on point of view. Malfont's position just outside Mercilla's presence chamber oddly prefaces the icon and trial and suggests that his crime may be outspokenness about their disparity.[36] Certainly the boldness of the poet who had openly changed his mind about the regime corresponds to the boldness of the poet who juxtaposes praise and satire in the proem.

Britomart at Isis Church and Radegone

Two episodes relevant to encomium in Book V remain to be noted: Britomart's vision at Isis Church and her victory over Radigund. Both allude in part to Elizabeth's dealing with the problem of Mary.[37] Aside from this topical aspect, Britomart's vision at Isis Church recapitulates two encomiastic phenomena discussed in the previous chapter: her meeting with Artegall in which adversaries become lovers; and her genetic role as mother of the British line and Elizabeth's ancestress. The vision presents these narrative events in a static and permanent manner. The two stages of Britomart's transfiguration—as Isis's priestess in linen stole and moon-mitre, then royally as the goddess herself in scarlet robe and crown of gold—encompass Britomart's double encomiastic identity in the poem as heroine-ancestor and type of Elizabeth. Her progress from moon- to sun-symbols and from priesthood to majesty indicates that Britomart-Isis, as well as epitomizing the equity that restrains justice from undue severity, also paradoxically contains the opposites, justice-equity, in herself. She both requires Artegall-Osiris as complement and simultaneously subsumes his meanings, just as Venus in the Temple of Venus—enwreathed by a snake as Isis is by the crocodile—contains within herself both male and female potentiality, even while the male element is externally symbolized.

It is in this sense that Britomart, having seen her destiny in a vision of clemency subduing severity, can nevertheless apply that vision by managing Radigund not with clemency but with "true Justice" (vii. 42). For both justice and clemency lie within her capacity. Indeed, the swift justice she administers to Radigund is the only clemency possible in this case (just as, for Elizabeth, true *misericordia* lay in Mary's execution).

At Radegone, Britomart finds the dream at Isis Church pervertedly realized by unnatural reversal of sexes. For Radigund takes on some negative meanings of the male crocodile in the dream, among them force and fraud.[38] As Terpin points out, Radigund subdues knights "by force or guile" (iv. 31); and she wins her fight with Artegall by a combination of fraud (playing dead) and force. Further, the crocodile "swolne with pride of his owne peerless powre" (vii. 15) tries to eat Isis. Radigund's pride is everywhere insisted on: she is "A Princesse of great powre, and greater pride" (iv. 33); her "belt of mickell pride" (v. 3), like the Amazon Hippolyta's, means libidinousness set against male authority.[39] Among the malleable aspects of the crocodile are "sterne behests, and cruell doomes" (vii. 22). But Radigund's Amazons are "like tyrants, mercilesse the more" (iv. 23), and their "proud law" (v. 22) an emasculating system that contradicts natural law. Indeed, Artegall's first glimpse of perverted Amazon justice mirrors the last stage of a legal process: Terpin "for the gallow tree prepard" (iv. 22).

The crocodile's most positive aspect is his erotic "game" that leaves Britomart-Isis "enwombed" (vii. 16) with the lion that ensures the British line. Britomart, however, sardonically recognizes Radigund's emasculation of Artegall as a "May-game" (vii. 40)—i.e. a perversion of the spring fertility festival. Spenser makes it clear that Radigund's "cruell hate" is sublimated erotic behavior (she vainly wooed "Bellodant the bold," iv. 30), and her secret advances to Artegall work out her association with Dido (her "Camis light of purple silke," v. 2, is Dido's "purpuream . . . vestem" of *Aeneid* 4. 139).[40] Like Dido's, her erotic ambitions are threats to dynasty and empire. When Artegall yields his "cruell minded hart" to "pitiful regard" and "ruth of beautie" (v. 13), he cooperates in sexually reversing and morally confounding the crocodile-Isis paradigm. Radigund thus uncontrollably acts out the crocodile's violence, while Artegall plays mercy-seeking Isis ineffectually. When Britomart refuses to hear Radigund's "streight conditions" (vii. 28) and decapitates her, she fulfills vicariously Artegall's derelict role as justiciar. But when she enters Radegone and "For very ruth" restrains the "hideous storme" of Talus's rampage (cf. the "hideous tempest" inflaming the crocodile, vii. 14) and her own "revengeful vow" (vii. 35–36), she realizes the paradigmatic vision in which "clemence . . . Restraines . . . cruell doomes" (vii. 22). As the vision shows, such behavior is closer to her own proper nature as an Isis figure.

It is worth noting how much more securely Britomart translates into action an ideal vision of justice and mercy than does Mercilla. While both are types of Elizabeth, Britomart is far more effective as a vehicle of encomium. In terms of the political allusion to the case of Mary Stuart, Britomart acts with clearheaded correctness, while Mercilla bungles and temporizes. But, because the Mercilla-Duessa episode matches historical fact and the Britomart-Radigund episode does not, the two episodes confront us with the opposition of fictive image and state of present time that recurrently damages the praise of Elizabeth in Book V.

In terms of encomium, Radigund, like Duessa in Book I, is a figure of *vituperatio*, a demonic parody of Elizabeth as ruler. Her government of Radegone elicits the famous stanza on women rulers according to which women are by "wise Nature" bound "T'obay the heasts of mans well ruling hand," "Unlesse the heavens them lift to lawfull soveraintie" (v. 25). This is the position taken by Calvin and the more moderate Genevans, who denied the right and ability of women to govern but (unlike Knox) allowed for divinely ordained exceptions.[41] The stanza does not necessarily mean that Spenser held the Calvinist position; rather, it eminently suits his needs as encomiast by making Elizabeth an example of special divine sanction. When in Radegone Britomart "as Princesse rained" (vii. 42), she does so as fictive type of the queen who is the successful exception to the rule.

Not much as been made in Spenser studies of the fact that Spenser borrows the name Radigund from a French saint (519–87) of the Merovingian period (herself the subject of encomia by Fortunatus).[42] He mentions her in *Mother Hubberds Tale* (497–99), where the priest advises the Fox to "seeme as Saintlike as Saint Radegund." Although the context is satiric, the reference to the saint's piety—"Fast much, pray oft, looke lowly on the ground, / And unto everie one doo curtsie meeke"—does not seem so. Certainly such attributes contrast sharply with Radigund's pride. In fact, Spenser exploits the irony inherent in Radigund's hagiological name. For instance, though wife to Clotaire, the saint was a virgin queen, "A wyfe and mayde as fewe other be."[43] Spenser emphasized Radigund's queenly rank, but her virginity results from displacement of desire to rage.[44] The saint escapes her lustful husband to found a convent at Poitiers. Radigund, her advances to Bellodant rejected, founds the Amazon city, Radegone. The saint is said to have shown special charity to prisoners. Radigund rather conspicuously does not.

In topical terms, Saint Radegund was a patroness of France—a role given a strongly anti-English cast in the Hundred Years' War during which the English lost nearly all French holdings.[45] Spenser has her pro-French, anti-English associations in mind when he makes her Amazon namesake a threat to the union of Artegall and Britomart and hence the British line. Here, the "Magnificke Virgin" Britomart (vii. 21) rescues Artegall from a Dido figure named after a French virgin queen, thereby helping to fulfill the prophecy that culminates in a true Virgin Queen. Ironically, one sense of Artegall's name may be "Art-de-Gaul," i.e. taken in by French wiles. (Interestingly, *Mother Hubberds Tale*, in which Spenser refers to Saint Radegund, satirizes the proposed French marriage.) The French threat to emasculate England by marriage, contrived in part by Catherine de Medicis, may thus be one sense of the episode.

Radigund is usually considered an allusion to Mary Stuart, and this is consistent with her saintly name, for Mary was briefly queen of France. Hence, the allusion to a virgin queen may satirically characterize Mary's loose living (Britomart suspects that Artegall has fallen into "harlots bondage," vi. 11). More precisely, the episode probably recalls the project (1563–65) of marrying Leicester to Mary, in which Leicester played the suitor's part most reluctantly. [46] Spenser does not suggest that Elizabeth and Cecil devised the scheme, but rather through Britomart makes Elizabeth the agent of Leicester's disentanglement. However, Britomart's unflinchingly assured handling of Radigund and especially her promptly decapitating the Amazon as soon as she can ("the wrothfull Britonese / Stayd not," vii. 34), so little resembles Elizabeth's vacillations in the case of Mary's execution as to insinuate criticism of the queen's behavior. As with his management of the Mercilla episode, Spenser appears here to be undermining the encomiastic statement of Book V.

CHAPTER SEVEN

1596
Pardon Thy Shepheard

Book VI is remarkable for its failure to praise Elizabeth, although Colin's beautiful apology for *not* including Gloriana offers praise by default. The sixth proem, however, like the first, begins with authorial assertion, proceeds to invocations, and climaxes in encomium. The mirror imagery, common to all three proems of 1590 (but significantly lacking in the defensive fourth and satirical fifth), returns in the sixth proem with the same sense of the queen as mediatrix that is found in the first proem: "The goodly praise of Princely curtesie" shows in her "pure minde, as in a mirrour sheene" and "doth inflame / The eyes of all, which thereon fixed beene" (VI. pro. 6). But there is a second mirror here, a "glasse so gay, that it can blynd / The wisest sight, to thinke gold that is bras" (st. 5). Contrast between truthful and flattering mirrors is a satirical convention in the long *speculum* tradition. In fact, in stanzas 4 and 5 Spenser heads toward a satirical impasse (as in the fifth proem) by opposing contemporary and ideal antique courtesy: when "matcht with plaine Antiquitie," courtesy is "now so farre from that, which then it was / That it indeed is nought but forgerie." Unlike the fifth proem, however, he resolves this impasse in the expected encomiastic way: the queen evinces a "patterne" of courtesy that outdoes "all Antiquity." Potential satire thus makes piquant the hyperbole essential to praise.

The last stanza voices encomium in broader terms that make the queen the pattern not only of courtesy but of all virtues: "Right so from you all goodly vertues well, / Into the rest, which round about you ring." This abstract concludes encomium in the poem: it is pointless to make the queen epitomize further virtues if she has been praised for all of them. The scheme whereby Elizabeth models the virtues, inspires their practice, and receives their achievement as "tribute" is a closed system, like the cycle of waters that is its metaphor. But it is a scheme in which the poet also participates. By deriving the book's thematic virtue from the queen and rendering it to her again, he implies that presentation of the poem is a reciprocal gesture of courtesy. In fact, the system of inspiring and receiving corresponds to the arrangement of the Graces at the book's matrix which means "That good should from us goe, then come in greater store" (x. 24). The "Faire Lords and Ladies" "which round about you ring" make the queen and her court analogous to the country lass of Colin's vision, surrounded by a hundred naked maidens "raunged in a ring" (x. 11, 12). But the point of the compliment is to compensate for the explicit absence of a royal type on Mount Acidale and apparently in Book VI at large.[1]

When conspicuous praise of Elizabeth occurs in the books of 1590, Spenser also makes us aware of his role as encomiast. As encomium of the queen becomes less and less evident in the books added in 1596, Spenser brings the role of the poet increasingly into focus; in one sense, the poet becomes the hero of Book VI. Hence, this chapter has two main subjects: the transfer of encomium from Elizabeth to other figures; and the poet's reassessment of his role, particularly with reference to Orpheus, the humanists' favorite archetype for the successful poet.

Pastorella and Colin's Lass as Private Figures

I have earlier shown how the private figure Serena replaces the expected royal type in the third canto of Book VI. Following the paradigm of Redcrosse and Una, we might look for royal allusion in Calidore's Pastorella. In fact, Calidore is first mentioned as a devotee of the queen's type, Florimell (III. viii. 28). Pastorella, however, is not only not a royal type, but actually blocks the Faery Queen's intentions, a difficulty the narrator probes in canto x: "Whilest Calidore does follow that faire Mayd," he must be "unmyndfull of his vow and high beheast, / Which by the Faery

Queen was on him layd" (st. 1). But criticism of the knight for substituting "Another quest" (st. 2) yields to exculpation by means of court satire: Calidore cannot "greatly blamed be" for preferring the shepherds' "happy peace" to the court's "painted show / Of such false blisse, as there is set for stales" (st. 3)." This combination of attitudes mirrors the epideictic opposition of praise and blame and leads to contradictions in stanza 4.

> For what hath all that goodly glorious gaze
>   Like to one sight, which Calidore did vew?
> The glaunce where of their dimmed eies would daze,
> That never more they should endure the shew
> Of that sunne-shine, that makes them looke askew.
> Ne ought in all that world of beauties rare,
>   (Save onely Glorianaes heavenly hew
>   To which can what compare?) can it compare;
> The which as commeth now, by course I will declare.

As an epithet for the court, "goodly glorious gaze" hints at Gloriana and reverses the satirical gesture. But the exaltation of "one sight, which Calidore did vew" over the courtiers' "sunneshine, that makes them looke askew" (a suspiciously ambivalent modifier) diverts the *comparatio* whereby the monarch outshines the sun to imply that the private sight outdoes the monarch. But before this comparison is complete, however, the parenthesis "Save onely Glorianaes heavenly hew / To which can what compare?" has reaffirmed her supremacy. To announce two different supremacies radically undermines encomium's fundamental claim that its subject exceeds all others. Spenser's stratagem here introduces the praise of Elizabeth as a means of amplifying the encomium of a private figure; at the same time, he denies any infringement on Gloriana's praise because that praise is distinct in kind. Such a stratagem, in a poem called *The Faerie Queene*, strains tact.

The "one sight, which Calidore did vew" is ambivalent, looking back to his courtship of Pastorella at the end of canto 9 and ahead to his imminent vision in canto 10. The ambivalence makes Pastorella and Colin's lass analogous. Both have attributes borrowed from the depiction of Eliza in *Aprill*. When Calidore comes upon Pastorella, she is the center of a pastoral court the details of which are transfigured in the revelation of the lass. Pastorella wears "a crowne / Of sundry flowres" (ix. 7) recalling the floral coronation of Eliza, while the lass is "Crownd with a rosie girlond" (x. 14). Whatever the lass's rose may mean, it matches Pastorella's real name Rose or Rosalind, for her old nurse Melissa (Greek, honeybee) identifies her by "The little purple rose" birthmark "Whereof her name ye then to her did give" (xii. 18). But neither rose seems to convey the Tudor associations of Eliza's rose. Pastorella is "Environ'd with a girland, goodly graced, / Of lovely lasses" (ix. 8), while the lass centers the dancing Graces and "An hundred naked maidens lilly white, / All raunged in a ring" (x. 11), and Eliza is a fourth among the dancing Graces. The arrangement aligns all three with Venus. Indeed, the shepherds take Pastorella for "their soveraine goddesse" (ix. 9), while the lass suggests "beauties Queene," Venus (x. 17), and Colin thinks her "a goodess graced / With heavenly gifts" (x. 25), a recapitulation of his "goddesse plaine," Eliza. Such parallels show that Spenser, as his poem nostalgically reverts to pastoral, is borrowing from *Aprill* to praise two private ladies.[2] From the perspective of Book VI, the informing figure in this interrelated set of passages is now Colin's lass. Certainly the sight of Pastorella enthroned anticipates the apparition of the lass only to be subordinated to it.

The apotheosis of Colin's unnamed country girl is the most luminous, magical, and haunting episode in the poem, effortlessly fusing fey Celtic lore, the allegories of Florentine Neoplatonism, and the Christian mystery of grace intermeddled, in the highest Renaissance fashion, with the pagan Graces. With each rereading it declares itself further. Although I must touch on the episode again before the end of this chapter, my topic fortunately does not demand an adequate account. On a more prosaic level, we may note that the *res gestae* exalting a country lass here are those used previously in the queen's praise: "Divine resemblaunce, beauty soveraine rare, /Firme Chastity, that spight ne blemish dare" (x. 27). Immediately following is the apology to Gloriana in which the voice speaking through Colin is not the narrator-persona but rather the poet-persona that speaks directly to Elizabeth in the proems:

Sunne of the worlde, great glory of the sky,
  That all the earth doest lighten with thy rayes,
  Great Gloriana, greatest Majesty,
  Pardon thy shepheard, mongst so many layes,
  As he hath sung of thee in all his dayes,
  To make one minime of thy poore handmayd,
  And underneath thy feete to place her prayse,
  That when thy glory shall be farre displayd
To future age of her this mention may be made.

This exquisite and moving apology is nonetheless an apology, overtly declaring that, at this most resplendent of the poem's allegorical matrices, the queen does not have pride of place. In fact, "one minime" greatly understates the private encomium just offered. The apology does reaffirm priorities: Gloriana is still "greatest Majesty" and the lass "thy poore handmayd." But, in apportioning praise here, Spenser has obviously given the greater part to the lass.

Through this apology Spenser retroactively confirms that, in the female quasi divinities who preside over the other allegorical cores—Caelia, Alma, Venus, and Isis—he is alluding to Elizabeth. By so managing each matrix, he has repeatedly presented Elizabeth as the ideal form of each virtue. In each such episode the hero experiences the model of the virtue, corrects his practice, and offers the achievement back to Gloriana: exactly the system presented abstractly in the sixth proem. But at the matrix of Book VI Spenser places, not an Elizabeth figure, but an unknown girl whose virtues epitomize those to be practiced in the book; for example, her "Firme Chastity, that spight ne blemish dare" corrects by example the questionable and easily slandered virtue of Priscilla and Serena. But her climactic virtue is courtesy, praised by outdoing *comparatio*: "all her peeres cannot with her compare, / But quite are dimmed, when she is in place" (x. 27). Calidore's first act after seeing her is not pseudopastoral but part of his Herculean role: he kills a tiger and so foreshadows the achievement of his quest. Thus, the apparition of Colin's lass stimulates Calidore's virtue just as Caelia does Redcrosse's.

The uneasy duality between outdoing praise of the lass and apologetic aside affirming Gloriana's supremacy shows particu-

larly in two astronomical images. One is the hyperbole that makes
the lass "the daughter of the day" who does "All other lesser lights
in light excell" (x. 26)—as Humphrey Tonkin suggests, probably
Venus in its morning-star form Lucifer or Aurora.[3] (The same
image works for Una in her apotheosis at the end of Book I.) The
typology agrees with the position of the lass in the Graces' dance
on Venus's mountain. However, the reaffirmation in the apology
that Gloriana is "Sunne of the world, great glory of the skye"
makes the lass ancillary to the queen as morning star is to sun, and
the tension is resolved.

But the other image, of Ariadne's Crown, apparently leaves the
tension unresolved. We take in the vision according to Calidore's
perception. First he sees the circle of maidens, then the Graces.
But *before* he sees the lass in the center there is a striking authorial
interpolation:

> Looke how the Crowne, which Ariadne wore
>> Upon her yvory forehead that same day,
>> That Theseus her unto his bridale bore,
>> When the bold Centaures made that bloudy fray,
>> With the fierce Lapithes, which did them dismay;
>> Being now placed in the firmament,
>> Through the bright heaven doth her beames display,
>> And is unto the starres an ornament,
> Which round about her move in order excellent.
>
> [x. 13]

This stanza with its mingling of myths has drawn much comment.[4] Frances Yates shows that Ariadne—deserted by Theseus,
crowned by Bacchus, stellified as the Corona borealis, and placed
in heaven near Virgo—was sometimes identified with Virgo-
Astraea and says that Spenser's "Virgo-Ariadne was also Eliza-
beth-Virgo." But her further assumption that this is the identity
of the girl in the vision[5] ignores Spenser's overt distinction between Colin's lass and Elizabeth's types in the apology to
Gloriana and also the structure of the heroic simile whereby the
stanza on Ariadne's Crown explicitly refers not to the lass but to
"the beauty of this goodly band" surrounding her. Only when the
simile is completed does Calidore perceive the lass in encomiastic
terms of outdoing that put both the goodly band and Ariadne's

Crown in the shade: "But she that in the midst of them did stand, /Seem'd all the rest in beauty to excell" (x. 14). Ariadne's Crown that rises above bloody fray may indeed compliment the queen. If so, it appears that Spenser has positioned one of Elizabeth's symbols to augment praise of a private lady, deliberately exacerbating the tension inherent in encomium of two subjects. While the apology claims that the lass is Gloriana's "poore handmayd," the use made of Ariadne does quite the reverse.

Tristram and Essex

Another figure who receives praise that, in the preceding books, would have been given to Elizabeth, is Tristram. In fact, in a book where the praise of the Faery Queen is nearly silent, Spenser deploys the encomiastic topoi freely to create an almost iconic portrait of this magnetic adolescent. Calidore's first glimpse of Tristram touches on *corporis bona* and *genus*: "A goodly youth of amiable grace," "tall and faire of face, / That sure he deem'd him borne of noble race" (ii. 5). Tristram later offers his own materials for *genus*: he is "a Briton borne, / Sonne of a King" (ii. 27), that is, *gens*; "the onely heire / Of good king Meliogras" and his queen "Faire Emiline" (sts. 28–29), that is, *patres*; his *patria* is Cornwall (st. 28) or "Lionesse" (st. 30). Calidore praises Tristram by a *comparatio* to "Latonaes sonne" Apollo (st. 25), playing on sun and son. But the dominant topos is one Spenser seldom uses, *educatio*, or signs of promise shown in youth: "For since the day that armes I first did reare," says Calidore, "I never saw in any greater hope appeare" (st. 26). In the darkening poem of 1596, hope is a rare quantity.

The redirection of praise topoi away from Elizabeth toward Tristram and his heroic promise is meant, I believe, to flatter the Earl of Essex, at the height of his brief career in the mid-1590s.[6] Two details make the connection, Tristram's age and his intense desire for arms. Spenser specifies Tristram's age with a precision unique in the poem: he "scarse did see / Yet seventeene yeares" (st. 5) and has been in exile since the age of ten (st. 30). Essex was in his seventeenth year when he first appeared at court, presented by his stepfather Leicester. His father, like Meliogras, "Untimely dyde" (st. 28), and he succeeded to the titles in his ninth year. Tristram's seven years of sylvan exile match the period Essex spent at Cambridge and on his estates.[7] Finally, Tristram's eagerness for "use of armes, which most I joy" (st. 32) squares nicely with Essex's attempts at conspicuous heroics and longing for glory.

The traditional identification of Calidore with Sidney seems operative when he dubs Tristram squire, for a codicil added to Sidney's will on his deathbed left Essex "my best sword"[8]—a transparently symbolic bequest to the then eighteen-year-old earl. At twenty Essex received from Leicester's will "the best armour I have . . . with a George and Garter, in hope he shall wear it shortly."[9] These gestures hand on a heroic role and appear obliquely here in Tristram's excitement at "despoyling that dead knight / Of all those goodly implements of prayse" (st. 34)— "gilden armes, with azure band / Quartred athwart" (st. 44), a reference to the gift of the Garter and Essex's installation in that order for his services during the summer of the Armada.[10] The rest of the device, "A Ladie on rough waves, row'd in a sommer barge," probably alludes to the queen's victory and the famous storm. These details correlate Tristram's *educatio* with anticipation of Essex's future brilliance.

In 1590 Essex married Sidney's widow, the beautiful Frances Walsingham. If we accept the Calidore-Sidney allusion, then some connections between Tristram and Calidore's Pastorella appear. Both are of the younger generation in Book VI, in exile from their true state, and dressed in green (ii. 5; ix. 7). Significantly, Calidore thinks Pastorella "a Princess Paragone" (ix. 11), and Tristram is a prince, as Calidore is not.

Some other details associate Tristram and Essex. Tristram is tall (ii. 3, 5) and "faire of face" (st. 5), two of Essex's conspicuous qualities. His origin in Cornwall and "Lionesse" hints at the Devereux's Welsh holdings. The *comparatio* like "Latonaes sonne, / After his chace in woodie Cynthus donne" (st. 25) alludes to his role as Elizabeth's favorite, since Cynthus is one of Diana's haunts (cf. II. iii. 31 and VII. iii. 50) and Apollo and Diana are brother and sister. But Apollo's most frequent association in Spenser is solar,[11] and when Tristram "Long fed his greedie eyes" on his new arms "shyning like Sunne rayes" (st. 39), the insistence on sun-armor hints at a royal role. The Tristram portrait may celebrate Essex as Leicester's successor in Elizabeth's favor. Yet Spenser salutes the earl in terms that ignore his total dependence on the queen.[12]

But why choose the well-worn name Tristram for Essex? Probably there is a pun on "Trist-*ramus*" or "sad branch" (Latin *ramus*) referring to his exile and promise of growth and related to his green forester's costume. In *Prothalamion* an epithet for Essex is "Faire branch on Honor." And in the proem courtesy, though on "a lowly stalke," "Yet brancheth forth to all nobilitie" (st. 4)—a perfect analogy to Tristram who, when dubbed by Calidore, reacts "Like as a flowre" that "Long shut up in the bud from heavens vew, / At length breakes forth" (ii. 35).

The name Meliogras also invites inquiry for Spenser deliberately changes Meliodas, Tristram's father in Malory.[13] It may mean "sweet grace" (Latin *mel*, honey). As Meliogras's "onely heire" Tristram would inherit this meaning: Calidore sees his "amiable grace" (st. 5) at once and his "graces" (st. 24) and "gratious goodly-head" (st. 25) as signs of noble *genus*. There may also be a sense "better grace" (Latin *melius*): Tristram certainly shows better grace than the knight he kills, and his princely rank transcends Calidore's fears of hierarchical discourtesy. Further, his natural courtesy more nearly approximates the Graces' than does Calidore's which, as practiced, depends more on nurture than nature (see ii. 2). In fact, Tristram's effect in Book VI resembles Belphoebe's in II: the figure who appears uniquely in a book to embody its deepest values. But in Book VI this figure is not a type of Elizabeth.

In Tristram, Spenser voices the popular enthusiasm for Essex in the mid-1590s which focused the growing restiveness, especially among the younger generation, with the aged and unpredictable queen. The minimization of royal encomium in Book VI and the ardent presentation of Tristram fit this mood exactly. With the Tristram portrait Spenser is also clearly making a bid for Essex's patronage. In 1590 a dedicatory sonnet promises Essex "more famous memory" in "the last praises of this Faery Queene" and requests patronage. Two other passages in the later works solicit Essex. *Prothalamion* (1596) juxtaposes the posture of a petitioner in "freendless case" who once had "gayned giftes and goodly grace" from Leicester, with a dazzling salute to Essex, fresh from the Cadiz expedition, as "great Englands glory and the Worlds wide wonder," rising "Like Radiant Hesper when his golden hayre / In th'Ocean billowes he hath Bathed fayre." The emphasis falls more precisely than with Tristram on Essex's brilliant promise as Britain's Hercules through whom "Thy country may be freed from forraine harmes." Here Spenser promotes the bellicose Spanish policy now centered upon Essex, which rejected the cautious diplomacy of Elizabeth and Cecil. A touch of royal encomium appears but couched to make "great Elisaes glorious name" dependent on Essex's "Wide Alarmes." The subject of the ensuing poem "Which some brave muse may sing / To ages following" would be Essex, not Eliza. The other passage, from the *View of the Present State of Ireland,* proposes the revival of the medieval lord lieutenancy (a viceregal office usually restricted to the royal family), to be filled by "suche an one I Coulde name upon whom the ey of all Englande is fixed and our laste hopes now reste."[14] There were many manuscript copies of the *View,* one of them found among the papers of Essex's secretary.[15]

Encomium of Essex in Book VI casts light on an often remarked oddity, the failure in 1596 to reprint the Letter to Raleigh. But the purpose of that Letter in 1590 may have been timeliness of address: it conspicuously associated Raleigh's name with the poem when his prestige was at its height. In the 1590s Raleigh's influence and credibility waned, and the competition between him and Essex was abrasive, so that republication of the Letter in 1596 would have compromised Spenser's bid for Essex's favor.

The Poet as Orpheus in Book IV

From the beginning we have seen how the poet's self-assertion usually accompanies encomium. But, as royal praise founders, the possibility of effective national poetry and perhaps poetry itself comes under doubt, causing the poet to defend and reassess his role. In fact, the 1596 installment bristles at either end with the poet's reactions to official dislike—outspoken in the fourth proem, cynical in the last stanza of Book VI. Both passages focus on Burghley's apparent displeasure with the poem's earlier books.

The first lines of the proem note overtly that Burghley "doth sharply wite" "My looser rimes" "For praising love." More remarkable is Spenser's astonishing counterattack on the most powerful man in England as one to whom "naturall affection" is a "thing unknowne": "Such ones ill judge of love, that cannot love, / Ne in their frosen harts feele kindly flame." Although, as Judson remarks, "we marvel at the poet's temerity,"[16] the defensive dedicatory sonnet to Burghley had anticipated "censure grave." Spenser seems at first to have avoided such a dedication, then added it hastily with six others during binding; at least eight copies lacking these seven sonnets exist.[17] The lord treasurer stood between Spenser and the crown of bays. To bypass him or to make him applaud the poem was equally impossible. In this frustrating situation the poet lashes out so recklessly as to thwart any further official recognition.[18]

The fourth proem's climax in encomium of Elizabeth as Venus "Queene of love" complements his praise of her as Diana in the third proem. But attack on Burghley rather than royal praise seems the point of the encomium. Spenser reverses the Virgilian *cano* formula—"To such therefore I do not sing at all"—while addressing it to the queen: "To her I sing of love, that loveth best." In the last stanza Cupid's invocation flaunts sensuality, setting "drops of melting love, / Deawd with ambrosiall kisses" over against the idea of rule. And the final line, "That she may hearke to love, and read this lesson often," not only scorns the supposed charge that erotic literature does not teach but also blatantly addresses the erotic lesson to the queen.

This embattled performance, perhaps composed as late as 1596, prefaces a book which reasserts the humanist claim that civilization depends on the great poet, just as (according to Horace) civilization originated with Orpheus. Spenser builds his defence of the poet in Book IV on two allusions to Orpheus: first, his pacification of the quarreling Argonauts (IV. ii. 1); and, second, his bringing Eurydice up from Hades (x. 58). These imply the poet's relevance to both heroic and erotic actions.

The Argonautic Orpheus is a maker of concord, the principle central to Book IV and to creation's order (i. 30). Concord's opposite is Ate, whose words incite "dreadfull discord" among the Argonauts, "That each of life sought others to deprive, / All mindlesse of the Golden fleece" (i. 23). The savior of the Argonauts is "None but a God or godlike man" "Such as was Orpheus" who "did take / His siluer Harpe in hand, and shortly friends them make" (ii. 1). Following patristic typology, Spenser parallels Orpheus with David calming Saul's madness with music and adds Menenius Agrippa (who controls the plebs with the fable of the belly in *Coriolanus*). These three exemplify the humanist defense of the poet's importance to the state. Spenser's quasi divine poet of concord corresponds exactly to Comes' Orpheus, whose pacifying eloquence makes him "the kind of man the rest of society must acknowledge as superior."[19]

The other allusion to Orpheus ends Scudamour's tale of how he "was emboldned" to seize Amoret, "That glorious spoyle of beautie," from the Temple of Venus. He boasts that Daunger threatened him no less than did "Cerberus, when Orpheus did recoure / His Leman from the Stygian Princes boure" (x. 58). Scudamour's identification with Orpheus is doubly ironic. First, there is irony of omission. By ignoring what happens next in Orpheus's story, he inadvertently draws attention to the next stage of his own story, the loss of Amoret to Busyrane. The Boethian allegory of Orpheus's loss of Eurydice as culpable surrender to desire (in Comes, Orpheus's *cupiditas*) reinforces the irony: neither Scudamour nor Orpheus control *cupiditas*. For although Scudamour claims himself "Cupids man" (st. 54) he does not apply his shield's motto, "Blessed the man that well can *use* his blis" (st. 8). This immoderation of desire and male sexual aggressiveness, symbolized by the cruel Cupid, separates and paralyzes the lovers. (In the 1596 edition Spenser does not reunite them, as he could easily do at the end of IV. ix).

If the erotic parallel between Scudamour and Orpheus is all too appropriate, the second irony rests on the inappropriateness of the identification. Scudamour has none of Orpheus's eloquence. He is instead a figure of impulsive physical action. He describes his courtship of Amoret as "bold," and that courtship more nearly resembles primitive marriage by capture than Petrarchan son-neteering. Scudamour's instinctive male boldness is not qualified by Orpheus's verbal arts, and it is not surprising that at their wedding Amoret should be carried off in a literary illusion, a masque based on Petrarch's *Trionfo d'amore* and filled with sonnet figures now become malevolent. The masque and the "most de-litious harmony" preceding it, which "The feeble senses wholly did confound" (III. xii. 6), are "charmes" of "the vile Enchaunter" Busyrane, who writes in a book with Amoret's "living blood" (st. 31). Busyrane is a vampirelike Orpheus. He replaces the inar-ticulate Scudamour, who was incapable of charming and reas-suring Amoret with verbal courtship or *Amoretti*. As the name *Amoretti* shows, Spenser deliberately contrasts in them the poet-lover's courting behavior with Scudamour's. Significantly, it is against Amoret's "intreatie" that Scudamour holds her "Like warie Hynd within the weedie soyle" (IV. x. 55), while the poet-huntsman of *Amoretti* 67 finds that his "gentle deare," elud-ing pursuit, still comes to him of "her owne goodwill."

The hymn in praise of Venus Genetrix, heard by Scudamour in the Temple of Venus (IV. x. 44—47), is not unlike the *Orphic Hymns* (particularly those to Natura and Venus) and, given the ironic identification of Orpheus and Scudamour, parallels the hymn Orpheus sings in Hades. Here, however, the hymn is sung by some anonymous, articulate lover who, unlike Scudamour, can express his passion. Furthermore, Scudamour is vulnerable to discord. The cacophony of Care's seven anvils (IV. v. 36) extends Ate's discordant effect on him and also opposes the concord of harmonious anvils that led Pythagoras to discover the principle of harmony intrinsic to cosmic order, the music of the seven spheres.[20] When Comes says that Orpheus's lyre had seven strings "in imitation of the seven planets," he implies exactly the kind of figure whose help Scudamour needs—the poet whose song adjusts reality by projecting spheral concord.

The Thames-Medway wedding procession is that sort of song, and it follows Scudamour's allusion to Orpheus almost at once. Invocation of a muse indicates a climax and draws attention to the poet's Orphic performance as he puts "In order as they came" (xi. 9) 170 rivers and marine figures. By ordering the floods, a natural symbol of mutability but also the sea that Elizabethans are wresting from Spanish control, Spenser proclaims himself as national poet—in "a festival piece celebrating a visionary England—and Ireland—united in friendly alliance, and married to a sovereign whose policy promises a strong and prosperous peace."[21] At the four-part procession's center is the legendary Arion, an Orpheus figure at whose music "all the raging seas for joy forgot to rore" (st. 23) and who orders the procession from within with a "most celestial sound" analogous to the perfect spheral music. Spenser's listing of the Irish "Mulla mine, whose waves I whilom taught to weep" (st. 41) identifies him with Arion through the mutual Orphic formula. Arion and the poet of Mulla are triumphant and plaintive types of the real poet who creates the set piece. Just before Arion appears Spenser mentions "rich Oranochy" and Amazon, thereby saluting Raleigh's planned expedition to Guiana and sounding an anti-Spanish imperial note appropriate to the post-Armada period: the "conquest of that land of gold" that "to you, O Britons, most pertaines" (sts. 21–22). Their positioning before Arion hints at the poet's vatic role as prophet of Britain's sea empire. But the weeping Orpheus of Mulla reminds Spenser's audience that their great national poet still lives rusticated in Ireland—"In savadge soyle, far from Parnasso mount," as Spenser complained in 1590 in the dedicatory sonnet to Grey of Wilton.

The paradox of a plaintive poet who is simultaneously triumphant is familiar from the *Calender*. The same paradox appears early in Book IV where Spenser announces his completion of the *Squire's Tale*, supposedly victim to "cursed Eld the cankerworme of writs" (ii. 33). If he can claim to be Chaucer's true successor "through infusion sweete / Of thine owne spirit, which doth in me survive" (st. 34), he can also claim the power to do what Chaucer cannot: he can repair the monument of Chaucer's fame by restoring his lost works—"I thy labours lost may thus revive." The superiority to Chaucer implied here makes Spenser the great English poet. His defense of the poet in Book IV is a defense of this claim. But in Book VI this yields to a reassessment of the poet's role touched with nostalgia and disillusionment. Again Spenser uses the Orpheus archetype as touchstone.

Orpheus and Hercules Gallicus in Book VI

Spenser orients the 1596 installment to Orpheus and Hercules, for the Renaissance the great archetypes of artist and hero. If Orpheus dominates Book IV, Hercules dominates Book V, where several adventures of Artegall and Arthur have Herculean analogues.[22] But Artegall's quest ends in frustration and his victimization by the Blatant Beast, who resembles the Hydra and Cerberus (VI. xii. 32, 35), both subdued by Hercules—although in one tradition the Hydra, always allegorized as envy, did not yield because envy dies only with death: "Post mortem cessat invidia."[23] Artegall's impasse indicates the limitations and vulnerability of the Herculean hero.

Although Colin is the preeminent Orpheus figure in Book VI, its protagonist also impinges on Orpheus's role. For the archetype behind Calidore (at least in canto iii) is not Hercules of twelve labors but Hercules Gallicus, a humanist phase of Hercules designed to show the eloquent man's superiority to the physical hero. Alciati's emblem "Eloquentia fortitudine praestantior" ("eloquence is superior to bravery") depicts Hercules still with club and lion skin, but also with delicate chains connecting his tongue to the ears of his willing captives. Achilles Bocchius points his version by seating Hercules on a triumphal car (see fig. 8).[24] Thus, Hercules Gallicus does easily with eloquence what Hercules did with brute effort. As Alciati says, "Cedunt arma togae; & quamvis durissima corda / Eloquio pollens ad sua vota trahit" ("Arms give place to the toga and, empowered by eloquence, [Hercules] makes hearts, no matter how hard, conform to his wishes"). Obviously, Hercules Gallicus is a hybrid between Hercules and Orpheus, with the balance tipped in favor of Orpheus.

Calidore's "every act and deed, that he did say, / Was like enchantment"; like Hercules Gallicus, he compels more by eloquence than by strength and "through both the eyes, / And both the eares did steale the hart away" (VI. ii. 3). The 1596 reading "every act and deed, that he did say" (usually misleadingly emended "deed and word") conveys precisely the sense of heroism achieved through speech, while its effect "like enchantment" reflects Orpheus's. The shift of hero from Hercules to

LIB. II.

HIC HERCVLES EST GALLICVS: INTELLEGAT, QVI AVRES HABET.

Symb. XLIII.

Figure 8. The triumph of Hercules Gallicus. From Achilles Bocchius's *Symbolicarum quaestionum libri quinque* (Bologna, 1574), by courtesy of the University of Toronto Library.

Hercules Gallicus brings the protagonist closer to the poet and implies the growing ascendancy in Book VI of poet over hero. That Orpheus subsumes Hercules is implicit in Spenser's continual borrowing of the Herculean word "labours" to designate the poet's activity (as in the 1596 additions to the royal dedication). In Book VI Spenser develops a persona that suggests an analogy between poet-voice and protagonist. Both grow weary. The poet becomes a wanderer or poet errant who pursues his "tedious travell" (punning on French *travail*, work) with "weary steps" (pro. 1); and Calidore tries to escape from his "quest, so full of toile and paine" (x. 2). Also, one senses that both are ageing: the poet has begun "to feele decay of might" (pro. 1); Calidore behaves paternally to young Tristram and turns out to be not of Pastorella's generation but her father's (xii. 11). In spite of this analogy, the knight remains the poet's creature, as in canto ix, 2 where "Calidores immortall name" depends on the poet-ploughman's willingness to go "Backe to the furrow which I lately left."

Although the hero of eloquence approaches the poet, he does not become Orpheus nor succeed as Hercules Gallicus. As Tonkin notes, Calidore shows in the first four episodes "a picture of diminishing success."[25] This is a normal feature of the hero's early performance: compare Redcrosse, Guyon, and Artegall. Here it is also a development from physical to verbal heroism. With barbarous Crudor and Briana, Calidore applies Herculean fortitude, although his sword's civilizing effect parallels Orpheus's civilizing rude men with song. (The name Briana betrays the usual Elizabethan disdain for Irish ways.) In the next episode Tristram saves Calidore from the potentially destructive collision of rank versus deed as criteria of courtesy and charms the knight with speech and looks so as to model Calidore's own virtue. In the third and fourth episodes, where Calidore acts as Hercules Gallicus, his solving problems through eloquence violates his own ideal of "simple truth and stedfast honesty" (i. 3). The "countercast of slight" he devises "To give faire colour" to Priscilla's shaky reputation, and the white lie he tells her father are hardly simple truth (iii. 16, 18), while his improvising a prop from the dead knight's head is a comically literal way of "adding comely guise"

(i. 2). The basic irony is that, if Calidore is to save Priscilla (and he does), he must compromise his own ideals.

The irony deepens when he breaks in upon Calepine and Serena. The repeated rhyme in "And pardon crav'd for his so rash default, / That he gainst courtesie so fowly did default" betrays undue protestation, as does the Herculean verb in "Him selfe thereof he labour'd to acquite" (iii. 21), for Calidore's labor here is an "act and deed, that he did say" typical of Hercules Gallicus. In that role "his gentle words and goodly wit" so enchant Calepine as to "allay that Knights conceiv'd displeasure" and cause Calepine to ask for the story of his adventures—a rehearsal which gives Calidore "delightful pleasure" (st. 22). Just when the hero of eloquence succeeds, the hitherto elusive Blatant Beast strikes. Calepine had thought himself "far from envious eyes that mote him spight" (st. 20), but it is now apparent that *invidia* is at work: for Calidore has seen something potentially scandalous; and he has sublimated his sexual envy into separation of the lovers. But the main irony is that the Beast eludes Calidore precisely because the knight contains it in himself. This is an extension of the irony latent in the Knight of Courtesy's insensitively sanguine and self-promoting mode of address, as here or when he greets Artegall or Colin (i. 4–5; x. 19). But there is also a sense—and one that troubles the end of the quest—that even the best-intentioned actions are inevitably destructive.

Calidore undoes the Hercules-Gallicus role in canto iii, and, as he pursues the Beast, he assumes the ordinary Herculean role of hero against monster. When he returns six cantos later, he is himself subject to the eloquence of two Orphic figures, Melibee and Colin.

Melibee is an Arcadian apologist who eloquently extols retreat. But his speech develops a peculiar cast when we note that, among many links connecting Books VI and I, it corresponds to Despair's.[26] Listening to Melibee's "pleasing tongue" and "melting mouth," Calidore finds that the "sensefull words empierst his hart" (ix. 26). Spenser describes the effect of Despair's rhetoric with identical images of the melting mouth and the pierced heart (I. ix. 31, 48). His egregiously sophistic eloquence leaves Redcrosse "charmed with inchaunted rimes" (I. ix. 48), a phrase suggesting that Despair, like Busyrane, is a diabolical Orpheus whose eloquence brings on destruction instead of harmony. In spite of pastoral simplicity and soothing platitudes, Melibee is like Despair a sinister Orpheus. His apology articulates an alternative to the now tiresome quest that permits Calidore to abandon it with salved conscience.

In himself, of course, Melibee is not malevolent, but rather an aged naif who has retained his youthful belief in simplistic escapist solutions: as a young man he "disdain'd" shepherding, but at court was "soone cloyd" (st. 25). He is equally deluded by the seeming security of his "lowly quiet life." To say that, contented with little, he is not "envyde of any one" (st. 21) ignores the knight's "certes I your happiness envie" (st. 19). This rationalized retreat, adorned with platitudes like "It is the mynd, that maketh good or ill" (st. 30), is shown up as beautiful nonsense by the brutal economic motive of the Brigants. Spenser has provided a touchstone for Melibee in the aged Hermit who "the art of words knew wondrous well, / And eke could *doe, as well as say* the same" (vi. 6). Though also living in withdrawal, the Hermit is alert to the Beast. His counsel avoids self-indulgent escape, recommending instead defensive self-discipline that corrects Melibee's simplistic fantasy of lowly invulnerability. In effect, the Hermit's "wise commaundements" (st. 15) redefine Melibee's Old Testament proverb "wisdome is most riches" (ix. 30)[27] from a subtler Christian perspective: "be ye therefore wise as serpents, and harmless as doves" (Matt. 10:16).

As Redcrosse incites Despair's speech, so Calidore initiates Melibee's, "drawing thence his speach another way" (ix. 18). In these episodes each knight unwittingly explores the destructive aspects of self that undermine the Herculean labor of quests. As Despair externalizes Redcrosse's too solemn sadness, so the fantasy of pastoral innocence reifies Calidore's indulgent capacity for self-deception, self-pity, and inclination to rest, apparent in his congratulation of Artegall as "happy man" because he has "Atchiev'd so hard a quest": "But where ye ended have, now I begin / To tread an endlesse trace, withouten guyde" (i.5–6). Calidore's self-pity is disguised envy. And these are exactly the emotions he projects on the pastoral. Further, his courtesy is partly a gift of birth: his "gentleness of spright / And manners mylde were planted naturall"; and partly cultivated: "To which he adding comely guize withall, / And gracious speach, did steale mens hearts away" (i. 2). The virtues Calidore has by nature are intrinsic, reflecting his name (Greek *kalla dōra*, beautiful gifts). But it is the extrinsic or acquired qualities of "comely guize" and "gracious speach" which he uses to charm and which he is himself enchanted by. For Melibee's "pleasing tongue" and Pastorella's "faire hew" together effect a "double ravishment" in Calidore that attacks his name and so "He lost himselfe" (ix. 26). By subjecting himself to Melibee's eloquence and Pastorella's beauty Calidore not only abandons his Hercules-Gallicus role; when he shirks his quest in favor of "the perfect pleasures, which doe grow / Among poore hyndes" (x. 3), he reverses the Choice of Hercules (virtue instead of pleasure) and thus rejects the ordinary Hercules role as well.[28]

Calidore's name also means cunning with gold (Lat. *callidus*, cunning). From the beginning, financial imagery hints that Calidore can use courtesy for profit: "The which in all mens liking gayned place, / And with the greatest purchast greatest grace" (i. 3). Ironically, it is the courtier's manipulation of the enchanting aspects of courtesy to gain advancement that Calidore, now rejecting court, introduces in reverse when he offers Melibee "much gold" (ix. 32). Though charmed by Melibee's speech, he seems not to have heard its disparagement of wealth.[29] In the shepherd's rejection of "That mucky masse, the cause of mens decay" (st. 33), however, we overhear Guyon's refusal of "worldly mucke" and recognize a reenactment of the Cave of Mammon. Though shallowly well-meaning as always, Calidore here takes Mammon's role, while Melibee is as unrealistic about money as is Guyon—high chivalry and base shepherding both pretending to be free of economics. Though the shepherds do not know the Beast, Calidore pursues it into their midst, where it disappears only to reemerge subtly through Calidore himself as envy of happiness, sexual competition, and proffered gold. Like the mercenary Brigants, Calidore is putting a price on the pastoral. As he regains his Herculean role he must pay for this episode by rescuing from them what little remains of the shepherd fantasy—Pastorella herself.

On Mount Acidale, Calidore is again enchanted by sound and sight, the media he has himself used to steal men's hearts away. But his attempt to enter that enchantment destroys it. One line before we see the hundred naked dancers we already have Calidore's reaction: "even he him selfe his eyes envyde" (x. 11). This puns on eyes-envyde-*invidia* (with its root *videre*, to see) and expresses the tradition that envy is "full of eyes" (cf. I. iv. 31) and feeds on itself.[30] Calidore, however, is as usual unaware of his destructive urges. The vision is a magically successful piece of art which vanishes when he tries to enter it, *invidia* here taking the form of conscious iconoclasm. Calidore at first recognizes the danger of "breaking of their daunce, if he were seene" (VI. x. 11), but later, deliberately "resolving, what it was, to know, / Out of the wood he rose" (VI. x. 17). As earlier, he tries to gloss over the damage with eloquence. While his back-slapping "Haile jolly shepheard, which thy joyous dayes / Here leadest in this goodly merry make" (st. 19) is simply inappropriate, the envious self-pity is authentic: "Right happy thou, that mayst them freely see: / But why when I them saw, fled they away from me?" Colin's rejection of these terms properly subordinates the failed hero of eloquence "which them thence did chace, / Whom by no meanes thou canst recall againe" (st. 20) to the vatic Orpheus. In response Calidore transfers culpability for his iconoclasm to "my ill fortune." Not until Colin expounds the vision can he acknowledge the element of the Beast in himself (st. 29).

Colin's exposition fuses the two features of matrix episodes or core cantos, modeling the hero's virtue and clarifying his identity, by reforming the meanings of "Calidore." In the epiphany of the Graces, who dispose "all gracious gifts" (st. 23), Calidore sees his own "beautiful gifts" transfigured and reordered. In their smiling, which means "That we likewise should mylde and gentle be" (st. 24), his natural gifts of "gentlenesse of spright / And manners mylde," ignored in his obsession with eloquence, are restored to preeminence. But the Graces' nakedness, which means they are "without guile / Or false dissemblaunce," "Simple and true from covert malice free," is a reproof of his verbal and visual deceptions, including his shepherd disguise. Most important, the Graces' arrangement in their dance[31] means "That good should from us goe, then come in greater store." Here "then" may mean both "rather than" and "subsequently." The ambiguity is important, for it indicates the grace involved in receiving as well as giving. This far transcends the courtly self-serving use of courtesy that "with the greatest purchast greatest grace." Under the pagan veil the Graces adumbrate God's gifts—i.e., the Christian concept of grace, while their Greek name, Charites, hints at the central Christian virtue of charity. Traditionally, charity is foe of envy: there is a Giotto diptych opposing them.[32] In this multilayered vision Calidore sees an ideal social paradigm immune from the Beast's malice, although the vehicle expressing it is vulnerable. In particular, he sees verbal courtesy transfigured from social manipulation to a system of creative giving and receiving in which Colin exercises his art to give encomium to his lass and the Graces respond by granting him vatic inspiration that transforms his gift into luminous apotheosis.

If we compare stanzas equidistant from each end of the book, some notable correspondences relevant to this episode appear. For instance, 115 stanzas from the beginning, Calidore dissembles to Priscilla's father (iii. 18), a fault corrected 115 stanzas from the end, when he learns that the Graces are "without guile / Or false dissemblaunce" (x. 24). Similarly, Calepine with Serena, thinking himself safe from "envious eyes," "In covert shade him selfe did safely rest" (iii. 20); in the corresponding stanza Jove begets the Graces, the antithesis of envy, on Venus's mountain of rest where he "In sommers shade him selfe here rested weary" (ix. 22). The most striking of these aligns Calidore's iconoclasm with the Blatant Beast, which first appears in the stanza (iii. 24) matching that in which Calidore shatters Colin's vision (x. 18).

As the Orphic Colin interprets his vision, Calidore by his ignorance is forced inevitably back into an ordinary Hercules role like Artegall's. As soon as he leaves Colin, the tiger episode occurs in which Calidore "had no weapon, but his shepheardes hooke" as an improvised club to kill "the monster" (x. 36)—a clearly Herculean epithet. A piece of patterning suggests the importance of this crux to Calidore's role. For, among several linked stanzas of the same number in cantos ix and x, it is in canto ix, 36 that Calidore is found "doffing his bright armes" and taking "In stead of steelehead speare, a shepheardes hooke"—the improvised weapon of x. 36. When the Brigants wipe out the pastoral world, Calidore "by diligent inquest" finds himself "a sword of meanest sort" (xi. 42). After killing some Brigants he earns himself "a sword of better say" (xi. 47): ironically, "better *say*" means a better tempered sword, not better eloquence. And his armed descent to the dark, candlelit Brigants' cave recalls not Orpheus's descent to Hell but Hercules'.

In Book VI two images of humanist culture founder: for, if Hercules Gallicus proves an impossibility, Orpheus is also vulnerable. Here Colin is no longer the triumphant Orpheus who can convoke a visionary assembly in *Aprill* or order waters for the Thames-Medway marriage. He cannot, as Calidore assumes, recall the vision by piping. The forces that bring on *furor poeticus*, that make the poem say more than the poet intends, that turn *poeta* into *vates*—these he can only supplicate: "none can them bring in place, / But whom they of them selves list so to grace" (x. 20). This is a humbler, more seasoned view of the poet than *Aprill* presents.

It is precisely because inspiration lies outside the poet's technical and even imaginative control, however, that Colin's vision— and any great art—manifests high courtesy. For the *poeta's* exercise of his verbal gifts, both natural and cultivated, brings on the *vates'* transcendent vision only when the Graces or divine grace vouchsafe their own mysterious gifts. The successful creative act thus mirrors the system of giving and receiving central to the model of courtesy. In this religious view of creativity, the artist's success depends on grace, which when given makes him analogous, in Sidney's phrase, to the "Maker of that maker." This paradox reduces to fundamentals the encomiast's earlier claim to both inability and power.

The evanescence of Colin's vision discredits the familiar Renaissance assertion of the poem's permanence (compare Eliza's encomium which Hobbinoll can "recorde"). Another Renaissance platitude about poetry—its double function of pleasing and teaching—is also qualified here. Colin's vision is in itself obviously *et dulce et utile*. One aspect of his teaching is the importance to courtesy of avoiding "guile / Or false dissemblaunce." As a result of the immediately subsequent tiger episode, Pastorella accepts Calidore as lover and rejects Coridon: "Yet Calidore did not despise him quight, / But usde him friendly for further intent" (x. 37). Clearly, dissembled friendship aimed at selfish manipulation contradicts the vision and contributes one more meaning to the knight's name: "cunning *(callidus)* with gifts." More alarmingly, the narrative justifies Calidore's guile. Controlled by feigned friendship, Coridon makes possible Calidore's rescue of Pastorella from the Brigants. In other words, if the hero is to achieve whatever good is possible, he must act with practical cunning antithetical to the ideal nakedness of the Graces. Painfully ironic doublethink is implicit here: for Calidore can rejoice in the model of courtesy but cannot afford its practice. His duplicity is more effectively altruistic. (Compare Britomart's conversion into action of the vision at Isis Church.) This intimation of poetry's social irrelevance implicitly opposes *dulce* and *utile*, and undoes the self-justifying idealism of the encomiast and the humanist promotion of Orpheus as civilizer.

Book VI ends cynically with the Triumph of Envy over both Hercules and Orpheus. The achievement of Calidore's quest reflects both the labor of "the hell-borne Hydra, which they faine / That great Alcides whilome overthrew" (xi. 32) and the alternate tradition that he failed (the ambiguity of "they faine" inclines to the latter). For the quest is ultimately unsuccessful. At first it appears that, "supprest and tamed," the Beast *"never more"* will "endammadge wight / With his vile tongue" (st. 38). But it soon escapes and becomes not only immune to capture ("Ne any is, that may him now restraine, / He growen is so great and strong of late") but escalating in destructiveness: "Barking and biting all that doe him bate, / Albe they worthy blame, or cleare of crime" (st. 40). The idea of heroism, and of worthy social action generally, here founders in impasse. For Calidore cannot escape his quest, though he tries. But to achieve it makes the world worse. The Renaissance archetype of Hercules as the altruistic hero who rids society of the monstrous is thus ironically reversed. Spenser implies that it is equally impossible to avoid action in this world and to make that action less than mainly destructive.

In the last two stanzas of Book VI, the Blatant Beast attacks *The Faerie Queene* itself. Defense from envy is the theme of the first words of Spenser's canon, the envoy to the *Calender*.[33] Now his major poem cannot "Hope to escape" (st. 41) from *invidia*, the special enemy of "all that ever writ" (I. iv. 32). Once again Spenser sees his poem's future in the light of Burghley's antipathy, and the resulting cynicism, with its sense of *dulce non utile*, is fatal to encomium: "Therefore do you my rimes keep better measure, / And seeke to please, that now is counted wisemens threasure" (VI. xii. 51). For the poem's concluding couplet means both that rewards come to canny poets who concentrate on metrics and that wise poets are paid for their silence. But the cynicism is also masochistic. In *October*, Orpheus's "musicks might" tames "the hellish hound" Cerberus. But here Cerberus's descendant triumphs over the poet, and the humanist symbol of civilizing, Orpheus, falls before the monstrous. In the seventeenth century, Orpheus dismembered by Bacchantes becomes a popular theme (as in *Lycidas*), but Spenser's self-mutilation at the end of *The Fairie Queene* already suggests it.

We can gain some perspective over the poem's evolution by noting how different the Blatant Beast is from an earlier figure of *invidia*, Braggadochio. By expressing "glory vaine" (II. iii. 4) Braggadochio travesties Gloriana: his first and last appearances in the poem threaten types of Elizabeth. Although this potentially destructive invidiousness shows his affinity with the Beast, his usual effect is expurgation of envy through comedy. In fact, Spenser often uses Braggadochio to externalize the poem's penchant for self-mocking gaiety. Surviving by verbal skills, he parodies chivalry's cumbersome athletic arrangements (e.g. III. viii. 17–18), its heroes' thirst for actions to validate their self-esteem (e.g. III. x. 24, 32), and even the poem's values, as in his scandalized rejection of Malbecco's bribe where allusions to Belphoebe's speech on honor and Guyon's to Mammon climax in a slather of alliteration at the inflexible Guyon's expense:

> But weete henceforth, that all that golden pray,
> And all that else the vaine world vaunt may,
> I loath as doung, he deeme my dew reward:
> Fame is my meed, and glory vertues pray.
> But minds of mortall men are muchell mard,
> And mov'd amisse with massive mucks unmeet regard.
>
> [III. x. 31]

When Artegall expels this wonderful *eques gloriosus* from the poem, its playfulness has already yielded to the sardonic moods of 1596. As J. Dennis Huston suggests, Artegall's mechanically legalistic treatment of Braggadochio promotes his monstrous mutation into the Blatant Beast.[34] In the Beast, Braggadochio's impudent boasting becomes "an obscene mass of tongues,"[35] and his latent but feckless malice becomes explicit and aggressive.

Ultimately, the Beast is the antagonist of man and God. As a monster it threatens *humanitas*—the rational, verbal, and creative values of society as conceived of in the Renaissance. "Blatant" (Spenser's coinage) is usually derived from the Greek *blaptō*, hurt, and perhaps Latin *blatero*, babble, but it also obviously relates to "blat"—i.e. speech distorted in a bestial direction (a pejorative form of "bleat"). The Beast's tongues are mostly human, but we learn this only at the end of the list of its animal tongues and their distorted sounds (VI. xii. 27). in the procession of Sins in Book I, Envy's last and climactic antipathies are his hatred of "all good workes" and his backbiting "famous Poets wit" (I. v. 32). The Beast's last two acts in Book VI parallel these: his attacks on monasteries, traditional agents of charity, and on the poem. Like Envy's, these are attacks on redemption and creation or recreation—i.e. on Christian history from Genesis to Revelation. The Beast is thus not only the enemy of the poet and his ordered words, but also an Antilogos set against the creating, redeeming, and recreating divine Word itself. In fact, the binding of the Beast, like the binding of Archimago in the same canto of Book I, alludes to the binding of "that old serpent, which is the Devil" (Rev. 20:2). In that vision, Satan is loosed briefly after a thousand years. In Book II Archimago escapes only to become ineffective. But the Beast escapes, devastating and uncontained, into this world. The distance between Braggadochio's buoyant insolence and the closing Triumph of the Blatant Beast measures the change in the poem between 1590 and 1596.

Mutabilitie: Through Dianaes Spights

The *Mutabilitie Cantos* are unarguably part of *The Faerie Queene*, not least because of their stanza (the Spenserian stanza would be more accurately named the "*Faerie Queene* stanza"), and serve as its final statement, mitigating the harshness and disenchantment of Books V and VI. Mutabilitie's evidence against the gods restates the fifth proem on the failure of planetary regularity, even echoing some of its phrasing. And when she "wrong of right, and bad of good did make" (VII. vii. 6), she reactivates its most radical statement of historical decline ("Right now is wrong, and wrong that was is right"). She is also an agent of *invidia*. Like Ate who tries to divide Concord's golden chain that binds "all this worlds faire workmanship" (VI. i. 30), Mutability "alter'd quite" "all this worlds faire frame" (VII. vi. 5). And, like the Blatant Beast, she attacks Cynthia because she begins "T'*envie* her that in such glorie raigned" (vi. 10). As well as *invidia*, Spenser epitomizes in Mutabilitie other antagonistic forces operative throughout the poem: Fortune, from whom Mutabilitie derives her wheel of change and who, according to Comes, once attacked Jove;[36] the shape-changer Archimago; and time that erodes the hero's attainment and the poet's fame. But these destructive energies reappear in Mutabilitie only to be contained. Her attack is pushed back into the latency by Nature's judgment and then seen in wider perspective through Nature's veiled prophecy and the Christian poet's further understanding of it. In this sense the *Cantos* extenuate the disillusionment in the books of 1596.

They express no encomium, however. Instead, of the two representations of the queen, one makes her the victim of change, the other its agent. In the first, Mutabilitie begins her rebellion by assaulting the moon, the only celestial body she succeeds in attacking, and one given Raleigh's encomiastic name for the queen, Cynthia. The moon's royal attributes are insisted on: a palace, a kingdom, an ivory throne drawn by black and white steeds (vi. 9)—Elizabeth's personal colors. But, unlike Humilta, "an aged syre, all hory gray" (I. x. 5), who guards the House of Holiness, and Awe, "one of mickle might" (V. ix. 22), who guards Mercilla's palace, Cynthia's feckless warder is "an hory / Old aged Sire" Tyme (VII. vi. 8) who "were he liefe or sory" cannot screen out Change. By flaunting the ambivalent lunar attributes—as it were, Jonson's "Queen and huntress chaste and fair" against Juliet's "inconstant moon"—Spenser imbues the allegory that had greeted Elizabeth's reign—*veritas filia temporis*—with a new ironic sense. As William Blissett points out, this episode subverts the cult of "Elizabeth's golden and perpetual youth, exempt from all variableness and shadow of turning."[37] By asserting that "Cynthia raignes in everlasting glory" (st. 8), then submitting her permanence to attack, Spenser employs his familiar stratagem of voicing, then destroying, an approving platitude.

The other passage, the Diana-Faunus digression, offers a paradigm of mutability in history, whereby an earthly paradise, "of old the best and fairest Hill" in a holy island, "Was made the most unpleasant, and most ill" (st. 37). Arlo was once the favorite haunt of Cynthia "that is soveraine Queene profest / Of woods and forrests" (st. 38). But, in her overreaction to Faunus's silly yet harmless voyeurism, the virgin goddess "There-on an heavy haplesse curse did lay," so that Arlo "Doth to this day with Wolves and Thieves abound" (st. 55). (Compare two invidious threats to pastoral in Book VI: the tiger and the Brigants.) In "Which too-too true that lands in-dwellers since have found" one hears an intense autobiographical note bespeaking Spenser's long Irish experience and referring particularly to Tyrone's rebellion of 1598, in which Kilcolman was sacked. (I assume very late composition or recomposition for the *Cantos* in 1598–99.)[38] Specifically, an Irish paradise is lost "through Dianaes spights" (st. 37)—an astonishingly candid phrase. (Later, in vii. 39, the poet goes a little out of his way to proffer another instance of "Dianaes doom unjust.") At the end of Book V, Spenser presents Elizabeth's Irish policies as vacillating and wrongheaded; here he makes them a particularly destructive aspect of Mutabilitie. This is not praise, but blame. Interestingly, the comic simile of the exasperated dairy wife who catches the creature who has been skimming her creaming pans and plans a horrible vengeance (st. 48), not only mocks Diana's overreaction to the revelation of her "somewhat" (st. 46), but also the cult of royal virginity.

Throughout this study we have come to expect the figure of the poet to emerge into prominence whenever encomium occurs, and this is no less so in these *Cantos* where encomium fails. He appears in several familiar postures: as the antiquarian delver "mongst records permanent" (vi. 2); as the dominating *poeta* who can command a change of muse (vi. 37); as the vatic vehicle of Calliope's will (vii. 1–2); as the narrator-commentator trying to advise Faunus (vi. 46, 49). But in the narrative the god of eloquence, Mercury, who once gave Orpheus the lyre, now finds himself powerless against Mutabilitie (vi. 18). And the poet's final posture, in the two stanzas of the eighth canto, similarly acts out his own helplessness in "this state of life so tickle" where Mutabilitie "In all things . . . bears the greatest sway." This voice is akin to that speaking in the proems, separate from the narrator and close to the actual poet. Its mood is contemplative and expresses the familiar stratagem of reviewing an assertion—in this case, Nature's judgment. While rejecting Mutabilitie's claim to alter astronomy, Nature affirms Pythagorean patterned change (as in the Garden of Adonis) as the means whereby creatures "worke their owne perfection." But the poet-contemplator, now playing *contemptor mundi*, resists this construction as subhuman, for in Nature's cycle the imagination feels itself incarcerated. The sense of being trapped appears in a syntactical pun, "And love of things *so vaine* to cast away," which recognizes both the need to reject the fleeting things of this world and the futility of the attempt. Similarly, the contemplator is able to go beyond Nature's premonition of a "time when no more change shall bee" to identify it with Christian expectation of a state when "all shall rest eternally / With Him that is the God of Sabbaoth hight"—the vision offered not to the vatic poet particularly but to Everyman. With the prayer of the last line—"O that great Sabbaoth God, grant me that Sabbaoths sight"—we reach the final topos of inability, for the first time devoid of any covert sense of self-assertion. Rather, *poeta* and *vates* fall into subordination before the ordinary visionary who is simply Christian man at prayer. Yet the last humble line cannot pass without the poet's punning on Hebrew *Sabaoth*, armies or hosts, and *Sabbaoth*, rest. In the pun resides a definition of eternity where God is both energy and repose and where the dichotomies the poem has engaged—quest and rest, epic and pastoral, vision and experience, art and reality, encomium and truth—resolve. But, as its heading notes, this short canto of eternity must be "unperfite" because as yet we see through a glass darkly.[39]

Retrospect

Underlying the last two stanzas of the *Cantos* is the Augustinian metaphor, central to medieval culture, of Christian man as a pilgrim seeking his heavenly home while journeying through the world's tribulations. The corresponding Renaissance metaphor receives its classical formulation in the ebullient *Oration on Human Dignity* where Pico urges man's potential for emulating the highest angels in honor and intelligence, to the point of assuming a place just beneath God himself. *The Faerie Queene* begins with just such humanist idealism. Its main encomiastic symbol is a British queen initially hymned as mediatrix between man and God. By naming her first type Una, Spenser implies that Elizabeth unites man's earthly and heavenly roles, and Contemplation explains Gloriana to Redcrosse in exactly these terms. Such idealism is essential to serious encomium. But the books of 1596 make us aware of increasingly urgent tensions in this idealism that undermine encomium and exacerbate separation of the hero from his goal and the real queen from her heavenly image. When great Renaissance attempts at synthesis founder, they sometimes fall back on old medieval certainties. A document of this sort appears at the beginning of northern humanism, Erasmus's *Enchiridion militis christiani* (1503). It attempts to articulate the assumed inherent unity of Christian and classical idealism by fusing their moral teachings. But soon the terms come apart, faith and grace sounding alien in a context dominated by wisdom and prudence, and Erasmus contrives a conclusion only by recourse to the medieval confessors' well-worn *remedia peccatorum*. In the *Enchiridion* the failure lies in the vehicle, not in the author's loss of conviction. But when the *Mutabilitie Cantos*, and, more broadly, *The Faerie Queene*, conclude with the authorial voice speaking as a pilgrim who sees earthly experience in terms of *contemptus mundi* and the heavenly Sabbath as his only true home, the failure that this betokens for the poem as encomium—as a unitive statement made possible by a queen who invites and fulfills idealization—lies in the collapse of the claim that England partakes in Jerusalem, and a concomitant return to the Augustinian sense that the City of This World opposes the City of God.

Spenser criticism has by now pretty much abandoned consideration of *The Faerie Queene* as the completed part of a projected poem of twelve or twenty-four books. One seldom any longer comes upon speculations that Spenser planned a denouement in some unwritten twelfth book. Rather, we now tend to accept the existing poem as a complete fragment. At the same time Spenser scholars are moving toward a perception of the poem's structure that will probably declare it a work of the most complex patterning. Such research, if it succeeds, will considerably further our appreciation of the paradoxical achievement of *The Faerie Queene*. For we will then have to recognize how Spenser has carried through an astonishingly intricate design while very nearly executing an about-face toward his encomiastic subject. From this point of view, the pull of evolving matter against fixed form is the poem's most basic and exciting tension.

List of
Abbreviations

CL   *Comparative Literature*
EIC   *Essays in Criticism* (Oxford)
ELH   *Journal of English Literary History*
ELN   *English Language Notes*
ELR   *English Literary Renaissance*
HAB   *Humanities Association Bulletin* (Canada)
HLQ   *Huntington Library Quarterly*
JMRS   *Journal of Medieval and Renaissance Studies*
JWCI   *Journal of the Warburg and Courtauld Institute*
MLN   *Modern Language Notes*
MLR   *Modern Language Review*
MP   *Modern Philology*
PMLA   *Publications of the Modern Language Association of America*
RN   *Renaissance News*
RORD   *Research Opportunities in Renaissance Drama*
SM   *Speech Monographs*
SP   *Studies in Philology*
Speculum
SpN   *Spenser Newsletter*
SRen   *Studies in the Renaissance*
TSLL   *Texas Studies in Language and Literature*
UTQ   *University of Toronto Quarterly*
WVUPP   *West Virginia University Philological Papers*

Notes

Chapter One

1. I use "rhetoric" in its historical sense, meaning the body of instructions about oratory that descend from Aristotle and the sophists, not in the loose contemporary sense where it means any verbal strategy. The only study of technical rhetoric in Spenser, Herbert D. Rix, *Rhetoric in Spenser's Poetry*, Pennsylvania State College Series, no. 7 (State College, Pa., 1970), does not venture beyond identification of figures. Paul Alpers, *The Poetry of "The Faerie Queene"* (Princeton: Princeton University Press, 1967) discusses the poem's rhetoric in the contemporary sense.

2. C. S. Baldwin, *Medieval Rhetoric and Poetic* (New York: Macmillan, 1928), chap. 1.

3. Theodore Burgess, *Epideictic Literature*, University of Chicago Studies in Classical Philology, no. 3 (Chicago, 1920), p. 93. On the Renaissance application of Hermogenes' stylistic precepts, see Annabel Patterson, *Hermogenes and the Renaissance: Seven Ideas of Style* (Princeton: Princeton University Press, 1970).

4. *Ars*, 1. 50–59. The texts of the *Ars* and the *Poetria nova* are printed by Edmond Faral, ed., *Les Poétiques du xiie et du xiiie siècle* (Paris: Champion, 1924).

5. *Medieval Rhetoric*, p. 189.

6. *De laboribus Herculis* 1. 11; ed. B. C. Ullman (Zurich: Thesaurus Mundi, 1951), pp. 61–63.

7. The importance of the Averroes Paraphrase is discussed by O. B. Hardison, Jr., *The Enduring Monument: A Study of the Idea of Praise in Renaissance Literary Theory and Practice* (Chapel Hill: University of North Carolina Press, 1962), pp. 34–35; and Bernard Weinberg, *A History of Literary Criticism in the Italian Renaissance (Chicago: University of Chicago Press, 1961)*, pp. 352–61, 586. On lyric as praise, see A. Leigh DeNeef, "Epideictic Rhetoric and the Renaissance Lyric," *JMRS*, 3 (1973): 203–31.

8. *Arte*, 1. 20, 1. 15; ed. G. D. Willcock and Alice Walker (Cambridge: Cambridge University Press, 1936), pp. 44, 33.

Notes

9. Hardison, *The Enduring Monument*, pp. 38–39. Sidney, *Defence of Poesie*, in *Prose Works*, ed. Albert Feuillerat, 4 vols. (Cambridge: Cambridge University Press, 1912, 1963), 3:23.

10. Hardison, *The Enduring Monument*, pp. 72–78.

11. *Poetices libri septem*, 3. 12; editio secunda (Heidelberg, 1581), p. 95.

12. *Defence*, in *Prose Works*, 3:30.

13. In Greek oratorical practice, for instance, encomium of a king *(basilikos logos)* readily converts to a treatise on ideals of kingship *(peri basileas)*. Significantly, a form named *paraenesis* mixes praise and counsel. See Burgess, pp. 137–38. On paraenesis, see as well Scaliger, 3. 105. An English poem actually titled as paraenetic is the *Paraenesis to Prince Henry* (1604) by Sir William Alexander, Earl of Stirling, *Poetical Works*, ed. L. E. Kastner and H. B. Charlton, Scottish Text Society, 2 vols (Edinburgh and London: Blackwood, 1921–29), 2:380–405. After Henry's death in 1613 it was readdressed to Charles. Groups of occasional poems, e.g. the verse epistles of Daniel or Donne, often run the gamut from encomium through paraenesis to counsel. Of Donne's, as edited by H. J. Grierson, *Poems*, 2 vols. (London: Oxford University Press, 1912), the first to Wotton (1:180–83) is deliberative, that to Edward Herbert (1:193–95) paraenetic, and the first to Countess of Bedford (1:189–90) encomiastic. Daniel's run more heavily to paraenesis.

14. Quoted in Lester K. Born's introduction to Erasmus's *Education of a Christian Prince* (New York: Columbia University Press, 1936), pp. 5–6. For the text of *Panegyricus*, see Erasmus, *Poems*, ed. C. Reedijk (Leyden: Brill, 1956), pp. 272–76.

15. "An Epistle to Selden," *Ben Jonson*, ed. C. H. Herford, Percy and Evelyn Simpson, 11 vols. (Oxford: Clarendon Press, 1925–52), 8:149. Since the poem proceeds to fulsome praise, the disavowal of flattery here becomes a means to hyperbole.

16. The idea of calling groups of occasional poems *silvae* is common in the Renaissance and apparently derives from Statius. For Tommaso Corea (1561) on *laus* and *vituperatio* in epigrams, see Weinberg, *Literary Criticism*, pp. 185–87.

17. For a mediaeval controversy on the morality of hyperbolic praise, see E. R. Curtius, *European Literature and the Latin Middle Ages*, trans. W. R. Trask, Bollingen Series, no. 36 (New York: Pantheon, 1953) pp. 163–64.

18. On the currency and impact of this textbook, which went through at least seventy-three printings between 1546 and 1689, see Donald Lemen Clark, "The Rise and Fall of Progymnasmata in Sixteenth and Seventeenth Century Grammar Schools," *SM*, 19 (1952): 259–63; and T. W. Baldwin, *William Shakespeare's Small Latine & Lesse Greeke*, 2 vols.

Notes

(Urbana: University of Illinois Press, 1944), chap. 34.

19. Aphthonius sophista, *Progymnasmata, partim a Rodolpho Agricola, partim a Ioanne Maria Cataneo Latinitate donata: cum scholiis Reinhardi Lorichii Hadamarii* (Frankfurt, 1598), pp. 157–58. *Votum* is mentioned in the mnemonic "Dispositio laudis tetrasticho comprehensa" designed to engrave the scheme on the student's mind, p. 173.

20. *Poems*, ed. F. M. Padelford, University of Washington Publications, Language and Literature, no. 5 (Seattle, 1928), pp. 83, 219–20.

21. Conversely, affected brevity could also contribute to the subject's dignity. See Hardison, *The Enduring Monument*, p. 228, n. 5. A good example is Jonson's "Epitaph on Elizabeth, L. H." which claims to show "what man can say / In a little."

22. *Arte of Rhetorique* 1560, ed. G. H. Mair (Oxford: Claredon Press, 1909), p. 17.

23. *Opera omnia*, 10 vols. (Leyden, 1703–6), 1:96b.

24. The bundling of several different (though often related) meanings under one term is typical of the confused terminology in Renaissance rhetoric. *Comparatio*, e.g., is used in at least three different senses in the Renaissance Aphthonius: as a special topos in the *laus* prescription, as a general topos of amplification, and as a theme in itself. *Locus communis* behaves even worse. Lee A. Sonnino, *A Handbook to Sixteenth-Century Rhetoric* (London: Routledge & Kegan Paul, 1968), untangles some of the terms but deals mainly with figures.

25. *Copia*, in *Opera*, 1:96b.

26. Thomas Wright, ed., *Political Poems and Songs from the Accession of Edw. III. to that of Ric. III.*, 2 vols. (London, 1859–61), 2:129.

27. *Poems*, ed. Agnes M. C. Latham (Cambridge, Mass.: Harvard University Press, 1951), pp. 5–7. In fact, the attribution of the poem to Raleigh relies on the citation of these apparently well-known lines as his by both Harrington and Drammond (ibid., pp. 93–98).

28. Burgess, *Epideictic Literature*, p. 132.

29. *European Literature*, pp. 83–85.

30. See Alain Renoir, *The Poetry of John Lydgate* (Cambridge, Mass: Harvard University Press, 1967), pp. 53–60. Curtius, *European Literature*, p. 84, discussing formulas of self-disparagement, notes that "in Rome of the Empire formulas of submission could not but develop as courtly glorification of the Emperor increased . . . To this exaltation of the Emperor there had to correspond an abasement of the individual."

31. On the history of the interpretation of the Orpheus myth, see John B. Friedman, *Orpheus in the Middle Ages* (Cambridge, Mass.: Harvard University Press, 1970); Kenneth R. R. Gros Louis's dissertation, "The Myth of Orpheus and Eurydice in English Literature to 1900"

Notes

(University of Wisconsin, 1964); and his "The Triumph and Death of Orpheus in the English Renaissance," *SEL*, 9 (1969): 63–80. See also A. Leigh DeNeef, *The Poetics of Orpheus: An Edition and Study of "Orpheus His Journey to Hell," by R. B.*, 1595, Seventeenth-Century Editions and Studies (forthcoming, 1978).

32. E.g. Augustine, *Civ. dei* 18. 37; Lactantius, *Inst. divin.* 1. 5.

33. Ed. C. de Boer (Amsterdam: North Holland Pub., 1915–54), 10. 2540–3008, 11. 179–80.

34. *De laboribus Herculis*, 4. 6; ed. Ullmann, p. 495.

35. *Genealogie deorum gentilium libri*, 5. 12; ed. Vincenzo Romano, 2 vols. (Bari: Laterza, 1951), 1:244–47.

36. *Ingeniosissimi metamorphoseos libri xv. In eosem libros Raphaelis Regii luculentissime enarrationes* (Venice, 1527), p. 112^v.

37. *Mythologiae sive explicationis fabularum libri decem*, 7. 14 (Venice, 1568), pp. 226^v–28^v.

38. "Le Personage d'Orphée chez Ronsard," *Lumières de la Pléiade* (Paris: Vrin, 1977), p. 278.

39. Spenser's uses of this formula are listed by C. Van Winkle, *Variorum Minor Poems*, 2:40. That Spenser associates the formula with Orpheus is clear in *The Ruines of Time*, 325–36.

40. A role made clear in *The Teares of the Muses*, 427–32. For discussion of Calliope in this role, see chapter 2.

41. *Odyssey* 11. 282–86. For Spenser on Amphion, see *The Ruines of Rome*, 25.

42. Spenser's most powerful statement of this Renaissance commonplace occurs in *The Ruines of Time*, 343–441.

43. See Scaliger, *Poetices* 3.109.

44. See E. C. Wilson, *England's Eliza*, Harvard Studies in English, no. 20 (Cambridge, Mass.: Harvard University Press, 1939), opposite p. 322; Frances A. Yates, "Queen Elizabeth as Astraea," *JWCI*, 10 (1947), plate 17e; Roy C. Strong, *Portraits of Queen Elizabeth I* (Oxford: Clarendon Press, 1963), p. 112.

45. See Wilson, *England's Eliza*, pp. 200–229; Yates, "Queen Elizabeth as Astraea," pp. 72–75. It is uncanny that the Virgin Queen should have been born on the eve of the Nativity of the Virgin (8 Sept.) and died on the eve of the Annunciation (25 March).

46. The total of twelve ladies probably reflects the twelve months, so that the woodcut in one sense portrays Colin composing the *Calender* itself.

47. See Strong, *Portraits*, painting no. 86.

48. The impossible mixed bouquet of flowers from spring to fall that is a common subject in Dutch Renaissance painting apparently conveys a

similar Edenic allegory. On the Golden Age in *Aprill*, see Patrick Cullen, *Spenser, Marvell, and Renaissance Pastoral* (Cambridge, Mass.: Harvard University Press, 1970), pp. 112–19.

49. Yates, "Queen Elizabeth as Astraea," plate 18c, shows Elizabeth portrayed as "Rosa Electa" in a floral border. On the provision of vast quantities of flowers for the queen's fêtes in the 1570s, see Elizabeth Jenkins, *Elizabeth the Great* (New York: Coward-McCann, 1959), p. 162.

50. *English Literature in the Sixteenth Century Excluding Drama*, Oxford History of English Literature (Oxford: Clarendon Press, 1954), p. 361. To some readers Colin's ode has no apparent structure. For Roy Daniells, e.g., "its organization could scarcely be looser. Apart from the queen's first sitting down and later rising to depart there is hardly any suggestion of sequence. The thirteen stanzas permit themselves to be arranged in several other ways without noticeable damage to the poem." *Milton, Mannerism and Baroque* (Toronto: University of Toronto Press, 1963), p. 137. Superficially, Colin's ode does convey this effect. But this is exactly the effect Renaissance poets commonly aim for: a sense of rhapsodic improvisation that belies the disciplined and intricate design. Similarly, for most readers, *Epithalamion* gave an impression of free composition until A. Kent Hieatt demonstrated its hidden structure in *Short Time's Endless Monument: The Symbolism of Numbers in Edmund Spenser's "Epithalamion"* (New York: Columbia University Press, 1960).

51. "Albee forswonck and forswatt" probably contains an "Albee"/Albion pun whereby Colin presents through himself England's devotion and even marriage to its native goddess, who at the beginning of her reign had claimed herself "bound unto a husband, which is the Kingdom of England." Such an implication would be intensely topical in 1579. See Jenkins, *Elizabeth*, pp. 76, 158. Virginia Tufte, *The Poetry of Marriage: The Epithalamium in Europe and Its Development in England*, University of Southern California Studies in Comparative Literature, no. 2 (Los Angeles: Tinnon-Brown, 1969), pp. 167–78, argues that the April ode is an epithalamium celebrating the marriage of Eliza and England. Alice S. Miskimin, *The Renaissance Chaucer* (New Haven and London: Yale University Press, 1975), p. 290, notes that Spenser takes the "Albee" line from the *Plowman's Tale*, attributed to Chaucer. (Cf. "the Pilgrim that the Ploughman playde a whyle" whom Spenser claims to "followe . . . farre off" in the envoy that ends the *Calender*.) Hence the line particularly connotes the native English tradition.

52. Yates, *Queen Elizabeth as Astraea*," pp. 37–56.

53. Edgar Wind, *Pagan Mysteries in the Renaissance*, revised ed. (Harmondsworth: Penguin, 1967), pp. 81–83. For the portrait, see Strong, *Portraits*, p. 79, no. 81.

Notes

54. However, encomium of monarchs was possible in pastoral from its beginning: e.g. Theocritus's seventeenth *Idyl* in praise of Ptolemy. On encomium in ancient pastoral, see Thomas G. Rosenmeyer, *The Green Cabinet: Theocritus and the European Pastoral Lyric* (Berkeley and Los Angeles: University of California Press, 1969), pp. 122–24. On Latin panegyrical pastoral in the Renaissance, see William Leonard Grant, *Neo-Latin Literature and the Pastoral* (Chapel Hill: University of North Carolina Press, 1965), chap. 11.

55. D. W. Robertson, *A Preface to Chaucer* (Princeton: Princeton University Press, 1962), pp. 128–34. Spenser's other important specification of the shepherd's pipe as bagpipe *(F.Q.* VI. x. 18) makes almost explicit the connection between eroticism and the poet's creativity.

56. See John W. Moore, Jr., "Colin Breaks his Pipe: A Reading of the 'January' Eclogue," *ELR*, 5 (1975): 3–24.

57. *Syntagma musicum.Volume Two, De Organographia, First and Second Parts*, trans. Harold Blumenfeld (New York: Bärenreiter, 1962), p. 37 (2. 2. 10).

58. Cf. its German name *zinke* of which the basic meaning is prong. The spelling cornett distinguishes it from the modern brass cornet.

59. Gustave Reese, *Music in the Renaissance*, rev. ed. (New York: Norton, 1959), p. 551. He notes, pp. 545–46, that Cellini was a virtuoso cornettist.

60. Jacopo Sannazaro, *Arcadia & Piscatorial Eclogues*, trans. Ralph Nash (Detroit: Wayne State University Press, 1966), p. 151.

61. On the *puer-senex* motif, see Curtius, *European Literature*, pp. 98–101.

62. Virgil, *Eclogues* 8. 55–56, sets Tityrus and Orpheus together in a set of impossibility topoi as poets of least and greatest ability.

63. The title itself may have as one of its senses "The Shepherd's Announcement" or perhaps "The Heralding of a Shepherd," for "calendar" has as root Greek *kalein*, call or summon. Miskimin, *The Renaissance Chaucer*, pp. 247ff., argues that Spenser's Chaucer was the Stowe folio of 1561. A. Kent Hieatt, *Chaucer, Spenser, Milton: Mythopoeic Continuities and Transformations* (Montreal and London: McGill-Queen's University Press, 1975), pp. 19–28, argues that Spenser used the Thynne editions of 1532–61.

64. In the topical sense the allusion is to be ecclesiastical abuse of pluralism.

65. I am indebted to Martin Howley and J. M. Richardson who independently made this observation to me.

66. The eclogue itself has 120 lines, the product of the tenth month and the year ("thys long lingring Phoebus race"—3).

Notes

67. Robert J. Clements, *Picta Poesis: Literary and Humanistic Theory in Renaissance Emblem Books*, Temi e testi, no. 6 (Rome: Edizioni di Storia e letteratura, 1960), pp. 57–59. Rabelais's *Gargantua*, V. 46–47, closes with a burlesque of the poetic fury vinously induced.

68. Erwin Panofsky, *Studies in Iconology: Humanistic Themes in the Art of the Renaissance*, Harper Torchbooks (New York and Evanston: Harper & Row, 1962), p. 142, with reference to Ficino's *Commentary on Plotinus' Ennead*, 1. 6.

69. It is important, however, to recognize Paul E. McLane's argument that Rosalind and Dido, as well as Eliza, are types of Elizabeth. *Spenser's "Shepheardes Calender": A Study in Elizabethan Allegory* (Notre Dame: University of Notre Dame, 1961), chaps. 3–4.

Chapter Two

1. *Virgil and Spenser*, University of California Publications in English, no. 2 (Berkeley, 1929), p. 318.

2. For the vituperative sense, see *F.Q.* II. ix. 25, "blazers of blame"; V. ix. 25, Malfont's "bold speaches, which he blazed had"; and *Teares of the Muses*, 102, "blazon out their blames."

3. See *Teares of the Muses*, 97–102, 451–68, and the dedicatory sonnet to Norris.

4. "Three proper wittie familiar Letters," in *Poetical Works of Edmund Spenser*, ed. J. C. Smith and E. de Sélincourt, Oxford Standard Authors (Oxford: Oxford University Press, 1912), p. 628.

5. Quoted by H. E. Cory, *Edmund Spenser: A Critical Study* (Berkeley: University of California Press, 1917), p. 73, n. 17. The *Theatrum* is usually thought to reflect Milton's opinions.

6. No source has been found for the epithet "Herculea proles" at the end of Sidney's *Apologie*. Either it is an allusion to Ariosto's "Ercolea prole" or (more likely) both are allusions to an unidentified common original. The phrase seems not to occur in classical Latin.

7. See Donald Cheney, *Spenser's Image of Nature: Wild Man and Shepherd in "The Faerie Queene"*, Yale Studies in English, no. 161 (New Haven and London, 1966), p. 81, n. 2; and Jane Aptekar, *Icons of Justice: Iconography & Thematic Imagery in Book V of "The Faerie Queene"* (New York and London: Columbia University Press, 1969), pp. 163–67.

8. Cupid's bow of ebony seems to imply another of a more propitious material, corresponding to his gold- or lead-tipped arrows which initiate, respectively, benevolent and malign erotic effects (cf. Ovid *Meta.* 1. 473f.). (In *March*, 83, Cupid has a silver bow.) In Chaucer's version of the *Romaunt of the Rose*, 918–38, Cupid's assistant Swete-Lokying holds

two bows, one "blak as bery or ony slo" and made from a tree with "fruyt of savour wykee," the other "of a plante / Without wem."

9. *Poetry*, p. 198.

10. See Wind, *Pagan Mysteries*, pp. 88–89.

11. See Alastair Fowler, *Spenser and the Numbers of Time* (London: Routledge & Kegan Paul, 1964), p. 5.

12. Vincenzo Cartari, *Le Imagini de i dei de gli antichi* (Lyons, 1581), p. 421.

13. The arguments of Padelford and Bennett are summarized in *Variorum F.Q.*, 1: app. 9. Lotspeich, *Classical Mythology in Spenser's Poetry* (Princeton: Princeton University Press, 1932), pp. 84–85. Starnes, "Spenser and the Muses," *TSLL*, 22 (1942): 31–58. Patrick Spurgeon, "Spenser's Muses," *Renaissance Papers* 1968, ed. G. W. Williams, Southeastern Renaissance Conference (Columbia, S.C., 1969), pp. 15–23, argues that both muses are involved.

14. This follows Boccaccio on the same subject almost verbatim: "For poets are not like historians, who begin their account at some convenient beginning and describe events in the unbroken order of their occurrence to the end . . . But poets, by a far nobler device, begin their proposed narrative in the midst of the events, or sometimes even near the end; and thus they find excuse for telling preceding events which seem to have been omitted." *Genealogiae* 14. 13; trans. Charles G. Osgood, *Boccaccio on Poetry* (Princeton: Princeton University Press, 1930), pp. 67–68. Boccaccio notes the tradition describing Lucan's *Pharsalia* as versified history rather than epic because of its chronological organization. Among the numerous anomalies of the Letter to Raleigh in relation to the poem it purports to describe is that whatever sense we may have of in medias res organization in *F.Q.* I and II is stimulated by the Letter and not the poem. Curiously, the Letter makes nothing of the unmistakable in medias res order of the first three cantos of Book III which mirror the device exactly as it appears in its locus classicus, *Aeneid* 1–3.

15. See Weinberg, *Literary Criticism*, pp. 41–42, 724.

16. In his April and November glosses E. K. accepts *De inventis* as Virgil's, although Robert Stephanus had correctly attributed them to Ausonius. Starnes, "Spenser and the Muses," p. 40.

17. Louis Réau, *Iconographie de l'art chrétien* 2 vols. (Paris: Presses universitaires de France, 1955–59), vol. 2, pt. 2, p. 617. Tasso's invocation alludes to Petrarch's famous canzone to the Virgin (*Rime*, 366) where the Woman Clothed with the Sun is clearly one of her types: "Vergine bella, che di sol vestita, / coronata di stelle." Strong, *Portraits*, p. 42, points out that the veneration of Elizabeth after her death as "Saint Elizabeth" and as the second Virgin in heaven uses the image of the queen as "a portent

in the skies, arrayed in the attributes of the Virgin as the Woman of the Apocalypse."

18. The difference between the two poets in these parallel passages points toward a broader contrast between their epics: Spenser's patriotism leads him to daring forms of the Christian-humanist synthesis; Tasso, alert to Tridentine strictures, is wary of heterodoxy. He seems to have altered his initial invocation at least three times: see Robert M. Durling, *The Figure of the Poet in Renaissance Epic* (Cambridge, Mass.: Harvard University Press, 1965,), pp. 195–96.

19. *Delle allusioni* (Rome, 1588), 3. 4. 2 (p. 176). Jewel, *An Apology of the Church of England*, ed. J. E. Booty, Folger Documents of Tudor and Stuart Civilization (Ithaca: Cornell University Press, 1963), p. 41; and ibid., Introduction, p. xv, for Alexander Nowell's use of the formula. I am grateful to Barbara Bernhart for drawing my attention to this formula and Fabricii's use of it.

20. Quoted by Jenkins, *Elizabeth*, p. 158, and by Wilson, *England's Eliza*, p. 4.

21. Roy C. Strong, "The Accession Day of Queen Elizabeth I," *JWCI*, 21 (1958): 92–93 and n. 48.

22. Garrett Mattingly, *The Armada* (Boston: Houghton Mifflin, 1962), p. 390.

23. Cf. the curious reinvocation at I. xi. 5–7 that *plays down* Redcrosse's fight with the dragon in favor of some later "worke . . . of endlesse prayse" that will depict the war "Twixt that great faery Queene and Paynim king." This seems to be another allusion to the Armada.

24. Strong, *Portraits*, pp. 39–40. This phenomenon in the Middle Ages is the subject of Ernst H. Kantorowicz, *The King's Two Bodies: A Study in Medieval Political Theology* (Princeton: Princeton University Press, 1957).

25. On the impresa and its relevance to Book V, see Aptekar, *Icons of Justice*, pp. 82–83, and René Graziani, "Philip II's *Impresa* and Spenser's Souldan," *JWCI*, 27 (1964): 322–24.

26. On triads in Spenser, see Alastair Fowler, "Emanations of Glory: Neoplatonic Order in Spenser's *Faerie Queene*," in Judith M. Kennedy and James A. Reither, eds., *A Theatre for Spenserians* (Toronto: University of Toronto Press, 1973), pp. 53–82. On intermediaries in the triad, the Renaissance locus classicus is Ficino's *Commentary on the Symposium*, 6. 1–6. The only complete translation is *Commentaire sur le Banquet de Platon*, trans. Raymond Marcel (Paris: Société d'Edition "Les Belles Lettres," 1956).

27. "Spenser and the Common Reader," *ELH*, 35 (1968): 618.

28. On the genre in the Renaissance, see Philip Rollinson, "The Ren-

aissance of the Literary Hymn," *Renaissance Papers* 1969, ed, G. W. Williams, Southeastern Renaissance Conference (Columbia, S.C., 1970), pp. 11–20. On elements of royal praise in *Fowre Hymnes*, see Elliott M. Hill, "Flattery in Spenser's *Fowre Hymnes*," *WVUPP*, 15 (1966): 22–35. Also, but more obliquely, Jon A. Quitslund, "Spenser's Image of Sapience," *SRen*, 16 (1969): 181–213; and Sears Jayne, "Attending to Genre: Spenser's *Hymnes*," a paper read at the 1971 Modern Language Association meeting and summarized in *SpN*, 3 (1972), no. 1, pp. 5–6.

29. *Prose Works*, 3:9–10, 25.

30. *Arte*, 3. 6; 1. 19; ed. Willcock and Walker, pp. 152, 41.

31. See *F.Q*. VI. x. 28 where Colin apologizes to Gloriana for omitting her from the central role in the vision of ideal courtesy. The apology indicates the presence of a royal type in each core canto in the preceding books.

Chapter Three

1. Graham Hough, ed., *The First Commentary on "The Faerie Queene"* (privately published, 1964), p. 9.

2. Ibid., p. 11.

3. As a rhetorical term in the Renaissance, *icon* means an extended verbal portrait realized mainly by use of similes. Both Puttenham and Peacham use it in this sense. See John B. Bender, *Spenser and Literary Pictorialism* (Princeton: Princeton University Press, 1972), pp. 38, 51. Bender's concept "focusing" somewhat overlaps with the sense in which I use "icon"; but his emphasis is on techniques of description, and mine on the revelation to which the icon gives rise. In addition to Bender's book, the specialized studies by Thomas P. Roche, *The Kindly Flame: A Study of The Third and Fourth Books of Spenser's "Faerie Queene"* (Princeton: Princeton University Press, 1964), and Aptekar, *Icons of Justice*, attest to contemporary interest in the iconography of *F.Q*. Alpers, *Poetry*, chap. 7, lays down important guidelines for critical use of iconography. C. S. Lewis, *Spenser's Images of Life*, ed. Alastair Fowler (Cambridge: Cambridge University Press, 1967), pp. 1–17, offers a succinct introduction to the subject. Richard Terrell Goode's dissertation, "Spenser's Festive Poem: Elizabethan Royal Pageantry and *The Faerie Queene*" (University of Texas, Austin, 1973) came to my notice too late for use in this chapter.

4. See Fowler, *Numbers of Time*, pp. 69–70.

5. "Una and the Clergy: The Ass Symbol in *The Faerie Queene*," *JWCI*, 21 (1958): 134–37. The satyrs' worship of Una's ass when she refuses their idolatry (I. vi. 19) shows Spenser's awareness of this emblem. Geoffrey Whitney included it in his *Choice of Emblemes*, 1585.

Notes

6. *The First and Second Prayer Books of Edward VI*, Introduction, E. C. S. Gibson, Everyman Books (London and New York: Dent, 1910), p. 283. In the second Book the office becomes the "Commination against Sinners," pp. 430–35. Spenser's phrase also echoes Isaiah 1:18 (quoted in the same office), "though our sins be red as scarlet, they shall be white as snow"—an allusion nicely epitomizing the opposition of Una and Duessa.

7. One as the number of both God and the church is a commonplace. See, e.g., Rabanus Maurus, *De universo libri xxii*, 18.3, in *Patrologia Latina*, 3:489.

8. See, e.g., Wilson, *England's Eliza*, pp. 244f., 250.

9. See Lawrence Rosinger, "Spenser's Una and Queen Elizabeth," *ELN*, 6 (1968–69): 13–18.

10. *Hymnarius Paraclitensis*, in *Patrologia Latina*, 178:1786.

11. *Duessa as Theological Satire* (Columbia: University of Missouri Press, 1970). Waters's point, though persuasive, is overstated: the Mistress Missa allusion does not begin to exhaust the meanings of Duessa nor does she (as he implies) express it at all points.

12. See Wilson, *England's Eliza*, pp. 200–229.

13. See Ivan L. Schulz, "The Maiden and Her Lamb," *MLN*, 46 (1931): 379–81. It is important to note that, after its appearance in the first icon of Una, Spenser never mentions the lamb again. Once its immediate relevance ceases he removes it from the poem simply by omission. The ease with which he does this suggests how *un*narrative a poem *F.Q.* is and how much instead it operates in terms of complex symbolic pictures.

14. First brought to bear on *F.Q.* by Frances Yates, "Queen Elizabeth as Astraea," pp. 37–56; see also Frank Kermode, *Shakespeare, Spenser, Donne: Renaissance Essays* (New York: Viking, 1971), pp. 33–49.

15. On these senses, see, e.g., William Nelson, *The Poetry of Edmund Spenser* (New York: Columbia University Press, 1963), pp. 157, 164–65; and John E. Hankins, *Source and Meaning in Spenser's Allegory: A Study of "The Faerie Queene"* (Oxford: Clarendon Press, 1971), pp. 13, 122.

16. *Figure of the Poet*, p. 114.

17. E.g. *F.Q.* I. ix. 29, 48; VI. ix. 26; *Colin Clouts Come Home Again*, 596–99.

18. Two subtle and far reaching discussions of this phenomenon, attention to which is essential if one is to read the poem perceptively, are by Jerome S. Dees, "The Narrator of *The Faerie Queene*: Patterns of Response," *TSLL*, 12 (1971): 537–68; and Stan Hinton, "The Poet and his Narrator: Spenser's Epic Voice," *ELH*, 41 (1974): 165–81.

19. Angus Fletcher, *The Prophetic Moment: An Essay on Spenser*

Notes

(Chicago: University of Chicago Press, 1971), discusses at book length the interpenetration of what he terms *templar* and *labyrinthine* symbols.

20. Jenkins, *Elizabeth*, p. 157.

21. *Variorum F.Q.*, 1:396–98.

22. Francis J. Grant, ed., *Manual of Heraldry* (Edinburgh: Grant, 1962), pp. 136–37; *Boutell's Heraldry*, rev. C. W. Scott-Giles and J. P. Brooke-Little (London and New York: Warne, 1963), p. 211. The supporters of Elizabeth and Henry VIII literally and structurally *support* Una in her wandering: she is first rescued by the lion and last by Arthur bearing Cadwallader's dragon.

23. Fowler, *Numbers of Time*, pp. 66–67.

24. Parts of Psalm 22, especially the lion verse, appear prominently in the various occasional forms of prayer authorized during Elizabeth's reign. Here the lion invariably means the Catholic foes of the queen and English church. One form issued in 1576 for annual use on Elizabeth's accession Day includes a cento of psalm verses arranged to narrate how the church, driven into the wilderness by enemies, was delivered by God. The early part of canto iii abounds with allusions to this cento. For the forms, see *Liturgies of Queen Elizabeth*, ed. W. K. Clay, Parker Society (Cambridge, 1847); for the cento, pp. 555–56. The day before her coronation, Elizabeth in a public prayer styled herself as Daniel divinely saved from "gredy and rageing Lyons: even so was I overwhelmed, and only by thee delivered." Sidney Anglo, *Spectacle, Pageantry, and Early Tudor Policy* (Oxford: Clarendon Press, 1969), pp. 345–46. Cf. Una's "he my Lyon, and my noble Lord," I. iii. 7. On Spenser's biblical allusions, see Naseeb Shaheen, *Biblical References in "The Faerie Queene"* (Memphis: Memphis State University Press, 1976). In my observations, however, the biblical allusion does not have much hermeneutic value until one becomes aware of the associations it derives from the liturgy and exegesis. For such use, see James Nohrnberg, *The Analogy of "The Faerie Queene"* (Princeton: Princeton University Press, 1976), Index to Scriptures, pp. 864–70.

25. John E. Hankins, *Source and Meaning in Spenser's Allegory: A Study of "The Faerie Queene"* (Oxford: Clarendon Press, 1971), pp. 106–7.

26. Ibid., p. 106.

27. Strong, *Portraits*, p. 66.

28. Interestingly, in the symmetry of these two cantos—the first beginning with its icon, the second ending with it—the lion's rage occurs in the fifth stanza (I. iii. 5) and Braggadochio's lust in the fifth stanza from the end (II. iii. 42).

29. This argument is usually associated with Josephine Waters Bennett, *The Evolution of "The Faerie Queene"* (Chicago: University of Chicago

Press, 1942), where it is part of a complex set of speculations about the development of *F.Q.* But the idea that the present, highly Ariostan Book III descends from an early form of the poem may be defended simply by appeal to Harvey's letter of 1580 where he recognizes, in some part of *F.Q.*, Spenser's attempt to "seeme to emulate, and hope to overgo" the *Orlando*. See Spenser, *Poetical Works*, ed. Smith and de Sélincourt, p. 628.

30. Northrop Frye points out that in *F.Q.* "impulsive action is really pseudo-action, a passion which increasingly becomes passivity." "The Structure of Imagery in *The Faery Queene*," *UTQ*, 30 (1961): 121.

31. *Apology*, ed. Booty, p. 74.

32. *Liturgies*, p. 578.

33. Ibid., p. 605. The prayer is part of a form occasioned by Leicester's expedition to the Low Countries, 1585.

34. See, e.g., Aptekar, *Icons of Justice*, pp. 204–17.

35. Orgoglio's *genus* from winds blowing through caves in the earth (vii. 9) is the ancient explanation of earthquakes, as in Pliny, *Natural History* 2.81. On "Geaunt" (vii, 8, 14) from Greek *gea*, earth, see A. C. Hamilton, "Spenser, 'well of English undefyld,' " in Kennedy and Reither, eds., *Theatre*, p. 111.

36. See John Foxe, *Acts and Monuments*, ed. Josiah Pratt, 8 vols. (London, 1853–70), 1:305–12, who claims, following Gildas, that Joseph of Arimathea, sent by the apostle Philip about 63 A.D., began the British church (p. 306). Constantine, "a Briton born, by his mother Helena, . . . by the help of the British army (under the power of God), which the said Constantine took with him out of Britain to Rome, obtained, with great victory, peace and tranquility to the whole universal church of Christ" (p. 312).

37. "Let Constantinus be never so great: yet wherein is your noble grace to him inferiour? in many things equal, in this superiour, for that Constantinus, being only an helper unto the persecuted, your highness hath dispatched that persecution from other, under which ye were so entangled yourselfe: and that chiefly (what so ever they pretended) for the truth of your profession, wherein your grace hath more to rejoyce than in any other thing els beside" (Ibid., p. 312).

38. 1563 ed., p. Bii[r]. Discussed by Yates, "Queen Elizabeth as Astraea," p. 41.

39. *Acts*, 1:310.

40. *Variorum F.Q.*, 1:308.

41. I. i. 29, where a series of pleonasms culminating in "voyde of malice bad" hints at the "aged Sire" 's true nature and his insecure grasp of the verbal enchanter's art.

Notes

42. On the interaction of seriousness with comedy (or at least playful-ness) in *F.Q.*, see William Nelson's wise and witty essay, "Spenser *ludens*," in Kennedy and Reither, eds., *Theatre*, pp. 83–100. Spenser always portrays Archimago in comic terms because he is, *inter alia*, genuinely diabolic—the Father of Lies—and, according to tradition, Satan cannot bear to be laughed at. See the epigraphs from Luther and Thomas More that begin C. S. Lewis, *The Screwtape Letters* (London: Bles, 1942).

43. *Numbers of Time*, pp. 58, 48.

44. The canto also seems to contain seven groups of six stanzas each. The central such group (st.s 19–24) begins with the idea of a six-year "terme," has two parallel lines at its exact center, and begins and ends with phenomena of mutability: the delayed marriage and the entry of the messenger. Such a design of seven groups of stanzas may reflect the groups of seven symbols in Revelation (messages to churches, seals, trumpets), a book which otherwise affects this canto strongly.

45. On sea- and ship-metaphors in *F.Q.* see Kathleen Williams, "Spenser: Some Uses of the Sea and the Storm-tossed Ship," *RORD*, 13–14 (1970–71): 135–42; and Jerome S. Dees, "The Ship Conceit in *The Faerie Queene*: 'Conspicuous Allusion' and Poetic Structure," *SP*, 72 (1975): 208–25.

46. John Dixon glossed the six years to mean "the time of the raingne of phil: and marye." *First Commentary*, pp. 9–10.

47. For this tradition, see Josephine Waters Bennett, "Britain Among the Fortunate Isles," *SP*, 53 (1956): 114–40.

Chapter Four

1. On wit in this passage, see Nelson's essay in Kennedy and Reither, eds., *Theatre*, p. 88. On its geographical speculations, see Michael Murrin, "The Rhetoric of Faeryland," in *The Rhetoric of Renais-sance Poetry from Wyatt to Milton*, ed. T. O. Sloan and R. B. Waddington (Berkeley: University of California Press, 1974), pp. 73–95.

2. Henry Peacham, *The Garden of Eloquence* (1577), translating Joan-nes Susenbrotus, *Epitome troporum ac schematum* (1540); quoted by Rix, *Rhetoric*, p. 43.

3. In the 1596 dedication of *F.Q.* to Elizabeth, Spenser adds Virginia to the list of lands over which she is "empresse."

4. *The Allegorical Temper: Vision and Reality in Book II of Spenser's "Faerie Queene,"* Yale Studies in English, 137 (New Haven, 1957), chap. 6.

5. Ibid., pp. 136–37.

6. See Wind, *Pagan Mysteries*, pp. 47–48.

Notes

7. Merritt Y. Hughes, "Virgilian Allegory and *The Faerie Queene*," *PMLA*, 44 (1929): 696–705, suggests that this icon, which draws allusively on the appearance to Aeneas of Venus disguised as a hunting nymph, reflects the Neoplatonic allegorization of Virgil's Venus as an Idea. To present a Diana figure by allusion to a famous passage on Venus is to invite complication.

8. On comedy here, see Nelson, in Kennedy and Reither, eds., *Theatre*, p. 92. To elaborate a simile or metaphor far beyond its point of departure is one of Spenser's favorite comic tactics. It occurs again in connection with Belphoebe's praise at III. v. 51–54 where Spenser adapts the rose image for her virginity from Ariosto's Angelica only to pursue it in stanza fifty-one with perversely sober horticultural literalness. See discussions by Alpers, *Poetry of "F.Q.,"* pp. 192–94, and Roche, *Kindly Flame*, pp. 139–42.

9. *The Historie of the Most Renowned and Victorious Princesse Elizabeth* (i.e. trans. of Camden's *Annales*) (London, 1630), p. 6.

10. The following section proposes that several topical allusions to New World mythology occur in the second half of Book II—a response to growing awareness, in the 1580s, of England's potential imperial destiny. Some readers will react suspiciously to any such suggestion, partly because the study of historical allegory in *F.Q.* was discredited by rigid and unconvincing approaches early in this century; of these, F. M. Padelford, *The Political and Ecclesiastical Allegory of the First Book of "The Faerie Queene"* (Boston: Ginn, 1911) is typical. More recently, however, Yates's famous article on the political meaning of Astraea, and Kermode's work on the mythology of Tudor propaganda (see above, chap. 3, n. 14, as well as Kermode, Stephen Fender, and Kenneth Palmer, *English Renaissance Literature: Introductory Lectures* [London: Gray-Mills, 1974], pp. 1–12) have rehabilitated topical allegory and shown its usefulness in interpreting some parts of *F.Q.*, especially Book I. Since strong parallelism between I and II is generally accepted, it is not unlikely that such allegory is present in II. Although what I advance below is to some degree tentative, it seems useful to include in a study of political encomium in *F.Q.* any topical material that bears on that encomium in an illuminating way.

11. For the details of Spenser's imitation, see Robert M. Durling, "The Bower of Bliss and Armida's Palace," *CL*, 6 (1954): 335–47.

12. Robert Ralston Cawley, *Unpathed Waters: Studies in the Influence of the Voyagers on Elizabethan Literature* (Princeton: Princeton University Press, 1940), pp. 3–15, notes that the Fortunate Isles were ordinarily identified with the Canaries in the Renaissance (pp. 4–7) as Tasso also seems to do: his Fortunate Isles are somewhere west of Africa (st. 37),

and Armida's isle is one of them. But by approaching them through an unmistakably American frame of reference and making the voyage anticipate Columbus's, he also gives his Fortunate Isle a New World coloration to which Spenser is demonstrably alert. Bennett, "Britain Among the Fortunate Isles," pp. 114–40, says that Calypso's isle, Ogygia, was anciently held most remote in the world. Armida detaining her lover in her remote American island is more in the tradition of Calypso than of Circe, although Spenser makes Acrasia overtly Circean.

13. See, e.g., Lewis Hanke, *Aristotle and the American Indian* (Chicago: University of Chicago Press, 1959), chap. 1; J. H. Elliott, *The Old World and the New*, 1495–1650 (Cambridge: Cambridge University Press, 1970), chaps. 1–2; Luis Weckmann, "The Middle Ages in the Conquest of America," *Speculum*, 26 (1951): 130–41. Peculiar though the relocation of these wonders in the New World may appear, it allowed the Renaissance mind, with its symbolic cosmic models and designed universe, to accommodate the revelation of America in inherited terms. Thus, the localization in America of the Golden Age, the four rivers of Eden, the devil's island-home, the seven enchanted cities, the fountain of youth, unicorns, wild men, mermaids and sirens, trumpet-playing apes, Mandeville's men whose heads do grow beneath their shoulders, and Amazons. Amazons were the object of several enthusiastic searches; in 1540 Francisco de Orellana permanently attached this transplanted myth to the Americas by descending what he proclaimed as their river (Weckmann, "The Middle Ages," pp. 132–33). In 1596 Raleigh in the *Discoverie of Guiana* can still confidently report the location and social customs of American Amazons. Jose Durand, *Ocaso de sirenas: manaties en el siglo XVI* (Mexico: Tezontle, 1950), reprints sixteenth-century Spanish accounts of manatees and dugongs which confused them with mermaids and sirens. A basic study of such New World mythology is Enrique de Gandia, *Historia critica de los mitos de la conquista Americana* (Buenos Aires and Madrid: Roldán, 1929). See also Fredi Chiappelli, ed., *First Images of America*, 2 vols. (Berkeley: University of California Press, 1976), especially the essays in part 2.

14. Hanke, *Aristotle and the American Indian*, p. 3.

15. Garcilaso de la Vega, el Inca, in his *Royal Commentaries of the Incas* (1606) explains the phenomenon thus: "The emerald grows to perfection in its mineral gradually acquiring the green color, as a fruit ripens on a tree. At first it is a dusky white with a greyish or greenish tinge. It begins to ripen or attain perfection on one of its four sides, probably that facing the east, as is the case with fruit which with I have just compared it: the good color then spreads from one side until it covers the whole emerald. It remains in the state in which it is mined, whether perfect or imper-

fect." 1.8.23; trans. Harold V. Livermore, 2 vols. (Austin and London: University of Texas Press, 1966), 1:530.

16. *The Discoverie of the Large, Rich and Bewtiful Empyre of Guiana*, facsimile, The English Experience, no. 3 (Amsterdam and New York: Theatrum Orbis Terrarum, 1968), p. 12.

17. "Of Coaches," in *Essays*, trans. John Florio, intro. George Saintsbury, 3 vols. (New York: AMS, 1967), 3:148. Augustin de Zarate's *History of the Discovery and Conquest of Peru (1555)* tells of similar gardens, containing, among other gold and silver reproductions, "all the kinds of grasses that grew in that land, with their ears and shoots and nodes copied from nature." 1. 14; trans. J. M. Cohen (Harmondsworth: Penguin, 1968), p. 58. A fuller account occurs in the *Royal Commentaries* of Garcilaso. Its association of real and metal plants, the botanical verisimilitude of the latter, and their many-seasoned effect, all have parallels in the garden of Spenser's Bower. "All the royal palaces had gardens and orchards for the Inca's recreation. They were planted with all sorts of gay and beautiful trees, beds of flowers, and fine and sweet-smelling herbs found in Peru. They also made gold and silver models of many trees and lesser plants: they were done in natural size and style with their leaves, blossoms, and fruits, some beginning to sprout, others half-grown, and others in full bloom. Among these and other splendors, they made fields of maize, copying the leaves, cob, stalk, roots, and flowers from life. The beard of the maize husk was done in gold and the rest in silver, the two being soldered together. They made the same distinction in dealing with other plants, using gold to copy the flower or anything else of a yellow tint and silver for the rest." 1. 6. 2; trans. Livermore, 1:315.

18. See Curtius, *European Literature*, pp. 198–200.

19. The coinage "Ingoes" makes "ingots" seem to derive from "Incas." The Elizabethan "Ingas" follows the normal form used in the Spanish chronicles of the Conquista (as in the passage from Raleigh's *Discoverie* quoted above). Such false etymology is an ancient means of allegory to which the synthetically archaic language of *F.Q.* lends itself effortlessly. On the subject of false etymology in the poem, see Martha Craig, "The Secret Wit of Spenser's language," in Paul J. Alpers, ed., *Elizabethan Poetry: Modern Essays in Criticism* (New York: Oxford University Press, 1967), pp. 447–72; the dissertations by Jay Belson, "The Names in *The Faerie Queene*" (Columbia University, 1964), and Alice Blitch, "Etymon and Image in *The Faerie Queene*" (Michigan State University, 1965); and A. C. Hamilton, "Our New Poet: Spenser, 'well of English undefyld,' " in Kennedy and Reither, eds., *Theatre*, pp. 101—33.

20. For an account by a conquistador who participated in the reduction of Montezuma's treasure, see Bernal Diaz de Castillo, *The Conquest of*

Notes

New Spain, trans. J. M. Cohen (Harmondsworth: Penguin, 1963), pp. 270–74; also the official historian of the Conquista, Francisco Lopez de Gomara, *La Historia general de las Indias*, Part 2 in *Biblioteca de autores espanoles* (Madrid: Atlas, 1946), 22:232–33; and W. H. Prescott, *The Conquest of Mexico. The Conquest of Peru*, Modern Library (New York: Random House, n.d.), pp. 965–67, 995. See Prescott, idem, p. 960, on the Incan temple plates.

21. Cited by William S. Maltby, *The Black Legend in England: The Development of Anti-Spanish Sentiment*, 1559–1660 (Durham, N.C.: Duke University Press, 1971), pp. 18–19. Las Casas's *Brevissima Relacion de la destruccion de las Indias* appeared in English in 1583 as *The Spanish Colonie*.

22. *Discoverie*, pp. 10–14. On the myth of El Dorado, see Gandia, *Historia critica*, chap. 7; and Constantino Bayle, *El Dorado fantasma* (Madrid: Consejo de la Hispanidad, 1943), especially chap. 10.

23. *Discoverie*, p. 10. Cf. Craig's comments on the meaning of "Idle Lake" and "Inland sea" ("The Secret Wit of Spenser's Language," p. 464) Gyon mentions the Caspian in terms of trade in st. 14.

24. Gomara's history of the Conquista appeared in English in 1578, Zarate's Peruvian chronicle in 1581, then Las Casas's diatribe against Spanish exploitation of the Indians in 1583. That these translations of Conquista materials should not appear until the 1580s indicates the topicality of the subject among Elizabethans during the decade when Book II of *F.Q.* was written. On the relations of Spenser and Raleigh toward the end of the decade, see Alexander C. Judson, *The Life of Edmund Spenser* (Baltimore: Johns Hopkins Press, 1945), pp. 135–37.

25. See Susan Snyder, "Guyon as Wrestler," *RN*, 14 (1961): 249–52; and A. D. S. Fowler, "The River Guyon," *MLN*, 41 (1960): 289–92.

26. Henry Reynolds, *Mythomystes*, in J. E. Spingarn, ed., *Critical Essays of the Seventeenth Century*, 3 vols. (Oxford: Clarendon Press, 1908–09), 1:159.

27. According to Dee, people from western colonies founded by Arthur had arrived in Norway late in the Middle Ages. A. L. Rowse, *The Elizabethans and America* (London: Macmillan, 1959), pp. 18–19.

28. David French, *John Dee: The World of an Elizabethan Magus* (London: Macmillan, 1972), p. 197.

29. *De Orbe Novo: The Eight Decades of Peter Martyr d'Anghera*, trans. F. A. MacNutt, 2 vols. (New York: Putnam, 1912), 1:75.

30. The supposed transmission of syphilis by Columbus's men is described in 1526 by Gonzalo Fernandez de Oviedo, *Natural History of the West Indies*, chap. 75; trans. Sterling A. Stroudmire (Chapel Hill: University of North Carolina Press, 1959), pp. 88–89. For a concise statement on the question of its American origin, see Francisco Guerra, "The

Problem of Syphilis," in Chiappelli, ed., *First Images*, pp. 845–51. See also ibid., pp. 835 and 879–80.

31. Though the image originates in *Iliad* 8. 19–22, it may also (given the New World allusions in *F.Q.* II) hint at the great gold cable of the Incas, a lost wonder recorded by Zarate, 1. 14 (p. 58), and Garcilaso, 1. 9. 1 (1:543–45) who says it is "famous throughout the world, but has still never been seen by any stranger, though many have desired it."

32. On the features of the terrestrial paradise, see Cawley, *Unpathed Waters*, pp. 30–31.

33. *Kindly Flame*, pp. 104–6. Cf. the use of similar psalm-tags with liturgical associations noted above in chapter 3. On the twins' birth and their complementary nature, see Isabel G. MacCaffrey, *Spenser's Allegory: The Anatomy of Imagination* (Princeton: Princeton University Press, 1976), pp. 271–90.

34. See Fowler, *Numbers of Time*, chap. 5. Like six, five is also a marriage number but, as I. xii and Book VI itself seem to show, Spenser prefers six for this association.

35. See William Nelson, *The Poetry of Edmund Spenser: A Study* (New York: Columbia University Press, 1963), pp. 229–30; Roche, *Kindly Flame*, pp. 81–82. The point was originally made by Warton in the eighteenth century.

36. Eric St. J. Brooks, *Sir Christopher Hatton, Queen Elizabeth's Favourite* (London: Cape, 1946), p. 173.

37. Jenkins, *Elizabeth*, pp. 224, 234–35, 249.

38. Iona and Peter Opie, eds., *The Oxford Dictionary of Nursery Rhymes* (Oxford: Clarendon Press, 1951), p. 179.

39. Judson, *Life of Spenser*, pp. 69–71.

40. See Conyers Read, *Lord Burghley and Queen Elizabeth* (London: Cape, 1960), pp. 208ff.

41. R. W. Beckingsale, *Burghley: Tudor Statesman*, 1520–1598 (London: and New York: Macmillan, 1967), pp. 16, 253ff.

42. See *Variorum F.Q.*, 3:303–4. But Roche, *Kindly Flame*, pp. 134–36, shows that the hermaphrodite is not unusual as an emblem of married unity. See also Donald Cheney, "Spenser's Hermaphrodite and the 1590 *Faerie Queene*," *PMLA*, 87 (1972): 192–200.

43. *Genealogie*, 3. 21, cited by Chauncey Wood, *Chaucer and the Country of the Stars* (Princeton: Princeton University Press, 1970), p. 66, who notes that the tradition of Mercury as a god of eloquence goes back to Martianus Capella's *Marriage of Mercury and Philology*.

44. P. 150. Although Roche rejects Upton's queer notion that Florimell represents Mary of Scots, he also curiously suggests that she cannot be related to Elizabeth (*Kindly Flame*, pp. 150–51).

Notes

45. On the snowy Florimell see Frye, "The Structure of Imagery in *The Faerie Queene*," p. 140; and William Blissett, "Florimell and Marinell," *SEL*, 5 (1965): 87–104.

46. Roche, *Kindly Flame*, pp. 152ff.

47. Fowler, *Numbers of Time*, p. 174. Cf. the well-known annual ceremony of the doge casting a ring in the sea to symbolize his marriage to Venice.

48. Jenkins, *Elizabeth*, pp. 71–73.

49. Ibid., pp. 62, 159.

50. Charles G. Smith, *Spenser's Proverb Lore* (Cambridge, Mass.: Harvard University Press, 1970), p. 285.

Chapter Five

1. For the range of meanings possible for "glory" in Renaissance literature, see Françoise Joukovsky, *La Gloire dans la poésie française et néolatine du xvie siècle* (Geneva: Droz, 1969).

2. *Evolution*, p. 48.

3. Ibid., p. 49.

4. *Allegory: The Theory of a Symbolic Mode*, Cornell Paperbacks (Ithaca and London, 1970), p. 272.

5. Isabel A. Rathborne, *The Meaning of Spenser's Fairyland*, Columbia University Studies in English and Comparative Literature, 131 (New York, 1937), 22ff.

6. Rathborne, ibid., chap. 1, argues that Cleopolis is an Augustinian worldly city. Although admitting that Gloriana is "in some sense a mirror of heavenly glory" (p. 20), she is uneasy with the idea.

7. One of the most illuminating pieces of close reading in Spenser scholarship is Harry Berger's comparison of these two histories. See his *Allegorical Temper*, chap. 4.

8. *Mythologiae*, 4. 6. See Lotspeich, *Classical Mythology*, pp. 102–3.

9. Jerry Leath Mills' "Spenser and the Numbers of History: A Note on the British and Elfin Chronicles in *The Faerie Queene*," *PQ*, 55 (1976): 281–87, argues persuasively that Spenser organizes his chronicles according to Jean Bodin's numerological schemes based on the physical and spiritual numbers—that is seven and nine, respectively. The Faery chronicle comprises seven nine-line stanzas, making it an ideal product of body and soul, like the ideal house of temperance, "Proportioned equally by seven and nine" (II. ix. 22), where the soul, or Alma, governs the body. I am grateful to Professor Mills for letting me read this article in manuscript.

10. See Bennett, *Evolution*, chap. 6, especially p. 68ff.

Notes

11. *Acts and Monuments*, 1:323.

12. Hughes, *Variorum F.Q.*, 1:484. Cf. Milton's consideration of an Arthuriad.

13. Beckingsale, *Burghley*, p. 215.

14. *Meaning of Fairyland*, p. 233. Cf. the Virgin's image on Gawain's shield in *Sir Gawain and the Green Knight*, 645–50.

15. *Source and Meaning*, p. 109.

16. "Secret Wit," in Alpers, ed., *Elizabethan Poetry*, p. 461 and n. 18.

17. Mills shows that, of Bodin's three "climacterics," or critical numbers in ageing (forty-nine, sixty-three, eighty-one), two are present in the British chronicle: Christianity arrives with the forty-ninth chronicle stanza (st. 53), and Arthur breaks off at the sixty-third (st. 68).

18. *The Prophetic Moment: An Essay on Spenser* (Chicago and London: University of Chicago Press, 1971), p. 88.

19. Alciati, *Emblemata* (Lyons, 1551), p. 226: "Herculeos crines bicolor quod populus ornet, / Temporis alternat noxque diesque vices."

20. Strong, *Portraits*, p. 21.

21. See *Variorum F.Q.*, 2:295, where Upton thinks the bird a cuckoo and Kitchin thinks it an owl; and the exchange between Graham Hough and Alastair Fowler, "Spenser and Renaissance Iconography," *EIC*, 11, (1961): 223–38. Fowler argues for the turtledove but, like the cuckoo and the owl, its connection with Pan is elusive. Spenser's "dight" may have the meaning "compose" in the sense of composing poetry. There may also be a connection between the nightingale and Pan through Philomela's father Pandareos (*Odyssey* 19: 516ff) or Pandion (*Metamorphoses* 6. 427).

22. On Minerva's relevance see Fowler, *Numbers of Time*, pp. 122–32.

23. Ibid., p. 132 and n. 2.

24. Cf. Elizabeth's famous performance as martial leader during the Armada's approach, when she appeared in armor before the troops at Tilbury and proclaimed that in the "body of a weak and feeble woman" was "the heart and stomach of a king." Jenkins, *Elizabeth*, p. 285.

25. Virgil's fourth *Eclogue* makes the idea of the return of the Golden Age corresponding to the coming of a ruler a standard theme in subsequent praise of monarchs. John Davies's *Hymnes of Astraea* is the striking Elizabethan example. But, in spite of a tendency in some recent criticism to refer to the Golden Age in Spenser, he does not (to my knowledge) anywhere use the theme of the Golden Age returned, his allusions to the myth being either nostalgic or ironic.

26. Strong, *Portraits*, painting no. 86.

27. *The Sources of the British Chronicle History in Spenser's "Faerie Queene"* (New York: Haskell House, 1964), p. 44 (original publication 1910).

Notes

28. In one of their senses, Britomart and Artegall are the same name, identical at the point where they overlap with Arthur's name: *Brit*om*ART*e*gall* (Briton and Gallic both meaning Welsh). Of the other three main erotic stories in *F.Q.* III–IV, two show similar overlapping of names: Scud*AMOR*et and, through rhyme as well as land-sea pairing, Flor*i*mell and Mar*i*nell. The fourth story, of Belphoebe and Timias, is frustrated and, significantly, their names are discrete: Timias (Greek, honor) merely expresses one of Belphoebe's attributes.

29. Harper, *Sources*, pp. 161–62.

30. For the sources, see ibid., pp. 168–78.

31. Mills notes that, when "Briton moniments" and Merlin's prophecy are read as one, the stanza proclaiming the advent of the Tudors, III. iii. 48, coincides with the third of Bodin's climacteric numbers of history, eighty-one.

Chapter Six

1. Cory, *Spenser*, pp. 254–325, attributes the decline to Spenser's disappointment in his career and "the shipwreck of his impersonal ideals" (p. 255). For Edwin Greenlaw's review, see *MLN*, 35 (1920): 165–77.

2. Roger Sale, *Reading Spenser: An Introduction to "The Faerie Queene"* (New York: Random House, 1968), chap. 4. The following articles comment variously on the failure of idealism toward the end of the poem: Harry Berger, "A Secret Discipline: *The Faerie Queene*, Book VI," in William Nelson, ed., *Form and Convention in the Poetry of Edmund Spenser* (New York and London: Columbia University Press, 1961), pp. 35–75; Richard Neuse, "Book VI as Conclusion to *The Faerie Queene*," *ELH*, 35(1968):329–53; and Joanne Craig, "The Image of Mortality: Myth and History in *The Fairie Queen*," *ELH*, 39 (1972): 520–44.

3. J. E. Neale, *Queen Elizabeth I*, Pelican Biographies (Harmondsworth: Penguin, 1971), p. 355.

4. On the iconographical background of lion-drawn chariots, see Roche, *Kindly Flame*, pp. 22–28.

5. On the meanings of the caduceus and its association with the olive wreath, see Fowler, *Numbers of Time*, pp. 157–62.

6. It is worth noting that Marinell is attacked by Britomart at his first appearance in the poem and at his last is rescued by Artegall.

7. Noted by Upton. See *Variorum F.Q.*, 5:187.

8. E.g. in II. iii. 43.7 Braggadochio sees Belphoebe's escape as a "foule blot" to knighthood; in V. iii. 37. 7 Talus "blotted out" Braggadochio's arms. In II. iii. 33–34 Trompart takes Belphoebe for a goddess, that is, Diana; in V. iii. 27–28 Florimell reassumes Venus's cestus.

Notes

9. *Source and Meaning*, pp. 179, 182. He also convincingly derives Calepine's name from Greek *chalepoi* to mean mansuetude or mildness in the face of aggression, p. 179.

10. See Northrop Frye, *Anatomy of Criticism* (Princeton: Princeton University Press, 1957), p. 148.

11. E.g. in I. iii. 4 Una takes her fillet "From her faire head"; in VI. iii. 23 Serena makes "a garland to adorne her hed." In I. iii. 5. 1–2 "It fortuned out of the thickest wood / A ramping Lyon rushed suddainly"; in VI. iii. 24. 1–2 "All sodainely out of the forest nere / The Blatant Beast forth rushing unaware."

12. *The Queen and the Poet* (London: Faber, 1960), p. 98, n. 2, and app. 3. The poem is no. 19 in Raleigh's *Poems*, ed. Latham, p. 20; see also her comment, pp. 118–19. Interestingly, Timias is the only other figure bitten by the Beast, and in III–IV he bears allusion to Raleigh. In VI. vi he and Serena seek the Hermit's aid against slander.

13. *Source and Meaning*, p. 174. In New Hierusalem are "Saints all in that Citie sam" (I. x. 57); and in *Maye*, 168, Piers asks "what concord han light and darke sam."

14. William Nelson, "Queen Elizabeth, Spenser's Mercilla, and a Rusty Sword," *RN*, 18 (1965): 113–17.

15. See Aptekar, *Icons of Justice*, chap. 4, on the iconography of this lion.

16. Fabricii's *Allusioni*, an emblem book lauding Gregory XIII, shows his device, a winged dragon, in each emblem. See above, chap. 2, p. 49.

17. T. K. Dunseath, *Spenser's Allegory of Justice in Book Five of "The Faerie Queene"* (Princeton: Princeton University Press, 1968), pp. 206–7.

18. In 1596 Elizabeth was sixty-three. Creighton Gilbert, "When Did a Man in the Renaissance Grow Old?" *SRen*, 14 (1967): 7–32, especially 30–32, puts this age in context when he argues that retirement in the late forties and death in the early fifties was the expected pattern (as with Shakespeare who retired at forty-seven and died at fifty-two) and that kings with their better life expectancy died on the average in their fifties.

19. *Allegory of Justice*, p. 217.

20. *Numbers of Time*, p. 197.

21. *Allegory of Justice*, pp. 217–18.

22. Neale, *Elizabeth*, pp. 278–83; Jenkins, *Elizabeth*, pp. 273–80.

23. "Elizabeth at Isis Church," *PMLA*, 79 (1964): 378–83.

24. *Poetry*, p. 267.

25. *Allegory of Justice*, p. 214, n. 42.

26. On the topos, see Curtius, *European Literature*, pp. 160–62. Spenser adapts it normally at II. x. 72.

27. H. J. Todd in his edition of 1805 assumed "Armericke" to be a misprint and conjectured "Americke." But "Armericke" is exactly the

kind of nonce-word pun Spenser uses brilliantly to undermine an easy, approving formula by insinuating a contrary sense, as when the girls swimming in the fountain show Guyon "th' *amorous* sweet spoiles" (II. xii. 64), a bilingual oxymoron which destroys the platitude "amorous sweet" by hybridization with Latin *amarus*, bitter.

28. Apart from the Garden of Adonis in III (which probably dates from pre-book composition), the matrix occurs in canto x, even in IV, which is otherwise of a piece with III. In II the matrix spreads over ix-x to contain the experience of exemplary house and revelation of identity that in I require only canto x.

29. *World of Glass*, p. 176.

30. Cited by A. C. Hamilton, *The Structure of Allegory in "The Faerie Queene"* (Oxford: Clarendon Press, 1961), p. 190, who puts his emphasis on the idealization: Spenser "sees the present as an antique Image." Mine is on the irony made possible by idealizing current events. In fact, II. pro. 4 declares the poem's "antique Image" to be a mirror of Elizabeth's regime; V. pro. 1 sets the "image of the antique world" against debased "present time." The disparity epitomizes the shift in idealism between 1590 and 1596.

31. *Numbers of Time*, p. 193.

32. Ibid., p. 196.

33. *Life of Spenser*, p. 109.

34. These lines invite us to search for an anagram in "BONFONT." In fact, the two meanings Spenser suggests for "Malfont" give approval to interpretation of names in the poem by multiple etymology.

35. *Arte of Poesie*, 1. 16 (p. 35).

36. The Malfont stanza is important as part of a system of correspondences connecting stanza 25 (st. 26 in I and VI) of each ninth canto. All these stanzas are about speech. The stanza matching V. ix. 25 is II. ix. 25, on the tongue as part of the body in the House of Alma. In II. ix. 25. 6 the tongue excludes "blazers of crime"; in V. ix. 25. 6 Malfont has "blazed" his "bold speeches."

37. René Graziani, *PMLA*, 79 (1964): 376–89, discusses the topical allegory fully.

38. On these as issues in Book V, see Aptekar, *Icons of Justice*, chap. 7.

39. Dunseath, *Spenser's Allegory of Justice*, p. 131. On Radegund's role as an Amazon, see Celeste Turner Wright, "The Amazons in Elizabethan Literature," *SP*, 37 (1940): 433–56.

40. Aptekar, *Icons of Justice*, p. 249, n. 2.

41. James E. Phillips, Jr., "The Background of Spenser's Attitude toward Woman Rulers," *HLQ*, 5 (1941): 5–32; "The Woman Ruler in Spenser's *Faerie Queene*," ibid., pp. 211–34.

Notes

42. J. H. Walter, "*The Faerie Queene*: Alterations and Structure," *MLR*, 36 (1941): 51, notes an allusion to Saint Radegund's married virginity. At Cambridge a community of Benedictine nuns under her patronage had been suppressed in 1497 to create a college named for Saint Mary, Saint John the Evangelist and Saint Radegund, soon known as Jesus College. A versified *Lyfe of Saynt Radegunde*, probably by Henry Bradshaw, a monk of Chester, was published somewhere between 1508 and 1527. See René Aigrain, *Ste Radegonde*, vers 520–587, 4th ed. (Paris: Gabalda, 1930); also his "Un ancien poème anglais sur la vie de sainte Radegonde et le culte de sainte Radegonde en Angleterre," *Etudes mérovingiennes: actes des journèes de Poitiers* (Paris: Picard, 1953), pp. 1–7; F. Brittain, *Saint Radegund, Patroness of Jesus College, Cambridge* (Cambridge: Bowes, 1925); and his edition of *The Lyfe of Saynt Radegunde* (Cambridge: Cambridge University Press, 1926), introduction.

43. *Lyfe*, p. 49.

44. In fact, there is probably an obscene sense of Radigund's name, suggesting "counsel from the pudendum." Britomart plainly corrects Talus's euphemism "wretched bondage" to "harlots bondage" (vi. 10–11).

45. Brittain, *Saint Radegund, Patroness*, p. 52. "In 1450 an annual procession was established by Charles VII as a mark of gratitude to Saint Radegund for her help in bringing the Hundred Years' War to a successful conclusion. The king had frequently invoked the aid of the saint against the English, and had been crowned at Poitiers on Saint Radegund's day. The capture of Cherbourg, the last English stronghold, on Saint Radegund's Eve, was regarded as a signal mark of the saint's powerful intercession, and the grateful Charles had his first infant daughter named after her." Aigrain, *Sainte Radegunde*, p. 177, notes that a vision of the saint had encouraged the defenders of Poitiers during the English attack of 1202.

46. Elizabeth Jenkins, *Elizabeth and Leicester* (New York: Coward-McCann, 1962), pp. 93–95, 106, 113–15; Antonia Fraser, *Mary Queen of Scots* (New York: Delacorte, 1969), p. 217.

Chapter Seven

1. Bennett, *Evolution*, p. 41, notes that Book VI is the only one in which Spenser does not mention the Order of Maidenhead. Arthur's search for the Faery Queen, however, is touched on rather forlornly: "with portance sad, / Devizing of his love more, then of daunger drad" (VI. vii. 6).

2. Tufte, *Poetry of Marriage*, pp. 172–74, points out that Spenser

adapts many phrases from the April ode for the private praise of the bride in *Epithalamion*.

3. *Spenser's Courteous Pastoral: Book Six of "The Faerie Queene"* (Oxford: Clarendon Press, 1972), p. 262, n. 60.

4. Lotspeich, *Classical Mythology*, p. 39; Cheney, *Wild Man*, pp. 231–36; Alpers, *Poetry of "F.Q."*, pp. 12–14; Tonkin, *Courteous Pastoral*, pp. 129–31.

5. "Queen Elizabeth as Astraea," pp. 69–70. She notes that the constellation Ariadne's Crown was culminant at Elizabeth's birth and made a device to honor her in Sir Henry Lee's entertainments. But cf. her reference to "The picture of Elizabeth seen by Sir Calidore" (p. 70).

6. See *Variorum F.Q.*, 6:351–54, for arguments by Long and Heffner that Calidore is an Essex figure. But the tired knight, apparently the contemporary of Pastorella's father (xii. 11), and whose attitude to Tristram is avuncular, can hardly bear timely allusion to the earl who was twenty-nine in 1596. In any case, as I shall show below, the tradition of finding in Calidore some hint of Sidney or Leicester or both makes sense from the perspective of this episode.

7. See G. B. Harrison, *The Life and Death of Robert Devereux, Earl of Essex* (London: Cassell, 1937), chap. 1; and Robert Lacey, *Robert, Earl of Essex* (New York: Atheneum, 1971), chaps. 2–3.

8. Harrison, *Essex*, p. 21; Lacey, *Essex*, p. 38.

9. Harrison, *Essex*, p. 34; Lacey, *Essex*, p. 50.

10. Harrison, *Essex*, p. 35.

11. See Lotspeich, *Classical Mythology*, pp. 37–38.

12. Essex's fortune was made in 1590 when Elizabeth granted him the right to tax Levantine wines and ruined when she did not renew the grant.

13. Caxton's *Morte d'Arthur*, 8. 1. Spenser must change Malory's name Elizabeth for Tristram's mother, but why to Emiline? Cf. "redoubted Emmilen," *F.Q.* III. iii. 54.

14. *Variorum Prose Works*, pp. 223, 428.

15. Judson, *Life*, p. 187. Whether Spenser ever received Essex's patronage is unknown. Charles E. Mounts argues that Essex had good reasons for not patronizing the poet. "Spenser and the Earl of Essex," *Renaissance Papers 1958, 1959, 1960*, ed. George W. Williams, Southeastern Renaissance Conference, 1961, pp. 12–19. The earl did pay Spenser's funeral expenses but apparently only upon persuasion. Judson, *Life*, p. 206.

16. Judson, *Life*, p. 177. Cf. the rigorous attack on Burghley in *The Ruines of Time*, 447–55.

17. Judson, *Life*, p. 142.

Notes

18. On the relations between Spenser and Burghley, see *Variorum F.Q.*, 6:271–72. On Spenser's pension for the 1590 poem and Burghley's probable hindrance of it, see Nelson, *Poetry*, pp. 6–17.

19. See discussion of Comes above, pp. 13–14.

20. On the tradition that Pythagoras invented music, see Isidore, *Etym.* 3.16. "The Greeks say that Pythagoras discovered the first principles of this art from the sounds of hammers and the plucking of taut strings." See John M. Steadman, "The 'Inharmonious Blacksmith': Spenser and the Pythagoras Legend," *PMLA*, 79 (1964): 664–65.

21. Fowler, *Numbers of Time*, pp. 174–75.

22. Discussed at length by Aptekar, *Icons of Justice*, and Dunseath, *Allegory of Justice*, both passim. See their indexes.

23. Aptekar, *Icons of Justice*, pp. 209–12.

24. Andreas Alciati, *Emblemata* (Lyons, 1551), p. 194. Achilles Bocchius, *Symbolicarum quaestionum libri quinque* (Bologna, 1574), 2. 43 (p. 92). Jean MacIntyre, "Spenser's Herculean Heroes," *HAB*, 17 (1966): 5–12, is to my knowledge the first scholar to note the relevance of Hercules Gallicus to Book VI (although she wrongly associates the figure with Colin). For extended discussion of Hercules Gallicus, see Marc-René Jung, *Hercule dans la littérature francaise du xvie siècle* (Geneva: Froz, 1966), chap. 3.

25. *Courteous Pastoral*, p. 51.

26. Nohrnberg, *Analogy*, pp. 717–18, notes parallels between Despair and Melibee.

27. On the biblical background of this proverb, see *Variorum F.Q.*, 6:241.

28. On the Choice of Hercules, see Wind, *Pagan Mysteries*, pp. 205–6.

29. As Calidore does not hear Melibee on gold, neither does Melibee hear Calidore on envy. Their dialogue is actually two monologues by self-absorbed speakers. It is not courteous speech or "civill conversation" (i. 1).

30. On Calidore as infected by envy, see Ronald B. Bond, "A Study of *Invidia* in Mediaeval and Renaissance English Literature" (Ph.D. diss., University of Toronto, 1972), pp. 188–201.

31. Not the usual arrangement which is described by Wind, *Pagan Mysteries*, chap. 2.

32. Bond, "A Study of *Invidia*," chap. 1, especially pp. 22ff.

33. For discussion at length of *invidia* as enemy to literature in the Renaissance, see ibid. (*The Theatre of Worldlings* of 1569 is hackwork and not properly part of the Spenser canon, which carefully follows the pastoral-to-epic pattern.)

34. "The Mock Hero in Spenser's *Faerie Queene*," *MP*, 66 (1969):

212–17.

35. Fletcher's phrase, *Prophetic Movement*, p. 290.

36. Lotspeich, *Classical Mythology*, p. 86.

37. "Spenser's Mutabilitie," in *Essays in English Literature from the Renaissance to the Victorian Age, Presented to A. S. P. Woodhouse 1964*, ed. Millar Maclure and D. W. Watt (Toronto: University of Toronto Press, 1964), pp. 31–34.

38. For discussion of the arguments as to date, see S. P. Zitner's edition of *The Mutabilitie Cantos* (London: Nelson, 1968), pp. 2–4.

39. See Fowler, *Numbers of Time*, pp. 58–59, who points out that in numerology eight can mean eternity, as in Augustine's *Epistles*.

Index to *The Faerie Queene*

(General Index follows)

Index to *The Faerie Queene*

General Index

Abelard, Peter, 61
Adonis, 107, 129
Aeneas. *See* Virgil
Aigrain, René, 213 n. 42, n. 45
Alençon, duc d', 18, 102–4
Alpers, Paul, 42, 189 n. 1, 198 n. 3, 203 n. 4, 214 n. 4
Amazon (river), 90
Amazons, 90, 151
America. *See* New World
Amphion, 15
Anglo, Sidney, 200 n. 24
Aphthonius, *Progymnasmata*, 6–7; *laus* prescription, 6–10, 15–18, 66, 73, 90, 114–15
Aptekar, Jane, 195 n. 7, 197 n. 25, 198 n. 3, 201 n. 34, 211 n. 15, 212 n. 38, n. 40, 215 n. 22, n. 23
Aristotle, 189 n. 1; *Poetics*, 4; Averroes Paraphrase of, 4; *Rhetoric*, 2–3, 9
Ariosto, Ludovico, *Orlando furioso*, 37, 39–44, 47, 63–64, 116, 124; Angelica, 42, 106, 202 n. 8; Bradamante, 124–25; Orlando, 40–41; Ruggiero, 40–42, 124–25; third-canto encomium, 71, 124–26; persona of poet, 63–64, 109; praise of Este dynasty, 41, 47, 116, 124
Armada, 51, 163, 168, 197 n. 23, 209 n. 24
Art and nature, 89, 92–94, 100
Arthur, as imperial hero, 116–17. *See also* Dee; empire, Elizabethan
Arthur Tudor (son of Henry VII),

115–16
Astraea (Virgo), 52, 100, 142, 148–49, 160 n. 10
Augustine, St., 53, 69, 113, 127, 184, 192 N. 32
Ausonius, *De inventis musarum*, 196 n. 16
Averroes, 4

Bagpipe, 25, 27, fig. 2
Baldwin, C. S., 3, 189 n. 2
Baldwin, T. H., 190 n. 18
Bayle, Constantino, 206 n. 7
Beckingsale, R. W., 207 n. 41, 209 n. 13
Belson, Jay, 205 n. 19
Bender, John B., 198 n. 13
Bennett, Josephine Waters, 44, 112, 200 n. 29, 202 n. 47, 204 n. 12, 208 n. 10, 213 n. 1
Berger, Harry, 86, 208 n. 7, 210 n. 12
Bernhart, Barbara, 197 n. 19
Blitch, Alice, 205 n. 13
Blissett, William, 182, 208 n. 45
Boccaccio, Giovanni, *Genealogiae*, 11–13, 43, 106, 196 n. 14
Bond, Ronald B., 215 n. 30, n. 32
Book of Common Prayer, 60, 69
Botticelli, Sandro, 15
Brittain, F., 213 n. 42, n. 44
Brooks, Eric St. J., 207 n. 36
Burgess, Theodore, 189 n. 2
Burghley, William Cecil, Lord, 63, 104, 117, 132, 154, 164–65, 179

Cadwallader, 68, 117, 127
Callimachus, *Hymns*, 55
Calliope, 11, 14, 31, 44–48, 183
Calvin, John, 153
Camden, William, *History of Elizabeth* [*Annals*], 89
Camoëns, Luiz Vas de, *Lusiads*, 125
Cartari, Vincenzo, *Imagini de i dei*, 44
Cawley, Robert Ralston, 203 n. 12, 107 n. 32
Circe, 82
Chaucer, Geoffrey, 29–31, 193 n. 51, 194 n. 63; *Parliament of Fowls*, 54; *Squire's Tale*, 168; *Romaunt of the Rose*, 195 n. 8
Cheney, Donald, 195 n. 7, 207 n. 42, 214 n. 4
Chloris, 15
Church calendar: Ash Wednesday, 60–62; Christmas, 101; Easter, 62, 77–78; Good Friday; 69; Lent, 78
Church of England, 74; Act of Supremacy, 79; antiquity of, 76; head of, 62; reformed clergy of, 60–61, 74. *See also* Foxe; Jewel
Church, Roman Catholic, 74, 76, 137; English Catholics, 137; Mistress Missa, 62; papacy, 49–50, 62–63, 67–75
Church, True, 58–59; Bride of Lamb, 59; Israel in Babylon, 61; and lamb, 61–62; Woman Clothed with the Sun, 68–69, 78. *See also* Una
Cicero, 8
Clark, Donald Lemen, 190 n. 18
Clemency. *See* justice
Clio, 44–47

Columbus, Christopher, 91–92, 101
Comic admixture in encomium, 78–79, 88–90, 108–10, 123–34, 128–30, 137, 179–80, 182, 202 n. 1, 203 n. 8
Constantine, 76–77, 201 n. 36, n. 37
Contemptus mundi, 183–84
Comes, Natalis, *Mythologiae*, 11, 13–14, 43, 166, 67, 181
Core cantos, 146, 159, 175, 212 n. 28
Cornett, 24 fig. 1, 26–28, 28 fig. 5
Cory, Herbert, 131
Courthope, W. J., 112
Craig, Joanne, 210 n. 2
Craig, Martha, 118, 205 n. 19, 206 n. 23
Cullen, Patrick, 193 n. 48
Curtius, Ernst Robert, 10, 190 n. 17, 191 n. 30, 194 n. 61, 205 n. 18, 211 n. 26
Cynthia. *See* Diana

Daniel, Samuel, 190 n. 13
Daniells, Roy, 193 n. 50
Davies, Sir John, *Hymnes of Astraea*, 209 n. 25
Dee, John, 98–99, 206 n. 27
Dees, Jerome S., 189 n. 18, 202 n. 45
De inventis musarum, 46
DeNeef, A. Leigh, 189 n. 7, 192 n. 30
Diana, 18–19
Diaz del Castillo, Bernal, *Conquest of New Spain*, 205 n. 20
Dido. *See* Virgil
Dixon, John, 59, 62, 71, 202 n. 46
Donne, John, 148; verse epistles,